BROADENING HORIZONS

Contemporary Social Work Studies

Series Editor:
Robin Lovelock, University of Southampton, UK

Series Advisory Board:
Lena Dominelli, University of Southampton, UK
Peter Ford, University of Southampton, UK
Walter Lorenz, Free University of Bozen-Bolzano, Italy
Karen Lyons, University of East London, UK
Joan Orme, University of Glasgow, UK
Jackie Powell, University of Southampton, UK
Chris Warren-Adamson, University of Southampton, UK

Contemporary Social Work Studies (CSWS) is a series disseminating high quality new research and scholarship in the discipline and profession of social work. The series promotes critical engagement with contemporary issues relevant across the social work community and captures the diversity of interests currently evident at local, national and international levels.

CSWS is located in the School of Social Sciences at the University of Southampton, and is a development from the successful series of books published by Ashgate in association with CEDR (the Centre for Evaluative and Developmental Research) from 1991.

Titles include:

Reflecting on Social Work: Discipline and Profession
Edited by Robin Lovelock, Karen Lyons and Jackie Powell

Beyond Racial Divides: Ethnicities in Social Work Practice
Edited by Lena Dominelli, Walter Lorenz and Haluk Soydan

Valuing the Field: Child Welfare in an International Context
Edited by Marilyn Callahan, Sven Hessle and Susan Strega

Social Work in Higher Education: Demise or Development?
Karen Lyons

Community Approaches to Child Welfare: International Perspectives
Edited by Lena Dominelli

Child Sexual Abuse and Adult Offenders: New Theory and Research
Edited by Christopher Bagley and Kanka Mallick

Broadening Horizons

International Exchanges in Social Work

Edited by

LENA DOMINELLI
University of Southampton and President, IASSW

WANDA THOMAS BERNARD
Dalhousie University

ASHGATE

Published by
Ashgate Publishing Limited
Gower House
Croft Road
Aldershot
Hants GU11 3HR
England

Ashgate Publishing Company
Suite 420
101 Cherry Street
Burlington, VT 05401-4405
USA

Ashgate website: http://www.ashgate.com

British Library Cataloguing in Publication Data
Broadening horizons : international exchanges in social
    work. - (Contemporary social work studies)
    1.Social service 2.Student exchange programs 3.Social
    service - Cross-cultural studies
    I.Dominelli, Lena II.Bernard, Wanda Thomas
    361.3

Library of Congress Cataloging-in-Publication Data
Broadening horizons: international exchanges in social work / edited by Lena Dominelli and Wanda Thomas Bernard.
    p. cm. -- (Contemporary social work studies)
    Includes bibliographical references and index.
    ISBN 0-7546-1945-1
    1. Social service--International cooperation. 2. Social service. I. Dominelli, Lena. II.
Bernard, Wanda Thomas. III. Series.

HV40.B85 2003
361'.0071'55--dc21

2003050266

ISBN 0 7546 1945 1

Printed and bound in Great Britain by MPG Books Ltd, Bodmin, Cornwall

Contents

List of Contributors

EDITORS

Lena Dominelli is Professor of Social and Community Development and Director of the Centre for International Social and Community Development in the Faculty of Social Sciences at the University of Southampton, England and current President of the International Association of Schools of Social Work. She is an established author with an extensive publication record, including several publications in the Ashgate series 'in association with CEDR'. This has now been re-launched as the Contemporary Social Work Series. Her most recent books are: *Feminist Social Work Theory and Practice* (2002); and *Anti-Oppressive Social Work Theory and Practice* (2002).

Wanda Thomas Bernard is Director of the Maritime School of Social Work at Dalhousie University in Canada. She was a founding member of the Nova Scotia Association of Black Social Workers and has worked as a practitioner and undertaken research in anti-oppressive social work. She has both national and international publications, including contributions to various books, one of which was *Valuing the Field* in the CEDR/Ashgate series.

CONTRIBUTORS

Helena Albertson was a social work student who undertook an international exchange placement on the *Child Abuse, Protection and Welfare Project*.

Constance Barlow is Placement Coordinator in the School of Social Work at the University of Calgary and has organised overseas placements for students. She has publications based on her experiences in this area.

Phil Beck was a social work student who undertook an international exchange placement on the *Child Abuse, Protection and Welfare Project.*

Christine Bennett was a social work student who undertook an international placement in India.

Kish Bhatti-Sinclair is Director of the Practice Teaching Programme at the University of Southampton. She has been a community worker and practitioner for a number of years. She has also written a number of published articles.

Cecilia L.W. Chan is Professor of Social Work in the Department of Social Work and Social Administration, Director of the Centre on Behavioural Health and Associate Director of the Centre for Suicide Research and Prevention at the University of Hong Kong. She has published more than a hundred articles and book chapters in her areas of expertise. Cecilia Chan has also been honoured by the community of international social work educators by being invited to give the Eileen Younghusband Lecture at the IASSW Congress in Montpellier, France in July 2002.

Ernest W.T. Chui is Associate Professor in Social Work in the Department of Social Work and Social Administration at the University of Hong Kong. He is also the Fieldwork Coordinator and has engaged in planning and promoting overseas placements for students since 1998.

David Colombi works at the Centre for Human Services Technology based in the Department of Social Work Studies at the University of Southampton and has been involved in creating a number of web-based courses, including the International Child Welfare Course which arose from the EU-Canada Project. He has a number of publications relating to the new information technologies and education and a book in the CEDR/Ashgate series.

Sally Cosstick is Team Manager, Child Protection Enquiry, in Southampton Social Services. She has written in the area of child welfare and domestic violence. Her team included the practice teachers that supervised the Canadian students who came to England.

Anne Davies is Service Manager, Assessment, for children and families, in Southampton Social Services. She has written in the area of feminism and domestic violence. She oversaw the team that housed the Canadian students who undertook their placements in Southampton.

Donna Dustin is Senior Lecturer and Pathway Leader in Social Work at London Metropolitan University. Her early social work experience was in the field of mental health. She has taught undergraduate social work in Canada. Her current research interest is the impact of care management on social work practice in local authority social services departments with implications for the professional status of social workers.

Joan Gilroy recently retired as Director of the Maritime School of Social Work at Dalhousie University in Canada. Her writings have focused on feminism in social work. She was a founding member and Chair of the Women's Caucus for both the Canadian Association of Schools of Social Work and the International Association of Schools of Social Work. She contributed to *Community Approaches to Child Welfare* and to *Valuing the Field*, both published in the CEDR/Ashgate Series.

Michelle Hammond was a social work student who undertook an international exchange placement on the *Child Abuse, Protection and Welfare Project*.

Greger Helin is Manager of the community-based team at Älvsjö Community Centre in Stockholm, Sweden. He is a practice teacher who has supervised Canadian students placed in Sweden. He also co-wrote a chapter for *Community Approaches to Child Welfare*.

Sven Hessle is Professor of Social Work at Stockholm University in Sweden. He has an extensive list of publications in the field of child welfare and is currently co-editor of the *International Journal of Social Welfare*. He also contributed to *Community Approaches to Child Welfare* and co-edited *Valuing the Field* in the CEDR/Ashgate Series.

Nicoline Isacson is a practice teacher working at Älvsjö Community Centre in Stockholm, Sweden. She supervised Canadian students placed in Sweden. She also co-wrote a chapter for *Community Approaches to Child Welfare*.

Madhubala Kasiram is Lecturer in Social Work in the School of Sports Science and Social Work, University of Durban-Westville, South Africa.

Sue Lawrence is Principal Lecturer in Social Work at London Metropolitan University and Course Co-Director of the MA Comparative European Social Studies (MACESS) delivered in Maastricht, The Netherlands. Her social work experience began in 1970 in London. Her current research interests are drawn from ten years of experience of networking, collaboration and teaching in a European context.

Anne LeBlanc was a social work student who undertook an international exchange placement on the *Child Abuse, Protection and Welfare Project*.

Andy Markland was a social work student who undertook an international exchange placement on the *Child Abuse, Protection and Welfare Project*.

Renee Meuse was a social work student who undertook an international exchange placement on the *Child Abuse, Protection and Welfare Project*.

Melanie Myles was a social work student who undertook an international exchange placement on the *Child Abuse, Protection and Welfare Project*.

Carolyn Noble is Field Co-ordinator and Professor in the School of Social Work at the University of Western Sydney in Australia. She has published in her areas of expertise.

Rubeena Partab is Lecturer in Social Work in the School of Sports Science and Social Work, University of Durban-Westville, South Africa.

Sheila Sammon is the Placement Co-ordinator in the School of Social Work at McMaster University in Canada. She has written on field supervision and placements and was a key member of the European

Union-Canada Project. She was involved in both sending students to Europe and receiving students from Europe.

Bethany J. Savoy was a social work student who undertook an international exchange placement on the *Child Abuse, Protection and Welfare Project.*

Vishanthie Sewpaul is Professor of Social Work at the Centre for Social Work at the University of Natal in Durban, South Africa. She is particularly interested in the areas of gender, HIV/AIDS, sexuality, globalisation, social policy reformed and emancipatory pedagogical strategies. She has played a key role in developing social work theory and practice in South Africa and has published in her areas of expertise.

Julia Waldman is Research Fellow in the Department of Social Work Studies at the University of Southampton. She has a number of publications on child welfare and contributed to *Valuing the Field.*

Walene Whitaker is the Placement Co-ordinator at the School of Social Work at the University of Victoria in Canada. She has written on field supervision and placements and was a key member of the European Union–Canada Project. She was involved in both sending students to Europe and receiving students from Europe.

Disclaimer

The views conveyed in this book are those of each of the authors concerned and not necessarily those of the editors, the universities involved in the EU-Canada Exchange Project, nor of the EU–Canada Project funders.

Acknowledgements

Writing this book has been an adventure shared with many others. To all of those who willingly gave of their time and talents in exploring an important issue for social work education and practice, we give heartfelt thanks. You are too numerous to mention, but our journey would have been incomplete without you. Nonetheless, we would like to highlight a couple of names for their special contribution to international student exchanges, who for lack of time were unable to write about their experiences in this book: June Tilling, Lesley Burt, Lena Cederlund and Marilyn Callahan.

We would also like to thank the European Union and the Canadian government for funding the *Child Abuse, Protection and Welfare Project*, because this made possible the experiences that lie at the core of this book. And, to David Whiteley, a deep appreciation for his endeavours in preparing the tables that challenged our computer skills.

We also thank the writers whose commitment to internationalism has made it possible for them to share their experiences with you in the hopes of improving both the planning and the services that are provided for overseas students, despite busy schedules. At the same time, we should stress that the views conveyed in this book are those of each of the authors concerned and not necessarily those of the editors, the universities referred to, the European Union–Canada Project, or the funders of the various projects covered in these many pages.

Lena Dominelli and Wanda Thomas Bernard

To all our sisters and brothers

Foreword

International social work has had a lengthy history in both the academy and in the field. There have been a number of endeavours that have sought to develop its theory and practice through various exchanges involving academics, practitioners and students. At the beginning of the twenty-first century there has been a renewed interest in international social work, especially its development following the impact of globalisation on professional working relationships involving clients and practitioners, and the relationship between the individual and the state.

Many of the initiatives promoting international social work have been conducted under the auspices of the International Association of Schools of Social Work (IASSW) and the International Federation of Social Workers (IFSW) which have taken responsibility for developing a global community of educators and practitioners respectively since 1928. These two organisations have also worked to get the profession of social work heard in the international arena, particularly with the United Nations and its associated bodies. Additionally, their local branches work to foster the interests of social work where services are delivered.

This book is timely. It describes the experiences of a number of people who have been involved in international exchanges in social work across a range of different countries. Although their programmes are different and the projects that they have organised and delivered are varied, there are a number of similarities that they share. These include the difficulties of securing funding for this work, creating an adequate and supportive infrastructure for both academic and fieldwork, and ensuring recognition of the knowledge, values and skills that the students demonstrate whilst on placement.

At the same time, these exchanges have provided students with enormous learning opportunities, developed their self-knowledge and enhanced their professional development. These positives alone would warrant the endorsement of international social work on all courses of social work world-wide. It would then ensure that the potential to secure a better understanding of global social problems, and seek local solutions that would take account of their broader social context would be more readily realised.

International social work has to find ways of building a unity amongst a wide range of professional groupings, professional structures, methods of working, political ideologies, and funding arrangements. Celebrating diversity within unity will be an enormous challenge for internationalists. But, as this book demonstrates, it is not an impossible mission. There are innumerable possibilities for being creative in developing new ways forward that meet the needs of today and tomorrow. In the quest to reach these, past lessons can be informative.

Past history can inspire future orientations without being a drag on people's inventiveness. After reading this book, if you have not already embarked on international exchanges, I hope that you will be moved to begin an exciting new chapter in your life and organise your own project. If you are a seasoned veteran of international exchanges, I hope that you will enthuse your activities in new directions.

Lena Dominelli

1 Introduction

LENA DOMINELLI and WANDA THOMAS BERNARD

Social work has had a tradition of being concerned with international issues (Addams, 2002; Salomon, 1937; Dominelli, 2000). But it has only recently begun to worry about theorising its position as an internationalising discipline within a global economy (Dominelli, 1998). Rising to the occasion will present quite a challenge to practitioners because their remit has traditionally been locality based. Social workers have been guided in their practice by local customs, traditions and legislative frameworks (Dominelli, 2000). This has been apparent in the literature where even a journal like the *International Social Work* has focused on reporting on activities within particular countries.

The meaning of international social work has been a contested one that has nonetheless encouraged exchanges of personnel. Although its predominant reflection in the literature has been one of placing a number of developments from different countries within the covers of one book, e.g., Brauns and Kramer (1989), Mayadas et al., (1997); Ledrer and Neal (1999). Recent publications such as Hokenstad and Midgeley (1997), Lyons (1999) and Healy, (2001) have begun to theorise the relationship between the local and the global in social work. However, a considerable theoretical space remains.

The authors in this book are contributing towards meeting this theoretical and practice gap in their consideration of the experiences of academics, practitioners and students involved in international exchanges in social work. One of these initiatives has absorbed a group of people who have participated in an international endeavour funded by the European Union (EU)–Canada Exchange Programme in Higher Education and collaborated on a Project entitled, *Child Abuse, Protection and Welfare*. The work undertaken in this Project underpins the writings of the majority of the writers who have contributed to this volume. The other authors have organised separate projects in various other countries including South Africa, the United States, China and Australia.

European Union-Canada Project

The *Child Abuse, Protection and Welfare Project* was one of 76 funded by the European Union and Canadian government during 1997 to 2000, and the only one dealing with mainstream social work issues, including student placements. One of its principle aims was 'to develop analytical frameworks and theories which facilitate international child welfare practice and thereby increase social workers' potential to practice in other countries' (Callahan and Dominelli, 1996). This publication, which draws on the experience of this Project and the attendant literature, constitutes an attempt to take this work further.

So, the *Child Abuse, Protection and Welfare Project* was created formally for the primary purpose of developing international social work theory and practice. As the experiences it provided form the core of this book, we describe the Project briefly below.

The Partners

The partners who participated in the European Union–Canada Project were schools of social work drawn from both Europe (three countries) and Canada (three provinces). The partners came together to form a network that was largely associated with the schools of social work located in the following institutions:

European Partners:

The University of Southampton, Southampton England (Co-ordinator for the European Partners and the overall Project)
The University of Stockholm, Stockholm, Sweden
The Professional University of West Brabant, Breda, the Netherlands

Canadian Partners:

The University of Victoria, Victoria, British Columbia (Canadian Co-ordinator)
Dalhousie University, Halifax, Nova Scotia
McMaster University, Hamilton, Ontario

Each of these institutions had its own set of regulations and ways of teaching and learning. Therefore, the partners encompassed diverse approaches to social work education, theory and practice.

Each school had extensive links with the field and so was able to bring in agency partners from each locale into the Project and thereby expand the newly formed network. These agencies provided the placements where the students were placed. Each university sent a minimum of 7 students so that by the end of the Project, a total of 45 students had undertaken placements in child welfare agencies. Of these, 22 were students from Canada placed in Europe and 23 were from Europe and placed in Canada.

In addition to the people who were directly involved in the Project, its scope and impact was increased through conferences involving academics, practitioners, students, and in some cases, service users, and in the seminars that the exchange students presented to the receiving institution at the beginning of their placement and the home one at the end of it. Furthermore, the Project sought to extend its influence through the creation of a web-based course on international child welfare and various publications.

The Project began with the intention of exchanging social work students on their final *assessed* placement at either undergraduate (Bachelors) or postgraduate (Masters) level. But, towards the end of the Project, several students undertook their first assessed placement instead of their final one overseas. This change was made to accommodate eligible students who would have missed the opportunity to undertake an international exchange because the Project was due to terminate during their first year of study.

In addition to the exchange of students, academic staff discussed their country's research in the field of child welfare and practitioners presented examples of best child welfare practice through Project conferences. Students also played major roles in these conferences, assisting with their organisation and presenting papers. The Project, therefore, had a number of outcomes other than that of exchanging students. In specific terms, these included: staff and practitioner visits, conferences, seminars, books and other publications, a video, a Project website, and an international child welfare course on the web.

International Exchanges: Issues for Consideration

Working across national boundaries presents a number of challenges. These are related to differences in language, culture, legislative framework, socio-political systems, and the organisational structures of higher education in their respective countries. The principles on which collaboration across these divides takes place become crucial to the success of such endeavours. In this Project, the guiding principles were reciprocity, social justice, recognising the dignity of others, equality and teaching social work students how to work with 'clients' in a respectful manner. These values underpinned the philosophies of all Project participants and made it possible for those involved to work with one another in ways that respected differences and valued collaborative and mutually supportive ways of working with each other.

In this particular Project, the guiding principles also had to examine closely the oppression of children – a form of age oppression that Dominelli (1989) terms 'adultism' because it involves adults abusing their power over children, and the affirmation of children's rights because its work was centred on enhancing the well-being of children. Agreeing the principles for co-operation can be a testing time in itself. However, we found that agreement was eased by virtue of the fact that most participants were known to the Project co-ordinators and they were able to pull together a group of people who had similar values and goals.

Respecting difference and not imposing one particular view or paradigm of practice or structure upon the others constituted an important part of the collaborative framework for this network. Looking at issues that arose through the prism of avoiding the oppression of one participant by another grounded our interactions with each other.

From the very first face-to-face meeting at the beginning of the Project, it was clear that the Project participants liked each other and got on well. This provided a reservoir of goodwill that enabled difficulties and disagreements to be resolved amicably and ensured that the gap between the resources available and those needed could be overcome. So, even though the Project was seriously under-funded, good-will, a strong desire to promote collaboration and social justice, and a commitment to providing the best possible experience for students contributed to the Project's overall success.

There were a number of issues which the participants needed to address early on in the Project's history which tested our practice of these principles. We consider these below under the headings, language, opportunities or opportunism.

Language

Language is a key aspect of communication that needs to be addressed when crossing national borders. Our Project involved people with English, Swedish or Dutch as their mother tongue. Within the Project, we found that the linguistic skills of those from predominantly English-speaking countries were less developed than those from the other countries. For us, this was because the participants from the non-English-speaking countries of Northern Europe were generally more proficient in their use of the English language than the English-speaking ones were of the other languages. Additionally, we inhabit a world in which a substantial amount of the literature written in English has been translated into other languages, including those involved in this Project, but the converse does not hold to the same extent.

With regards to social work, English texts have been translated into Swedish and Dutch. However, very little of the Swedish literature and even less of the Dutch one have been translated into English. Consequently, a range of interesting publications addressing conceptual and practice concerns, but written in Swedish and Dutch were unavailable to those who could not speak, read or understand these languages. However, Project resources were not sufficient to enable us to translate many of these materials into the other languages.

Language was acknowledged as an issue that needed to be addressed during the first Project meeting. Dealing with it proved to be more problematic than we anticipated. Initially, the main preoccupation of the Project participants referred to the role of English as the lingua franca because we worried that might disadvantage participants from Sweden and the Netherlands going to Canada, and students from Canada going to Sweden and the Netherlands. However, it quickly became apparent that there were several other dimensions that had to be taken into account.

We had not calculated sufficiently for the funds to cover translation costs for the materials from each of the three Project languages to be translated into the other two. Another problem was the difficulty in training either academic staff or students in a language they did not already possess because pressured schedules meant that the time for learning to become proficient in another language was not available prior to the student going on their placement overseas. Thus, the burden for translating documents fell onto those Project members, who spoke the relevant languages fluently. In the main, these were academic staff. But, given all their other commitments, they could only do a limited amount of this type of work.

Language also proved to be problematic for those speaking English. English and Canadian English are two different versions of the same language, and we needed a 'glossary' to help us deal with those differences. For example, people might be aware of a truck being the same as a lorry, or even a pavement as depicting a sidewalk. But, even in the social work lexicon, there were important terminological differences. A 'field instructor' in Canada was a 'practice teacher' in England. A 'practicum' for Canadian students became a 'practice placement' when they crossed the Atlantic. 'Academic staff' in Britain became 'faculty' in Canada.

However, there was an up-side to this issue. We found through the course of the Project, that students compensated for their lack of verbal facility in a language by drawing on their non-verbal skills. This in turn heightened their awareness of a range of coping strategies that they used to meet the challenge of feeling disempowered through language. This gave them some empathy for the feelings of those disadvantaged by language in their own country. They also realised the importance of abilities that had often been masked when doing social work in their own country.

Additionally, Canadian students working with Swedish-speaking and Dutch-speaking clients were able to make a virtue of their inability to speak the relevant language. Instead of dividing the student practitioner from the 'client', the language barrier became a source of role reversal and empowerment because it provided a space in which the 'clients' could teach the students something that they did not know. Thus, working in an unfamiliar culture without knowledge of the local language can help students become more sensitive to power differentials between them and those they intend to serve.

Opportunities or Opportunism?

Globalisation has shrunk the planet metaphorically on the spatial dimension because technology has made it possible to overcome the barriers of time and geography to a considerable degree by speeding up travel and communication times (Deacon et al., 1997). This has encouraged both more inclusive forms of communication and labour mobility. Working in the international arena provides wonderful opportunities for expanding our horizons as we learn about other peoples and subject our own cherished understandings of the world to critical scrutiny.

Globalisation has facilitated these sorts of possibilities by encouraging interaction across borders, making travel relatively cheap and accessible, improving communications through internet connections, and providing the technologies that enable us to condense time and space into more manageable entities. At the same time, globalisation is a contradictory force in that it enables a greater degree of exploitation to occur alongside opportunities for closer collaboration, development and growth. In an attempt to capture the distasteful exploitation of others this implied, this capacity was termed, 'opportunities or opportunism' (Dominelli, 1996).

Consequently, in picking up the positive aspects of the challenges fostered by globalisation, steps must be taken to counter its negative impact. This is because globalisation privileges those with greater access to the world's material resources and the dominant or what has been termed the 'global' culture or McDonaldisation of society (Dominelli, 1992, 1996; Ritzer, 2000).

In this more mobile world, professionals have access to labour markets other than those in their countries of origin. Consequently, they may find that during their working careers they may end up working in a country other than that in which they trained. Steps need to be taken beforehand to prepare them for this. Otherwise, opportunism may easily gain the upperhand in their dealings with those from other cultures. Additionally, the internationalisation of social problems and the increased levels of interdependence between countries are spreading their influences across a broader geographical expanse.

As a result, problems that originate in one country may have repercussions for another. These interconnections become evident for practitioners located in a different geographical location, for example, in work involving child prostitution, inter-country adoptions and refugees and asylum seekers and form what Khan and Dominelli (2000) call the 'internationalisation of social problems'. Natural disasters, poverty, and wars intensify these trends. Social workers require training to address these issues proficiently and fairly.

Social work education has an important role to play in equipping practitioners to practise in globalising social situations and environments. Internationalising social work to accommodate the local to the global will enable educators to foster the positive aspects of globalisation (Dominelli, 2001). At the same time, globalisation has increased the danger of education becoming a plank in a neo-colonialist agenda in which other territories and their cultures become another site for those from privileged backgrounds to ensure their cultural dominance.

This opportunistic approach to international encounters was eschewed by the Project as we sought to uphold our commitment to equality and social justice in everything we did together. Living up to this ideal required us to become sensitive to each other's requirements and differences, whatever their source, and find ways of accommodating our diversities so that we were each able to flourish within and through this collaboration.

Collaboration thereby became a path to growth rather than an obstacle course to be surmounted. An illustration of this is that we did not seek to develop a common assessment framework for our students. We decided instead, that we would respect the assessment framework provided by the student's home institution. This meant that the practice teacher (faculty liaison or agency supervisor) in the receiving institution became proficient in applying a teaching approach and an assessment framework other than the one that they were familiar with, and learnt to do so in a fairly short period of time.

Although this was a noble aim, the practicalities meant that practice teachers were often inadequately briefed in the new framework and were called upon to use it before they, the academic staff or the student, would have liked. Moreover, because the briefing sessions on each other's courses were provided by the academics at the beginning of the Project, there was a time-lag between the briefing session and the student's appearance on placement.

Consequently, explanations which appeared clear at the point of reception became more fogged when transmitted further down the line at some later point in time, and often by different people as a result of staffing changes. Staff turnover, both in the field and the academy had an impact on the Project's continuity.

Students who go abroad have the opportunity to grow and develop if their interactions with others are conducted in accordance with the principle of valuing others and being valued themselves. This meant that those who went abroad had to feel supported in what they were doing in order to work with others on a reciprocal basis. Therefore, we sought to place students in supportive environments that had the capacity to respond to their needs. But, even with careful preparation, the outcomes were not necessarily those that were anticipated.

Students were placed singly, in pairs or in threes on occasion, depending on placement availability and the number of successful applicants for places. Our initial thoughts suggested that having at least two exchange students from each institution being sent abroad at the same time and being placed in the same setting would encourage mutual support and be advantageous to both. This proved not to be the case for some.

Several students, interested primarily in their own experience, found being placed with another student from their home institution difficult, particularly if they had nothing else in common. And what started off being perceived as an opportunity became a barrier. Others who had been placed singly felt the opposite and wished they had been able to share their time with someone from their home base in order to reduce their isolation. Some of these points are examined by students in their contributions later in the book.

Fortunately, we also had examples of students who took advantage of the opportunity to be with others from their course. These enjoyed sharing placements with their colleagues because it meant that they were with someone who understood the constraints that they were under and with whom they could share their experiences more effectively and is referred to in the students' writings in part one of the book.

It was difficult for either staff or students to predict the responses of particular students until they were on placement, by which time it was not always possible to offer alternatives. Opportunities, in this sense, are a scarce commodity. Additionally, exchange students wanted extensive contact with the students in the receiving institution.

Practically, this wish was not always easy to accommodate because the focus on placement work meant that student timetables could not readily be aligned, and so students might go directly into their placement, having only the briefest of visits to their new academic institution. As a result, the student might not be as fully integrated into the receiving institution's academic programme and student cohort as either they or the Project organisers would have liked.

For instance, the different timetable requirements for each of the courses that they had registered for meant that exchange students might arrive at a point in the term when the students in the receiving institution were already out on placement, or if it was a vacation period, they might find the availability of both students and academic staff was limited. Thus, what appeared to be opportunities were often missed.

Harmonisation and Diversity

Managing the tension between harmonisation and diversity was one of the tasks that the Project partners had to grapple with early in the process. Recognising the global trend towards harmonisation, and the pushing of diversity into a homogeneous mould, especially in the cultural arena, we worried that harmonisation would limit the creativity that diversity offers. For example, the European Union suggested the use of the European Credit Transfer Scheme (ECTS) as a model that could be followed in the interests of harmonising courses and standards. Whilst the EU favoured harmonisation of standards, such as uniform structures and regulations to allow for the easy transfer of units from one place or setting to another, we preferred to recognise each other's regulations and work as they applied to specific course offerings.

In this Project we were able to recognise the unique ways of working that we each had without imposing a uniform structure on one another. Furthermore, we would suggest that the approach of embracing the diversity among us facilitated richer learning experiences as we were each able to engage students, practitioners and academic staff in critical reflection of the strengths and limitations of our own programmes and to compare these with those of our colleagues. For the exchange students, this meant that although their programme of study was guided by the regulations of their home universities, they were able to benefit from access to the programme offered by their receiving university.

Local Specificities and Commonalities

That all of the Project participants respected and valued diversity helped to counter the tendencies towards the homogenisation of our activities under the forces of globalisation. This meant that we had to acknowledge and validate local specificities, looking for both commonalities and differences. The local specificities such as language, culture and traditions, legislation and social policies, provided the context within which the social work students engaged in practice. As a result, we were able to develop better understandings of the different policies that guided social work interventions in each country and their particular approaches to child welfare.

Paying attention to the local specificities caused us to stop and reflect upon our own taken-for-granted ways of working with children. For example, the Swedish emphasis on the rights of the child made a number of us pause to consider the limited attention given to these in the framing of practice in the United Kingdom and in Canadian jurisdictions, where the dependency of children upon their adult carers rather than their autonomous personhood permeates the work that is done with them (for a detailed consideration of this point, see the Project contributions in Dominelli, 1999). This strengthened Project participants' conviction in supporting citizenship based approaches to working with children.

We found common ground in our shared values, particularly those that underpin social work practice – promoting social justice, client-centred practice, and human rights, citizenship and anti-oppressive approaches.

We shared similar visions of and goals for social work education in preparing students for critical and reflective practice aimed at empowering clients to develop to their full potential as citizens and challenge the oppressive barriers that impact upon them.

In addition, the shared history of social work between the Canadian and British partners at early points in their evolution provided common understandings for students from these two countries. The three Canadian partners shared legal and cultural history. However, because child welfare issues are under provincial jurisdictions, policies and practices varied from each other in many respects. Finally, guided by the more recent European Union directives, the three European partners shared commonalities, particularly around children's rights and civil liberties.

Isolation and Networking

Effective and efficient communications amongst the Project partners, amongst students on the Project and between the students, their placement overseas and their home base were crucial to the success of the Project and essential to overcoming student isolation when overseas. Students and partner institutions made good use of the modern information technologies, to ensure regular and frequent communication with and amongst each other.

Students were able to have quick access to their home tutors, and each other, via emails, providing that the technology was available, and they were comfortable using it. This helped to reduce student isolation and many developed networks that continued after the Project was completed.

The ease of communication via email proved to be particularly important for the students at the receiving university prior to their arrival, making the transition on arrival much easier for them. In some instances, we were able to pair students from the home and receiving institution, which is one way of formalising these arrangements. However, these opportunities must be carefully organised to ensure that the students are well-matched and that alternative arrangements can be made quickly when necessary. Communication between partner institutions was also necessary to ensure that exchange students were meeting the requirements of their home institution whilst on placement overseas.

The students had to overcome a number of hurdles to achieve success. As they grappled with the isolation that comes from being in another country, with a different language, culture, customs, and traditions, they had to simultaneously deal with a different education system and the stress of being on an assessed placement in unfamiliar terrain. The stakes were high for these students and they had to navigate their way quickly around obstacles to ensure the successful completion of their placement within a prescribed timeframe.

In addition, the students carried the special burden of being ambassadors for their home country. As one student put it, 'The strain is harder. We are not here simply to visit'. The on-site placement supervisor, the home supervisor, and the receiving institution are crucial players in such situations, as the students need encouragement, support and the quick resolution of identified problems.

However, there is no guarantee that those responding will always get it right. For example, in this Project, one student (included in the figure of 45) was unable to successfully make the transition from home to receiving country, and returned home after only three days. Others left their placements after two months because they did not feel that the learning experience was able to prepare them for practice at home, and the available supports in the receiving institution were insufficient to meet their needs for an assessed placement preparing them for social work practice at home.

For the majority of the students in this Project however, the overseas placement experience was very positive and both personally and professionally rewarding and challenging. Many of these students have gone on to work in child welfare, even those who were initially uncertain that this was their preferred field of practice. The spirit of camaraderie and collaboration amongst Project partners – academics, practitioners and students, appears to have helped strengthen the network and break the isolation that individual students faced when they began their exchange placement. And, all those involved in the exchange endorsed its continuation after the EU-Canada government funded period ended.

Communications

As noted above, the need for excellent communications was essential for the success of both individual students and the overall Project. That we made effective use of the available technology is also worth repeating here. International student exchanges are dependent upon strong links between the home base and the overseas institution, at all levels. The new information technologies have a major role to play in facilitating cheap, quick and easy to use technologies that enable communications to transcend time and space.

In the case of this Project, contact involved regular and open communication between the staff within the universities, the universities and their field agencies, the receiving and sending universities and between students and the staff at both the receiving and sending universities, with their placement supervisors and their home tutor. Students had to be creative in finding cost effective access to the internet and email. For example, local Internet Cafés were a good substitute when they could not get to the local university. Some academic staff used web-based technology to maintain links between their students on overseas placements and those on placement in their home country. This enabled the rich learning experiences gained on the international placements to be shared with a wider group of students.

The Project as a whole attempted to communicate via Web CT around the construction of a course on international child welfare, but this was less successful for technical reasons which are described by Julia Waldman later in this book. The range of communication links and networks that were possible in this Project illustrate some of the potential benefits of information technology in today's global society.

Recording the experience

Student exchanges were a central part of this Project. Hence, the actual recording of those experiences was one of the requirements for those going abroad. The purpose of the recording was two-fold: to convey the experience to those who had not attended the placement, and to provide a basis for future reflection and learning. Therefore, students were asked to keep a diary or log of their experience, including their thoughts and feelings about the practice overseas. These will provide a rich source of data for our future involvement in international social work and student exchanges. Additionally, they became a base for students' reflections of their learning on placement and for the seminars and written work they had to produce.

At the completion of their placement, each student was required to present a seminar on their learning experience, critically reflecting on the lessons learned and the implications for future placements. Students also had to present a seminar describing the child welfare system at home to the receiving institution at the beginning of their placement. For the students with limited child welfare experience, this meant that they had to become well-versed in their country's legislation, policies and practices in social work in general and in child welfare in particular prior to departure.

We noted earlier that each partner institution maintained its own assessment criteria for student placements. Whilst this was a positive initiative for the partners, it presented some challenges for the students who worried about the possibility of failing their placement because their home institution's requirements might not be met, or because the practice supervisor might have different expectations about what constituted acceptable practice. These fears were usually addressed through dialogue involving the students, the practice teachers and the academic staff.

Some institutions required the students to complete a written assessed assignment based on their experience in the overseas placement, while others required an unassessed assignment. In addition, a number of students had to complete other course work requirements, depending on where they were in their individual academic schedules and the home university's timetable. This created additional pressures and stress for some students, which had a potentially negative impact on their overall learning experience.

Several students have argued that they should have been exempted from some of the home assignments that applied to all students given the additional work and skills they were required to acquire to successfully complete an international placement. Still others suggested that there should have been more consistency in terms of the expectations regarding the requirements for students' recording of their experiences. Future exchange programmes will benefit from some discussion and dialogue about the tensions presented here.

Practicalities

Although the academic challenges contained tensions, many of the students found the practicalities of living and studying overseas even more stressful. Academic staff doing the selection and recruitment of students for scarce placements abroad, realised, for example, that many students who were interested in participating in the Project could not do so because of either financial or domestic responsibilities at home. Those caring for young children or ageing relatives could not easily go overseas for an extended period of time. Likewise, those with limited access to financial resources could not fund such a venture.

The overall Project Co-ordinator tried to address the financial issue with the funding body, but to no avail. This resulted in the disadvantaging of some eligible students who, through no fault of their own, missed the opportunity to participate in the international exchange programme. Consequently, the majority of the exchange students carried a single status without responsibility for anyone but themselves.

Those who did go overseas had to contend with other practicalities of living abroad, such as finding affordable and safe accommodation, managing different transportation systems, dealing with immigration issues, surviving unexpected expenses, having enough money for the duration of their stay, and being separated from family and friends. For a number of students, these issues consumed much of their energy when they would have preferred to be getting on with their placement. In some instances, accommodation at the local university did not materialise and alternate arrangements had to be made on-site fairly quickly.

Students were advised to arrive a week before their placement was to begin, to deal with the unexpected practicalities. However, time and/or money made this impossible for most students. Project partners in the receiving university usually helped students deal with these and similar time consuming practicalities, despite their other workload demands. This raises the contentious issue of institutional support and workload credit for academic staff members who participate in international exchange projects. The view that overseas ventures are voluntary activities undertaken by staff without institutional commitment or support is prevalent in academia. The failure of the EU-Canada funders to support infrastructure costs did not alleviate this problem for this Project. Colleague's goodwill can only go so far in making up the shortfall.

A number of Project participants found that though promised, such support was slow in coming forward. This also created sources of tension for those who were unable to explain or do much about such difficulties. Despite the structural shortcomings we encountered, goodwill and extra effort on the part of those formally responsible for students – other students, academic staff and practitioners, meant that in most cases these obstacles were eventually overcome.

Structure of the Book

A key objective of those writing this book is to assist those intending to embark on international student exchange ventures plan their journey and deal with key opportunities and difficulties that they are likely to encounter. This manuscript will take the readers on a journey of reflection and vicarious experiences, thereby enabling them to appreciate the pleasures and pain of living and studying overseas. Through the text, we seek to provide access to the experiences and voices of the different participants in international student exchanges involving work placements abroad.

Key to increasing our understanding of the processes encountered are the stories that are told by the students, practitioners and academics who recount what they did, the things they learnt and how they did so. Thus, we have not attempted to speak for the students, practitioners or academics involved in this Project. By the same token, they do not speak for us. The views expressed in each individual contribution represent the opinions and experiences of the particular author(s) concerned.

We have divided the book into three parts to give primacy of voice to each of the main groups involved in the exchanges: the students, the practitioners and the academics. Consequently, Part One focuses primarily on the students' experiences and what they have to say about the personal growth and professional development that occurred in and through these exchanges. These students volunteered to have their stories go into print when we asked for contributors. Central to their tales are explorations about themselves as individuals as well as the language, cultures and traditions of the other country that they had to integrate into their lives. Their stories enable the reader to make comparisons between their varied experiences – trials, tribulations and elations.

Part Two highlights the practitioners' views, particularly those in the field who have had responsibility for practice placements. Social workers play key roles in teaching students about social work practice in their locale, and in helping students meet their needs as human beings – their transport and accommodation difficulties, finding networks of support, responding to their loneliness and so on. And, they are often called upon to support students completing academic work for the home university.

Part Three has the academics talking about their work with students and practitioners who were both sent overseas and received in their own programmes of study. Also covered are their responsibilities with regards to the administration of international exchange projects and the key task of sustaining these projects and their participants over time.

We leave it to you the reader to choose those elements that are most helpful in your preparations for going to another country to learn about and do social work. Although the book concentrates primarily on the experiences of social work students, practitioners and academics on specific projects in specific locations, we think that what they have to say will resonate with others taking a path into what might be for them, unfamiliar territory. We think that it will also assist in highlighting areas of interest and concern that will require planning prior to going abroad, regardless of the discipline that is being studied.

Conclusion

Participation in an international project such as the European Union–Canada Project and the others described in this book provide exciting and rewarding opportunities for practice. However, international exchanges should not be entered into lightly, nor should those involved assume that they will not have to work hard to ensure their success and avoid falling into the trap of opportunism. But we think the journey will be worth it.

2 Internationalising Social Work: Introducing Issues of Relevance

LENA DOMINELLI

Introduction

Social work has tended to be a locality specific discipline that has focused on geographically bounded legislation, political configurations, economic frameworks, culture and norms (Dominelli, 2000). Its local specificity has given social work a rich diversity of forms throughout the world (Garber, 2000). At the same time, social work educators and practitioners have felt a need to internationalise their local curricula and practices, desiring to learn from other people's experiences and the knowledge acquired in other places. Hence, a number of social work educators and practitioners set about establishing organisations that would facilitate their engagement with the international domain (Kendall, 1998).

Through their endeavours, bodies such as the International Association of Schools of Social Work (IASSW), the International Federation of Social Workers (IFSW), and the International Council for Social Welfare (ICSW) were established in Paris, France in 1928 to facilitate these exchanges of information and enable people to visit one another's countries to discuss matters of mutual concern (Kendall, 2000). A range of activities facilitated the exchange of materials and contributed towards their ambition of internationalising social work.

These international encounters included the holding of international congresses, conferences and seminars international seminars, conferences and congresses for people to meet to consider particular topics on a regular basis. These produced new understandings of what constituted social work, innovations in curriculum materials, and the publication of books and journals alongside the formation of formal structures through which to influence policymakers at the national and international levels. The networks created through the endeavours of IASSW, IFSW and ICSW have remained active in the intervening period, and today, these three organisations play key roles in advising governments and international bodies such as the United Nations and its associated agencies.

In this chapter, I examine international social work, with an eye to how it has been defined and how it might be fostered through international exchanges.

International Social Work: The Interplay between Local and Global Tensions in Education and Practice

The tension between the local and the global continues to shape developments in social work theory and practice. The growing importance of the subject matter of this book is reflected in the push towards the inclusion of an international component in educational developments within specific nation states and regional blocs. An increasing number of educators and practitioners are becoming interested in international matters, as is evidenced by the growing attendances at international conferences, and in the demand for international issues to be considered in local curricula. For example, in England, growing integration within the European Union (EU) prompted the then Central Council for Education and Training (CCETSW) to foster seminars and the creation of curriculum materials on European Social Work during the 1980s and 1990s.

The European Union has begun to promote the recognition of professional qualifications acquired in one European country in another by issuing directives aimed at governing the conditions under which this would occur. These have included criteria that could lead to the harmonisation of professional qualifications. The latest initiative on this front, the Bologna Declaration envisages a common model of and infrastructure for education at tertiary level within Europe.

Additionally, the EU has set up mechanisms to facilitate discussion of such developments and funded student and academic staff exchanges that would hasten their evolution. As a result, the European Credit Transfer System (ECATS) has been put in place, and student exchanges in tertiary level education within Western Europe have been ongoing for some time through schemes such as ERASMUS and subsequently, SOCRATES.

Other programmes such as TEMPUS and PHARE have nurtured academic relationships between Eastern and Western European scholars. Schemes such as LEONARDO encourage the formation of partnerships involving universities, business, non-governmental organisations (NGOs) and representation from civil society in the formation of curricula for occupations with a vocational orientation. Furthermore, the European Union has developed two programmes that link students in Europe with those across the Atlantic – one addressing Canadian institutions of higher learning, the other American and Mexican universities.

More recently, the Council of Europe has started to show a renewed interest in the subject of harmonising qualifications in social work. It is exploring the possibility of a European-wide accreditation agency involving bodies such as the European Association of Schools of Social Work (EASSW). Regional developments of this nature have much to commend them, e.g., facilitating cross-border comparisons of qualifications obtained in a specific country for practice in another.

However, when used to prescribe developments in educational theories and practice, and in work undertaken with clients in the field, they carry the dangers of homogenising courses and reducing the richness and variety with which practitioners respond to local problems in their own unique ways, and must be guarded against.

Practitioners and educators in industrialising countries, particularly those living in countries that have had a colonial past have begun to challenge the imposition of Western hegemonic models of social work in their localities and create their own 'indigenous' models that are more suited to the needs of the people they work with. In this, their major focus has been that of *localising* social work to produce a locality specific variant which rejects hegemonic elements inherent in Western models of social work that have obliterated the local as they crossed borders to impose a common model of practice globally. The development of Family Group Conferences (FGCs) by the Maori peoples of New Zealand (Tait-Rolleston and Pehi-Barlow, 2001) is an extremely successful example of a locality specific development that has spread world-wide.

FGCs have been replicated in a range of countries, including England, Sweden and Canada.

I question the use of the term 'indigenous' to describe these innovations to social work theory and practice. I do so because the term 'indigenous' is a contested one. To begin with, it carries colonialist nuances linked to relations of domination that privilege the 'non-indigenous group(s). Secondly, it raises the issue of meaning: Which population group is encompassed by the concept, 'indigenous' people? The lengthy and complex history of human migration and the undocumented nature of much of it, make the determination of the 'original' inhabitants of any geographic locale an arbitrary matter.

Additionally, thinking in terms of 'indigenous' people in the context of human migration begs the question of how long do a people have to live in an area to be considered to belong to the geographic area in which they live. Will one generation, two, ten, or more be needed? I prefer to refer to these developments as the creation of locality-specific models.

This seems to me to transcend the exclusionary elements inherent in the term 'indigenous' and argue for forms of inclusionary social work that involve negotiations amongst all the people who live in a particular locality to arrive at models of practice that work for them and adhere to their specific needs and concerns.

At the same time, social work educators and practitioners engaged in internationalising social work must not lose sight of the central message of those wishing to 'indigenise' social work. That is, their widespread critique of the opportunistic and neo-colonialist practices of Western academics and practitioners that have prompted the exploitation of difference to establish hegemony for a dominant form of social work that disparages diversity and prospers at the expense of those it encounters.

Enforced homogeneity can also endanger local practices and traditions in favour of 'high tech' alternatives which may not necessarily meet the needs of local people, but which are more convenient for bureaucrats and managers who wish to monitor and control practitioner performance and their use of scarce welfare resources.

This technocratisation of social work constitutes part of the 'new managerialism' that accompanies the penetration of global market forces on the provision of social services (Dominelli and Hoogvelt, 1996, 1996a). In promoting the technocratisation of social work (Dominelli and

Hoogvelt, 1996a), globalisation promotes the values of efficiency, calculability, predictability and control through technological means (Ritzer, 2000). This development counters the values of relational social work, imposes homogeneity on different structures and practices, and reifies and commodifies welfare relationships and service provision (Dominelli, 2002, 2002a).

Another problematic element of the 'new managerialism' revolves around the imperatives of neo-liberal ideology. This constituent feature of the new globalising economy aims to subordinate human needs and intellectual development to market forces. These affirm the reduction of complex tasks to tick box and checklists that ignore process considerations and relational dimensions of social work interventions to stymie creativity and anti-oppressive practice (Dominelli, 1996).

Encompassed by the 'new managerialism' (Clarke and Newman, 1997), these approaches endorse corporate priorities and deeply implicate the state and its operatives in the spread of market-led social services provisions that are compatible with globalisation and its attempts to extract profits from welfare services and those who use them (Dominelli, 2002, 2002a, forthcoming) rather than promote facilities that respond to human needs.

In some country specific developments, internationalisation has been promoted beyond the curriculum and the concern of a few individuals interested in it. In the United Kingdom, for example, the issue has gained prominence in contemporary research evaluations. For example, the top rating in research in its nationwide Research Assessment Exercise (RAE) for all academic disciplines is only accorded to those whose research has had an international impact. In other countries, the equivalent dynamic has been more direct. For instance, in the United States, the Council for Social Work Education (CSWE) has recently adopted a policy requiring accredited social work programmes to include an international dimension in their teaching.

The demand for international placements and other forms of study abroad is, therefore, likely to increase significantly in the foreseeable future. These exchanges are likely to occur amongst industrialised countries, amongst industrialising countries, and between industrialised countries and industrialising ones such as India and Zimbabwe alongside those in the English-speaking westernised world.

Adding to the trend towards internationalisation is the impact of globalisation on population movements. Globalisation is increasing the need for labour mobility and, therefore, has implications for social work education and training. Students may find that they study and qualify in one country, but take up employment in another. In this context, it is advantageous if students experience study in countries other than their own. Globalisation has also contributed to the shrinking of national borders and to making people aware that what happens in other countries can have a substantial impact on their own (Dominelli and Hoogvelt, 1996, 1996a).

Social workers may have to respond to the aftermath of violent conflicts in other countries. This has happened with regards to Bosnia, for example, where social workers have been called upon to provide a relevant service to refugees and asylum seekers from that country in their own. Responses to the movement of people across borders can be enhanced by the broadening of horizons that occurs when students have themselves gone to live in a different country. These students can utilise the experience of being an outsider in a context where others are different from them to facilitate their capacity to empathise with the obstacles that have to be surmounted by those facing challenging situations when away from their home base.

International experiences often challenge students to grow personally and professionally when their taken-for-granted assumptions about daily life and their professional behaviours undergo scrutiny because they are in unfamiliar circumstances. Additionally, working in another country enables students to examine their commitments to other people in an internationalising world and can encourage them to become less parochial in their thinking. This capacity is particularly important in a discipline like social work, which is bounded by its own national concerns and legislative remits. In this situation, their location can result in practitioners, who are embedded within their local context failing to respond to the diversities that can already be found within their midst at home.

Preparing students to undertake study abroad is, therefore, an important part of the new agenda for social work educators and practitioners. However, the urgency with which educational institutions are responding to this new set of demands is patchy and some countries are more involved in international exchanges than others.

Despite the knowledge that has been acquired about the organisation and management of overseas study experiences over the years since IASSW, IFSW and ICSW came into being, the literature on this topic is limited. Those wishing to learn from the experiences of others in organising and managing international exchanges have few options to draw upon.

There are several books which consider international student exchanges. *Academic Mobility in a Changing World* by Blumenthal et al. written in 1995 and *Open Doors* by T Davis written in 1998, essentially provide statistics on the number of international students studying in the USA. *International Educational Exchange* by Klineberg covers some of the areas addressed in the contributions to this book, but it does not examine the specific needs of social work students and was written in 1976, thus making it rather dated.

This identified gap in the literature is also replicated in the journals, where few articles explore the experiences of students on study programmes overseas. In the few journals that have covered international student exchanges, the experiences of social work students and the complexity of their needs in having to link theory and practice in their study alongside learning material abroad that will have applicability at home is rarely considered. Catering for these two elements is essential in a professional discipline embedded in day-to-day realities like social work because it has its legitimacy to practice rooted in national legislation, social policies, cultural norms, traditions and values.

The journal, *International Social Work*, which is jointly sponsored by the IASSW, IFSW and ICSW, has been committed to the development of social work in the international arena for some time and brings discussions and projects from different countries for consumption by a broader professional public. However, it too struggles with issues such as the dominance of the English language in published works in the profession and with theorising international developments. Additionally, each of these three organisations has other publications which seek to disseminate social work policy and practice world-wide. These too encounter similar difficulties in moving beyond the dominance of Western models of social work and the English language.

Moreover, the theorisation of international social work and its impact on international exchanges in linking the global and the local has not been given high priority and much of the existing 'international' work focuses on describing front-line projects in specific localities, leaving it to the reader to do the work of thinking about the significance of a particular project for theory and practice within their own country (Dominelli, 1998). Examples of this approach are varied, and many are influential. These include Brauns and Kramer (1989), Gilbert (1997) and Mayadas et al. (1997).

This limited approach to internationalising social work has short-changed the profession by hindering its capacity in terms of marking out its own terrain in global discourses on welfare practice. This is a matter of concern given the appropriation of social work activities by other professionals and the haemorrhaging of its ability to influence international developments in its domain as a profession committed to social justice and personal well-being.

There may be books in other languages covering the topics of retheorising social work within the global arena, but these are not easily accessible to English speakers. So, this book aims to contribute towards filling the gap that we have found and is, therefore, timely. A number of contributors have based their writings primarily on the experiences arising directly from their involvement in one of the programmes referred to above – the European Union–Canada Higher Education Exchange Programme for Co-operation in Higher Education and Training.

In these, they examine the processes involved in international student exchanges from the beginning of the process – the bringing together of a group of people interested in setting up international exchanges – to a student's successful completion of a programme of study. By sharing these experiences and the lessons learnt from them with the readers, individual authors hope that they will enable those embarking on such an enterprise to draw inspiration for their exercise and avoid making mistakes in areas that can be identified beforehand, even if we have had to resort to writing in English because we lack the funds to translate our words into other languages.

The *European Union-Canada Project*, as the *Child Abuse, Protection and Welfare Project* became affectionately known to convey its international flavour, covered a particular experience of organising and managing international exchanges for social work students involving six institutions in four different countries across a three-year period. Additionally, I have commissioned chapters from academics involved in other international exchanges so that readers may make comparisons between the different ones that are considered within the leaves of this text. The authors in this work have also used the wider existing literature to draw parallels with other experiences and 'generalise' from their own.

Moving Forward on Internationalising Social Work

I (Dominelli, 1998) have argued that the internationalisation of social problems needs to be problematised to take account of globalisation, our interdependent world, and the fact that human migration has meant that national borders have been permeable for some time, and that the 'international is here, not only out there'. In other words, the global is local and the local is global. These developments, I believe make the retheorisation of international social work a matter of urgent priority.

Fortunately for the discipline, recent publications have begun to lay the foundation for this retheorisation. For example, Karen Lyons (1999) and I (Dominelli, 1996, 1998, 1999, 2001) have begun this task by linking international social work and globalisation. Lynne Healy (2001) has articulated an interesting analysis in this respect and argued that international social work is about acknowledging the interdependence that exists in the work.

Lynne Healy (2001, p. 7) defines international social work as:

'international professional action and the capacity for international action by the social work profession and its members. International action has four dimensions: internationally related domestic practice and advocacy, professional exchange, international practice and international policy development and advocacy'.

Whilst I agree that these four components are important elements in international social work, I think they omit one essential ingredient: the penetration of the local by the global and vice-versa.

Taking my perspective further suggests that conceptualising the international in relation to the national, in a binary relationship to it is inadequate. The two have permeated each other to form the other in a much more complex relationship than is allowed for in a binary dyad. There is a dialogical relationship between them which means that the one develops through its interaction with the other, and in turn is implicated in forming the other. They are not inseparable.

Theorising this relationship is, for me, a major concern for internationalists in social work who seek to uphold diversity within a framework of social justice and human rights in an interdependent world. At the same time, identifying and not losing hold of commonalities is an essential dimension of this task. In other words, it has to celebrate diversity within a non-oppressive unity. Heterogeneity, not homogeneity, is central to this process and outcome.

If international social work is to eschew relations of domination and subordination between different countries and their approaches to social problems and not become part of the neo-colonialist agenda inherent in a homogenising globalised capitalist socio-economic system, its adherents have to ask a number of awkward questions at the local, national and international levels (Dominelli, 1992).

These range from questioning the legitimacy of a socio-economic system and political rulers that allow poverty to exist on a massive scale both within countries and between countries (Wichterich, 2000) to undermining structural inequalities that perpetuate the oppression of people on the basis of social divisions such as 'race', gender, class, age, disability, religion, culture and sexual orientation and preventing the ascendancy of market-led responses to people in need.

Additionally, the global reach of multinational companies that are changing social work practice in countries with different cultures and traditions has to be interrogated for relevance and sensitivity to human aspirations. The damage to human welfare and well-being that the homogenising bureaucratic exigencies and forms of service delivery that are promoted by corporate managers has to be exposed. These have to be subsequently supplanted with rights-based, needs-led forms of practice.

Movement in this direction is particularly important in preventing the exploitation of poor people by overseas-based companies. This is because these firms pay workers low wages for the caring work they do and perpetrate the casualisation of waged labour for people who have little other than their labour to sell when earning their living and providing for themselves and their dependants throughout their life course.

At the same time, this retheorisation has to take on board the fact that social work education and practice in the world is incredibly diverse (Garber, 2000). Different theories, models, methods, policies and practices will make coming together to retheorise its international focus a substantial challenge. However, the outlook is promising.

The IASSW and the IFSW have been working together to strengthen the voice of the profession in the international domain. As a result of their collaboration, they have agreed a common definition of social work for the first time in their respective histories. This definition can be found in full on the IASSW and IFSW websites. Its essential features are quoted below:

> 'The social work profession promotes social change, problem-solving in human relationships and the empowerment and liberation of people to enhance well-being. Utilising theories of human behaviour and social systems, social work(ers) intervene(s) at the points where people interact with their environments. Principles of human rights and social justice are fundamental to social work' (www.iassw.soton.ac.uk).

Achieving a joint definition has marked the beginning of further developments in the ongoing collaboration between these two organisations. These initiatives will have a significant impact on the development of social work as an international global profession. Work is currently being undertaken to formulate jointly agreed global qualifying standards, common ethics and values, and support for human rights. These initiatives are challenging both social work educators and practitioners to put into practise their values of respecting diversity within a unity that strengths the profession so that it can better serve the people who rely upon its services.

International exchanges at the level of educators, practitioners, and students can assist in retheorising their activities, including their role and purpose in a rapidly changing world. And, they can help develop new models and methods for practice. Its value comes in giving people space to think differently, that is, challenge their taken-for-granted assumptions by experiencing novel ways of thinking, doing and reflecting upon their work. At the same time, they should not fall into the trap of thinking that the international is 'out there' and only accessible when they cross borders into other countries.

The contributions to this book demonstrate the interdependence between the local and the global. They also highlight how individual academics, students and practitioners, have attempted to deal with the issues this raises, sometimes alone, sometimes in formal partnerships with others, but always with a commitment to realising the dream of engaging with others who are different from themselves and assisting them in realising their citizenship.

Conclusions

Internationalising social work is a challenge that faces social work educators, practitioners and students on the emotional, practical and intellectual levels. Not all those involved in the profession see becoming involved in international activities of addressing the implications of internationalising social work for theory, policy and practice as priorities. But the interdependent nature of the world makes it an imperative dimension of contemporary practice. Delivering services to the range of people who live in the same localities as those paying for them requires practitioners to understand the links between the local and the global within a social justice, human rights-oriented framework of practice. Social inclusion has to be worked for by challenging the structural inequalities that keep people in their place and promote hardship in a global context.

Social workers have a major role to play in creating a world that safeguards the well-being of all those living on this planet. This includes that of developing international forms of social work that respect diversity, celebrate unity within diversity and transform hegemonic models of social work to ensure that these do not suppress the creation of locality specific forms of social work theories and practice. At the same time, these models have to strengthen the profession at the global level.

PART I

BEING AN INTERNATIONAL STUDENT – OPPORTUNITIES AND LESSONS LEARNT

3 Learning about my Professional Self through an International Placement

MICHELLE HAMMOND

Introduction

An international placement can be a profound experience that provides considerable opportunities for learning about myself as both a person and as a practising professional. As part of the European Union-Canada Project, *Child Abuse Protection and Welfare*, I was fortunate enough to be chosen as one of the students from the Maritime School of Social Work from Dalhousie University in Canada to go and study at the University of Southampton in England.

During my time in Southampton, I completed the final field placement of my Bachelor of Social Work at a child welfare placement, and in so doing, fulfilled the final requirement for my degree. This experience has had a considerable impact upon my life and professional training.

One of the goals of the Project is to share information and ideas pertinent to child welfare among the six Canadian and European universities involved. With that goal in mind, I will highlight some of the most crucial contrasts and comparisons between child welfare in Nova Scotia and England and will provide an overview of my experience in this chapter.

Beginning Placement

On 8 January 1999, I left my family, friends and home for a new country; a new life; and what would in the end become the experience of a lifetime, both personally and educationally. The unfamiliarity with where I was going and uncertainty about what lay ahead of me was initially daunting and felt overwhelming. However, my anxieties were lessened somewhat because I was going to England with a fellow student. Sharing experiences with my classmate helped to quell some of my fears about the coming three months. Ultimately, I gained from my student colleague a considerable degree of support, encouragement and friendship. I feel fortunate to have been able to share this experience with her.

On 11 January 1999, after a weekend of familiarising myself with Southampton, the city which was to become my temporary new home, I began my placement with the Southampton Social Services Child Protection Enquiry Team. I walked into placement that Monday filled with the trepidation and nervousness that comes with beginning something new and unknown.

At home, worries about going somewhere new would have been reduced by being familiar with the place, at least. For there, I would have walked into a new placement with the benefit of some knowledge about the agency, their mandate and responsibilities, the policies and legislation which guides their work. Also, I would have had some knowledge of the people who worked there and the community in which they operated.

In Southampton, I felt I was without the benefit of such information, and this served to compound my anxieties about starting my placement. My qualms made me aware of the amount of learning I would need to do in order to successfully work with the Enquiry Team. But, they helped to prepare me to rise to this challenge.

My concerns about the transitions from one place of study to another lasted throughout the duration of my placement, but were especially acute during the first few days. However, these were made much easier by the staff of the Enquiry Team. I arrived at placement that first day to find a desk had been allocated to me, literature on child welfare policies and legislation in Southampton had been prepared for me and my name had been placed on the Team's sign-in boards. These efforts did not go unnoticed by me and went a long way in reducing my uneasiness and in making me feel accepted as a new member of the team.

The staff in the Enquiry Team were most welcoming and their enthusiasm about having two Canadian students was very evident. Their efforts to guide me, include me as a team member and provide me with learning opportunities not only facilitated my transition to the placement, but also my learning as a social work student. The Team's continuous guidance, support and willingness to play a role in my learning, particularly the efforts of my practice teacher Carmel Rutledge, will not soon be forgotten.

Looking back, they impacted greatly on my experience and played an influential role in making my period of study with them the memorable one that it was. I believe that their efforts embodied the true essence of international cooperation and education and made them principle players in the European Union-Canada Project.

The Child Protection Enquiry Team

The Enquiry Team of Southampton is comprised of 14 members: a team manager, two clerks, two senior practitioners (both social workers), one of whom was based out of Southampton General Hospital and nine front-line social workers. The Child Protection Enquiry Team is based at Oakhill House in an area of Southampton called Shirley, and is a city-wide team providing services to children and families throughout the catchment area of Southampton.

Having a city-wide remit contrasts with other Children and Families Services Teams, which provide services to separate geographical areas of the city. For example, one of three assessment teams each services the east, central and west areas of Southampton. Given such a wide jurisdiction, it is not surprising that the volume of referrals to the Enquiry Team is high and workloads of team members correspondingly large.

The mandate of the Enquiry Team is to co-ordinate all new child protection enquiries and joint investigations with police following the principles set out in Section 47 of the Children Act (1989). The Enquiry Team also implements services if needed and appropriate to the findings of the child protection investigation. However, child protection referrals concerning a child who already has an assigned social worker from another Children and Families Services Team, are dealt with by that practitioner and Team, with the Enquiry Team involved and consulted as necessary.

In this respect, the Child Protection Enquiry Team has a role comparable to Nova Scotia's Intake Social Workers. However, a crucial difference between Southampton's Enquiry Team and a Nova Scotian Intake Team relates to the amount of time practitioners spend in court. Intake workers in Nova Scotia are in court a fair amount of the time. Enquiry Team workers in Southampton attend court primarily to obtain Emergency Protection Orders. Otherwise, they are not involved in court proceedings. In their situation, cases requiring court attendances are quickly transferred from the Enquiry Team to the Child Protection Support Team, which is the team that undertakes all court work.

Child welfare work in Southampton is a comprehensive and inter-disciplinary endeavour. Workers from education welfare, teachers, schools, health visitors, school nurses, family centre workers, and police doctors all play a crucial and inter-locking role in promoting a child's welfare. They are involved in investigations, participate in conferences and formulate child protection plans together.

In order to gain an understanding of the roles of these professionals, I was encouraged by my practice teacher to seek contacts and meetings with professionals from the other disciplines. As a result, I spent days or half-days with the police, education welfare, a family centre, a health visitor, Women's Aid, other children and families services teams, SCAMP (a day project providing support and outreach to parents) and a hospital social worker. I quickly came to see how the roles of all professionals were interwoven and I gained a deep appreciation of the importance of working co-operatively and closely with all the professionals involved in a child's life.

Based on and committed to the approach of working in partnership with children and families, Southampton's Enquiry Team makes decisions as to whether cases will proceed to a Child Protection Conference after an investigation is completed. If a decision is made to proceed to a Child Protection Conference, Enquiry Team workers prepare and present the relevant cases at the Conference.

Child Protection Conferences are inter-disciplinary meetings involving education, welfare, police, health visitors, schools, doctors, the social worker, and the child and family concerned. These occasions are designed as a forum to share information about the case, solicit the child's (if old enough) and family's thoughts and feelings about the situation and in the end, decide whether the child's name will be placed on the Child Protection Register.

The Child Protection Register is a compilation of the names of children who have been or are deemed 'at risk of being harmed'. All children on the Register have child protection plans designed at the Child Protection Conference to ensure their individual safety, and Enquiry Team workers hold the responsibility of implementing, monitoring and ensuring that the plan is upheld. The Enquiry Team holds these cases until the first Child Protection Review Conference is held approximately three months later. At that time, if further action is necessary, the case is transferred to the appropriate team within Children and Families Services.

Thus, like Intake Teams in Nova Scotia, the Child Protection Enquiry Team is based on a reactive approach. The Enquiry Team workers stay involved only long enough to see that the child is safe and the situation is stabilised. Ideally, cases are held approximately four months, but in reality, this period of time can be extended accommodate the high caseloads of all social workers and subsequent delays in transferring the case.

During my placement I realised that child protection procedures in Southampton and Nova Scotia differ in many respects. But a significant feature that is common to both and that underpins the child welfare system in England and Nova Scotia is that of protecting the children concerned.

Guiding Legislation

Child protection workers in England work under the auspices of the Children Act (1989). More specifically, however, the work of the Child Protection Enquiry Team is informed and guided by Section 48 of the Children Act (1989). Section 47 of the British 1989 Children Act is similar to Section 22 of Nova Scotia's Children and Family Services Act (1990). Both prescribe the circumstances under which a child protection investigation can take place. Yet, while the primary basis of Section 47 and Section 22 are the same, in that the initiation of investigations is dependent upon harm that has or may potentially come to a child, a fundamental difference distinguishes the two sections.

Section 22 of Nova Scotia's Children and Family Services Act (1990) specifically delineates and defines 14 circumstances under which a child is in need of protective services, whereas Section 47 of the Children Act (1989) is more general, and therefore, more open to an individual practitioner's interpretation of the circumstances they investigate.

Nonetheless, British social workers can also avail themselves of specific guidance. In Southampton, *Protecting Our Children* (Hampshire Area Protection Committee, 1997–1998) outlines policy and procedural requirements that describe significant harm. It defines 'significant harm' as:

i   the impairment of physical or mental health

ii   the impairment of physical, intellectual, emotional, social or behavioural development; and

iii   ill treatment which includes sexual abuse and forms of ill treatment which are not physical (Hampshire Area Protection Committee, 1997–1998).

Despite this definition of significant harm, Section 47 seems to me to be more open to interpretation than Nova' Scotia's Section 22. As such, child protection investigations undertaken under Section 47 may be more influenced by a worker's approach, perhaps giving a practitioner more freedom to find, or alternatively, not find, a child in need of protective services. And although the purpose of this paper is not to debate the merits of one section over another, the difference between Section 47 and Section 22 highlights for me the debate between subjective and more objectively defined definitions of children in need of protection.

Family Group Conferencing

An innovative development in the British system of intervention in child protection issues is the Family Group Conference (FGC). Family Group Conferences are child-focused meetings, usually convened upon the referral of a social worker, which provide families with the opportunity to become involved in developing plans that address a particular child's welfare needs. Family Group Conferences originated with the Maori population in New Zealand. As decisions in their culture had traditionally been made through a family network, the Maori people had become increasingly concerned and dissatisfied with the excessive amount of state intervention in their children's lives when they came to the notice of non-Maori practitioners in the child protection system and the failure of these practitioners to take account of their cultural traditions.

To reverse the trend of large numbers of Maori children becoming subjects of official state interventions and to provide more culturally appropriate services for children in need, Family Group Conferencing was born and developed. While the use of Family Group Conferencing in New Zealand has become mandated through legislation, their use in England is represented on a smaller scale and voluntary.

Although not explicitly mentioned in Britain's Children Act (1989), Family Group Conferences are given brief attention in the policy and procedure manual, *Protecting Our Children* (Hampshire Area Protection Committee, 1997–1998), indicating that they are growing in prominence within the field of child welfare in Southampton.

A central objective of England's Children Act (1989) is the development of a different balance between the rights of the child, the responsibilities of the parents and the role of the state as represented by social workers. One of the means used in achieving the goal of reducing state power in these matters, is that of working in partnership with families and facilitating the increased involvement of families in decision-making processes that affect them (Lupton, et al., 1995). Family Group Conferences are a prime example of partnership between families and social workers, and for this reason, Family Group Conferencing is becoming an accepted and encouraged approach to child welfare practice in Southampton.

Family Group Conferences are organised and run by an independent co-ordinator. Once convened, three phases comprise the process followed within them. These are: a) information sharing by the social worker and identification of what services agencies are able to offer the family; b) decision-making and plan development with only the family present; and c) plan review with the social worker and the co-ordinator present.

Within the model, built-in protection measures ensure a child's safety. Although families have the responsibility to develop plans, the social worker involved maintains the final say as to whether a plan becomes implemented, with a plan being rejected or modified only if it places a child at risk. There is also a review conference to monitor the progress of the plan. While such measures may be seen as reducing a family's power in the process, the overall approach ultimately helps to guarantee a child's well-being, which is the overriding responsibility of child protection workers.

For me, the appeal of Family Group Conferencing is rooted in its methods of working. The principles which are paramount to the process and success of Family Group Conferencing – partnership, empowerment, openness, self-determination, the belief in and focus on a family's strengths and enabling a family to use their strengths, are of major appeal to me. Furthermore, a plan that is developed by a family ensures that the family's culture, 'race' and language are included within it. A further crucial consideration for me is how Family Group Conferencing aligns itself with collective processes of decision-making. And, it occurs to me how much we have to learn from Canadian First Nations people where decisions are also made collaboratively within their communities.

Despite the obvious benefits to families, fairly low referral rates to these in the UK suggest that workers are resisting moves favouring the utilisation of Family Group Conferencing. This may be attributable to the conflict between high caseloads and the time commitment required for Family Group Conferencing. It is also possible that workers are reluctant to yield their decision-making role and the powers that emanate from their professional position to families (Jackson and Nixon, 1999). Nevertheless, the knowledge I gained of Family Group Conferencing in Southampton has led me to the belief that it is a viable and successful model of practice and would be advantageous for use amongst clients within Nova Scotia's child welfare system.

Duty to Report

Unlike Nova Scotia, England does not have mandatory reporting laws. Rather, reporting and referrals are dependent upon the general public's and professional's knowledge that child abuse is wrong and warrants reporting to the police or child welfare authorities. Referral sources to the Child Protection Enquiry Team represent a diverse cross-section of individuals. These range from professionals involved with children and their families, to the general public and family members, perhaps indicating that knowledge of the illegality of child abuse is widespread.

A focus on the duty to report in Nova Scotia during my final presentation in Southampton generated a great deal of interest and seemed to raise the question of whether mandatory reporting laws are beneficial. The Child Protection Enquiry Team is currently overwhelmed with referrals, and those attending wondered whether the volume of referrals to the Enquiry Team would increase further if a duty to report were to be implemented. Additionally, we posed the question of whether there would be an increase in false reporting in Nova Scotia if the penalties for false reporting were abandoned. Discussion of such questions is beyond the scope of this chapter. However, the differences in reporting between England and Nova Scotia present matters worthy of debate.

Similarities between the Nova Scotian and British Child Welfare Systems

While there are numerous differences between the child welfare systems of England and Nova Scotia, some of which are obvious and others that are subtle, similarities between the two systems abound. What follows will be a brief discussion of some of the characteristics that Southampton and Nova Scotia share.

Although legislative provisions between England and Nova Scotia differ, in both instances the paramount consideration is the 'welfare of the child'. So, though the means and processes of protecting children may be influenced by differences in the wording of legislation, workers in England and Nova Scotia are guided by the common goal of protecting the welfare of children, ensuring their safety and providing them with a safe environment in which to develop. Similar to this point is the recognition in both pieces of legislation of the importance of a child's culture.

Like Nova Scotia, England considers culture and background when determining what is in the 'best interests of the child' and demonstrates this belief in practice by making efforts to place children in environments which will meet their needs culturally. However, Southampton also shares with Nova Scotia, a lack of culturally diverse foster and adoptive homes which ultimately results in children being placed with families who do not share their cultural background.

Clients in Southampton and Nova Scotia share some demographic features. An overwhelming number of clients are faced with issues of poverty, and a lack of quality affordable housing. In general, lone mothers are disproportionately represented in the child welfare system.

This trend was replicated in my own caseload. Of the five families I was involved with, four were headed by single parent mothers who struggled daily to meet the physical and emotional needs of their children. The problems they faced were not necessarily due to lack of ability, knowledge or motivation, but rather to structural barriers including low incomes that stood in their way.

For example, clients in Southampton who required services would often encounter waiting lists in most agencies for resources. Therefore, clients can be left being unable to receive the help they need at the time they need it most. This can compound the stress of their situation and intensify the gravity of their involvement with the child welfare system. This is not only frustrating for clients, but also for the workers who struggle to best support their clients in an environment of economic restraint and limited resources. Obtaining resources for clients can become a daily struggle for practitioners, which in the end, adds additional pressure to the ever-present stress of carrying and managing large caseloads.

When I left Nova Scotia, I was unsure of what would confront me in the field of child welfare in England. What I discovered was that the two had crucial denominators in common. Despite being separated by an ocean, clients and workers in Southampton and Nova Scotia face issues and challenges that are comparable. They both encounter similar structural barriers when seeking to establish the collective nature of their plight and engage in daily struggles to make their lives less harsh. Their similarities made me realise that the circumstances of social workers and clients require collective responses. Ultimately, for me, this realisation emphasised the global nature of the common issues facing us all and therefore, the need for global solutions.

My Personal Learning and Experiences

I was able to reflect fully on my experience in Southampton only after I had returned to Nova Scotia. From my reflections, I am aware that my time with the Child Protection Enquiry Team has provided me with diverse opportunities to learn and gain experience in the field of child welfare. Due to the nature of the Enquiry Team's work, I was not able to hold cases for which I was fully responsible from that Team. However, I was able to observe investigations and conferences, spend days on the duty desk taking referrals, and observe other team members perform their duties. These activities contributed to my developing a sound knowledge and understanding of the Enquiry Team's work across the breadth of its roles.

My practice teacher was extremely committed to my learning and recognised the importance of my having the opportunity to carry my own caseload. Towards this end, she actively sought out a diverse range of cases which I could hold and for which I could be held accountable through her. In the end, I worked with a cross-section of clients, from a male teenager, with whom I completed individual work, to direct work with a young child and work with several families in different circumstances around a range of problems.

I was also fortunate to have some of my cases come from other Children and Families Services Teams, namely the Assessment Team which is mandated to carry out preventative work and the Children with Disabilities Team which has specific responsibilities for working with children who have disabilities and their families. These sources enhanced the possibility of my working with issues other than child protection ones.

Working with the Assessment Team and the Children with Disabilities Team also enabled me to become familiar with their responsibilities and mandates. Through the Assessment Team, I saw directly the benefits of preventative child welfare work, and through the Children with Disabilities Team, I was able to discern the advantages that addressing and meeting the needs of a child with a disability can bring, not only to that child, but also to the family as a whole. Additionally, interventions based on this diverse caseload, provided me with an opportunity to put into practice the skills and knowledge I had previously gained as a social work student and also allowed me to further develop my skills as a social worker and acquire new ones.

I have returned from Southampton with a great deal of knowledge about the field of child welfare, both in Southampton and Nova Scotia. I have gained and shared ideas and knowledge with others, and fulfilled my own goals as a student. Professionally, this experience will have tremendous impact and influence on my future career, wherever it takes me. However, I have returned to Nova Scotia having learned about more than just child welfare. I have returned with the knowledge about myself.

Going to England to live and work was a challenge, one that I successfully met. As a result, I have come home with the knowledge that I am capable of so much more than I have ever given myself credit for in the past. I have returned home with a profound sense of self-confidence and accomplishment. This is perhaps my most valuable piece of learning and will serve me well in my future practice as a professional. Also, I will never forget the personal lessons and insights that I have acquired from participating in the EU-Canada Project.

4 Learning what I didn't know about Myself as a Person

ANNE LEBLANC

Introduction

Undertaking a placement overseas can provide unexpected learning opportunities. These are not only about how interventions are carried out in other countries, but include discovering new insights into the self. In this chapter, I reflect upon my personal learning experiences in Sweden and become aware of aspects of my beliefs and behaviour with regards to my interactions with others who are different from me that I had not been aware of previously.

I spent four months on placement in Sweden absorbing every bit of knowledge that I could. I have seen many things and learned a lot. I visited a number of social welfare agencies, read many articles, watched several videos about Swedish social welfare and attended a number of seminars. I have learned about Just Therapy, Brief Therapy, Solution-Focused Therapy, Network Therapy, Milieu Therapy and Family Group Conferencing. This paper will give a brief overview of the organisation of the Swedish Welfare State, then move on to a description of the Framnäs School and Therapy Centre.

I will then make some comparisons between Framnäs and Halifax's Youth LIVE. I will conclude the paper with a description of some of the miscellaneous and sometimes unexpected learning that occurred while I was in Sweden and describe some concepts that I think would be useful and applicable in Canada.

The Organisation of the Swedish Welfare State

The Swedish Ministry of Health and Social Affairs has four legislative Acts that govern social work: the Social Services Act, the Care of Young Persons Act, the Law of Special Services and the Care of Abusers Act. The Social Services Act was built upon the principles of respect for others and free will. Section 1 of the Act states that:

> 'Public social services shall, on a basis of democracy and solidarity, promote people's economic and social security, equality of living conditions and active participation in the life of the community. With due consideration for the responsibility of the individual for his own social situation and that of others, social services shall be aimed at liberating and developing the innate resources of individuals and groups. Activities shall be based on respect for people's self-determination and privacy. When measures affect children, the requirements of consideration for the best interests of the child shall be specially observed' (Act, 1997: 313; MHSA, 1998, p. 1).

I think that this is a strong statement with which to begin the Act. It demonstrates the responsibility of the state for its citizens while recognising their right to self-determination. But, as will be demonstrated later, the Act also at times contradicts itself with regards to the ideal of self-determination.

The legislation states that 'the municipality is ultimately responsible for ensuring that persons residing within its boundaries receive the support and assistance they need' (MHSA, 1998, p. 2). It ensures that municipalities provide financial assistance for those who need it, certain basic services such as daycare or drug rehabilitation programmes for the people of the community who may require these, and special services for certain groups such as persons with disabilities. The legislation does not specify the precise programmes that should exist.

These decisions are left to the individual *kommuns* (municipalities). All social welfare type services are the responsibility of the *kommuns* with the exception of anything related to medical care which is governed by *länstnings* (a form of county government that deals only with medical health services).

The elected officials of the *kommuns* chair the many committees that ensure the smooth running of the community. The other members of these committees are citizens appointed by the government. They delegate the everyday work to supervisors who in turn give direction to individual social workers working for the *kommun*.

Before making any comment on the legislation, I should state that my knowledge and understanding of this and the laws discussed below is limited. Therefore, my comments have to be taken with some degree of circumspection. I consider the language used in the four Acts I discuss here to be generally paternalistic and sexist. However, I have been able to access only their translations, and some of the more subtle uses of language could be lost in the process of translation.

In my mind, The Social Services Act seems very vague. It also grants a lot of power to professionals, and putting a lot of faith in the governments of the *kommuns*. Many residents of Stockholm commented to me that their *kommun* and the some of the ones in the vicinity had recently elected more conservative governments which promised to change existing welfare arrangements. Their rule has led to a notable decrease in funding for social programmes.

I wondered whether enacting a more specific law governing expenditure could prevent this from occurring when more rightwing municipal governments are elected. I think that the same problem holds for Canadian legislation that impacts on social programmes. The ongoing battle between the federal and provincial governments over the funding levels and minimum standards of services is also contributing to the erosion of Canadian social programmes.

I think Canadians need to create and maintain legislation, describing minimum standards and designating who provides specified funding, that eliminates the vagaries of ideologically-based interpretations of the services that should be made available to people in need.

In Sweden, the Care of Abusers Act provides legislation that centres on helping a person with addictions. It has overcome some of these vagaries. It states, among other things that a person with an addiction can be forced into treatment when:

1. seriously endangering his (sic) physical or mental health;
2. running an obvious risk of ruining his (sic) life, or
3. liable to inflict serious injury on himself (sic) or someone closely related to him (sic). (MHSA:1998, p. 56)

Critique of Act

This Act has some strong points, but others make me feel very uncomfortable. One of its strengths is that everyone who wants treatment has a right to treatment. In Sweden a person with an addiction can only be dismissed from their job if they refuse treatment. The employer must give the person time off for treatment and, may be required to finance this treatment. The statement authorising intervention when a person is in danger of ruining his or her life seems highly paternalistic to me.

I think that this provision contradicts Section 1 of the Social Services Act. How can one individual judge whether or not a person is in danger of ruining his or her life? On what basis can anyone be given the right to pass such judgments? Giving professionals the power to answer these questions in the affirmative without further accountability worries me.

The Law of Special Services ensures several rights for persons with disabilities. These include the right to: a care assistant for 24 hours a day; reside in her or his own residence; and a taxi service at a nominal charge. Parents of children with disabilities also have a right to respite care.

I think this legislation is excellent. It recognises the right to autonomy for persons with disabilities and the special provisions they may need to achieve it. I also endorse its provisions for parents with children with disabilities to have respite care because making these resources available recognises that these families are doing demanding work. It also acknowledges that the well-being of children is not only the responsibility of parents but one for society as a whole.

The legislation with the greatest relevance for those involved in the European Union-Canada *Child Abuse, Protection and Welfare Project*, is the Care of Young Persons Act. Sections 2 and 3 of this Act are the equivalent to Section 22 of the Nova Scotia Children and Family Services Act. However, the Swedish version is not nearly as elaborate as that of Nova Scotia. The Swedish Act states:

> *Section 2* A care order is to be made if, due to physical or mental abuse, exploitation, deficiencies of care or some other circumstance in the home, there is a palpable risk of the young person's health or development being impaired.

Section 3 A care order is also to be made if the young person exposes his health or development to a palpable risk of injury through the abuse of addictive substances, criminal activity or some other socially degrading behaviour.

A care order is also to be made if a young person sentenced to closed institutional care under Chapter 31 section 1 of the Penal Code, in connection with completion of the sentence, is not considered to be in manifest need of continued care so as not to run the risks referred to in paragraph one. (Act, 1998: 616; MHSA, 1998, p. 39–40)

The Swedish Act is not specific and, in my view, is more open to personal interpretation than that of Nova Scotia which clearly defines the circumstances under which a child should be removed from the home.

Sweden, like Nova Scotia, has two ways to remove a child from the family. There is the option of voluntary care, where parents and social workers agree that the removal of the child is in his or her best interest. In this case the approval of the municipal Social Welfare Committee is required in approving the choice of a particular foster family.

The other option is compulsory care. When the family and social worker cannot agree on the best course of action, the social worker must take the case to the municipal Social Welfare Committee and it is this body that decides whether or not the case should go to court where the matter will be decided. An investigation must be completed and a decision made within four months.

Unlike Nova Scotia where the child, if aged twelve or over, has a say in his or her placement, the Swedish child only has some say in the matter if he or she is aged 15 years or older. Everyone involved, including the child if his or her needs differ from those of the parent(s), has a right to a lawyer.

If a child is to be taken into care, it must be before his or her 19th birthday. If parents remain involved in the child's life, the child can remain in care until he or she is 18. If they are not, the child can choose to remain in care until the age of 21. This differs greatly from Nova Scotia's legislation where children cannot be taken into care after the age of 16.

A child can voluntarily remain in care in Nova Scotia beyond 18, if he or she is in school. In Sweden, young people are considered children until the age of 18. In Nova Scotia, this stage ends at 16 as far as the provision of services goes. I think that Swedish legislation is better in this regard. Most young people need extra support, at the very least, until the age of 18.

Framnäs School and Therapy Centre

Framnäs School and Therapy Centre is a place where 'at risk' children, aged 12 to 16 years, and their families go when the children have voluntarily left the regular school system or have been asked to leave. The families are referred by Social Services and Social Services pays for their education there. The reasons that bring the children to Framnäs are varied. Some of the children who are currently students there have committed crimes, some are using drugs, some have learning disabilities, and one has Aspberger's Syndrome.

The Centre has much to offer these families. The children who attend the school daily are surrounded by supportive adults. There are two classes, each of which holds eight children. There are two teachers and two school therapists in attendance at all times. The school therapists are educated in social work and family therapy. The school setting is used as a framework for Milieu Therapy. Every opportunity for learning and personal growth is utilised within it.

One example of this is the use of the Pedagogic Kitchen, where twice a week, on a rotating basis, two children prepare lunch for the other children and teachers. The children choose the dish themselves and, with the assistance of a school therapist, plan and prepare the meal. The children are learning so many wonderful and necessary skills while they create and have fun. They learn to plan, cook, and co-operate with each other. Also, they work on their maths skills when they double or triple a recipe or measure out ingredients. They also learn to accept praise when they prepare a great meal and they also learn to hear criticism when someone does not like it, and maybe they learn to be a little kinder the next time they do not care for a meal someone else has prepared for them.

Framnäs has a philosophy which has been developed over 25 years of working with children 'at risk'. It is one that believes that the Swedish social welfare system has taken the powers of parenting away from the parents of children who have become involved with the system. Framnäs wants to give that power back and it is refreshing to see this. They believe that 'working arm in arm' with parents is the appropriate way of proceeding with work that is done with their child(ren).

From the very first encounter between the parent and the Centre, the decision-making is left to the parents. The managing director meets with them and tells them about the Centre and the strong commitment it requires from the parents. The parent then decides whether the Centre is the right place for his or her child.

The parents are involved in all aspects of the interventions undertaken during their child's time at the Centre. For the first weeks that the child is in the school, a parent or family member must be there too. Even after the initial period, parents can be asked to be present if the child is experiencing a difficult period. They are expected to be available to their child whenever the child or the school calls.

One of the reasons behind this requirement of constant parental availability is the Framnäs philosophy that parents and families are the most important people in a child's life. They are the ones whose opinion children respect. The relationship between them will in all likelihood last a lifetime while the relationship with Framnäs is only short term. Rather than create an artificial bond with the child, Framnäs works to strengthen the one that already exists. Whenever a child is asked to do something it is demonstrated to be the parent's will; for example, a therapist would say 'your mother has said she wants you to do this'.

Another aspect of Framnäs philosophy that has made a strong impression on me is the phrase 'making a hen out of a feather'. No small thing is allowed to pass without being addressed. Every little argument is talked over and sorted out. This is part of the Milieu Therapy. The children are being taught constructive conflict and anger management as they go about their daily lives.

Framnäs has a solution-focused orientation. That is, it does not believe in pathologising the children but in helping them and their parents find and capitalise upon their strengths to solve individual problems that they encounter. Family counselling is available to the families who request it and family meetings with the child's team, usually involving a teacher, a family therapist and the child's main school therapist, are frequent so that everyone is aware of the child's progress. Meetings also take place with the child's social worker so that he or she is kept aware of the child's progress.

Framnäs and Youth LIVE

Being at Framnäs and seeing the work done there led me to wonder if similar programmes existed in Halifax. I had not heard of any except Youth LIVE which targets groups of young people aged 12 to 30 years of age. It differs greatly from Framnäs, but has similar goals in that it works to keep youths in school and helps them to become confident and feel good about themselves.

Youth LIVE is an initiative that draws support from the community-at-large, all three levels of government (municipal, provincial and federal) in Canada, and the business community. It offers job training, entrepreneurial ventures, leadership training and a variety of life-skills training. The emphasis is on youths taking part in their community. One of their major initiatives is a recycling programme driven and managed by the young people in the programme.

Like Framnäs, Youth LIVE offers an alternative education programme. But the two initiatives differ in a number of ways. The Youth LIVE programme, while it does offer support programmes for parents, does not necessarily have the parental involvement that Framnäs does. While Framnäs youth live at home, many of the young people in Youth LIVE groups reside in group homes or supervised apartments. Therefore, I believe that the success of the young people in the programme depends on their initiative and motivation as well as the relevance and quality of the curriculum offered.

Youth LIVE's educational programme attempts to be relevant to the needs of today's youths. It provides junior high school and accredited high school programmes as well as outdoor and wilderness training for about 100 youths deemed 'at risk' every year. It helps prepare them for adulthood by teaching them life skills, career preparation and exploration, on top of their academic training. The Framnäs programme provides alternative junior high classes and life skills training but is limited to fewer students who must be between the ages of twelve and sixteen. An exciting aspect of Youth LIVE is that its staff and programmes reflect the diversity of the Halifax community. There are a number of African Canadians and Aboriginal people on the staff and culturally relevant programmes have been developed for all students (Youth LIVE brochure, undated).

A key difference between the two is that Youth LIVE does not have the therapeutic focus that Framnäs has. Youth LIVE also has a much broader mandate than Framnäs and includes community involvement, career planning, and entrepreneurial programmes. In my view, both Youth LIVE and Framnäs do great work for the youths in their respective communities.

Learning Experiences

Some Unexpected Learning within Framnäs

What follows is a discussion of the unexpected learning experiences that I was able to engage with. Living and working in Sweden for a few months gave me a small glimpse of what it means to be an immigrant. I say a glimpse because a number of factors made my life a whole lot easier than the life of an unsupported immigrant who could anticipate living in another country for a lengthy period of time. These include:

- my having a place to go every day where I could interact with Swedish people
- the prevalence of English-speaking amongst most Swedish people
- my white skin
- my coming from a wealthy country that is in many ways similar to Sweden, particularly with regards to climate, culture and sense of societal responsibility for its members.

Additionally, I knew that I could and would return to my home country at the end of my placement. Nonetheless, despite the privileges identified above, everyday things that Swedish people could take-for-granted were new to me. Simple things like trying to buy groceries or getting a subway pass or ordering a meal in a restaurant are done differently in Sweden. For the first couple of months that I lived there, every day presented new challenges. It was fun facing these challenges but there were times when I wanted my old life back where everything made sense to me and I was always aware of what was going on around me.

I expect that being an immigrant in Sweden is similar to being one in Canada. Thus, this experience was important to my growth and development both as a social worker and personally. It has helped me to understand the difficulties that immigrants face when they enter an unknown country. And, it helped me understand that it is possible to assist immigrants in ways that make them feel more welcome and comfortable in their adopted country.

Much of this response centres upon positive everyday contact with people from the country in question. Such contact not only makes people feel included into a new culture but it also helps the immigrant become familiar with language, customs and the everyday workings of the new country. I found such contact essential, and I was very fortunate to become friends with some very special Swedish people who made a great effort to show me 'what Stockholm was all about'.

Another bit of unexpected learning came from my interaction with the teenagers at Framnäs. It was easy for me to relate to them as regular teenagers any from a western country, regardless of the specific challenges that they were facing. Their interests were similar to those of most of the teenagers that I know: music, parties, and friends. Their concerns are also similar: fitting in, sexuality and relationships, disagreements with parents.

Watching these children reminded me that most teenagers approach their lives with passion and drama. I think that anyone who wants to work effectively with teenagers needs to bear this insight in mind.

Many of the teenagers at Framnäs showed great concern for me and my situation there. They felt some sympathy toward me as an outsider who did not quite fit in. They wondered how I was getting along without knowing Swedish. Some had even taken it upon themselves to teach me a few Swedish words. Most of which, I regret to say, will not be very useful in polite company.

It was interesting to watch them try to figure out what I was all about and where I stood in their Framnäs world. They did not quite see me as a staff person because they knew I was a student there. But in the past they had seen other students there and recognised that they held some position of power and authority over them. They learned very quickly that because I did not speak their language, they had considerable power over me. And, they took advantage of that power. Sometimes they pretended not to understand me when I spoke to them. Some, as mentioned earlier, taught me naughty words while telling me that they meant something else. In many ways, I became a sort of game to them. I happily went along with it, enjoying their harmless antics. It was fascinating to watch them relate to me in their varied ways.

Other Learning Opportunities and Observations

My visits to other agencies and many conversations with Swedish people and fellow Canadian students brought up many concepts and nuggets of information that greatly interested me. Some of these I experienced in a positive way; others, I did not. Some of these will be discussed below.

During my placement, I had the opportunity to visit the union headquarters for professional social workers. The Swedish Social Workers Union was formed forty years ago and has a membership of about 40,000, which encompasses about 85 per cent of Swedish social workers. The Union is working very hard toward a few goals. These are better salaries, a better quality education at schools of social work and the creation of an official process of licensing.

The government has been slow to respond to all these issues. The Union has decided to take action itself and created its own procedures for licensing. In order to obtain the certificate that the Union provides, persons with a social work degree must work for three years following their studies and two people must write letters of support stating that the person has followed ethical norms in practice and demonstrated knowledge of the relevant legislation.

I think that it is noteworthy that social workers in Sweden face many of the same issues and questions as those in Canada when it comes to professional issues such as salaries and licensing. However, one thing that does not seem to be as big a topic of discussion with Swedish social workers is the issue of developing a code of ethics, even though Swedish social workers do not have a formal one.

I believe a code of ethics is essential for a group of professionals who want to be distinguished from others doing similar work. I think it is also necessary to promote a sense of unity and common goals, and a work ethics within the profession. It is also necessary for the protection of both clients and workers, when a worker's actions are questioned. It is also a useful guide to action when a worker encounters ethical dilemmas. When in doubt, a code of ethics can provide guidance as to which path to take. I am very grateful that as a future social worker in Canada, I have a code of ethics to guide me.

Another matter I that I noted and which I found hard to understand was the strong hold that psychodynamic theory still has within Swedish social work. Family therapists in Sweden must go through a specified number of hours of psychotherapy before they can become certified. The issue arose for me when I met several therapists. One of these was a woman who works with children who have suffered emotional trauma. Her practice was based on psychodynamic theory. At another agency I visited, one therapist talked about her clients' transference upon herself.

Among others, a major reason for my reservations about psychodynamic theory is that it is so individualised and tends to blame individuals for all of their problems. Thus, I do not personally find it a useful theory for social workers. Yet, all of those workers mentioned above use it and are social workers. This left me feeling somewhat confused about the issue.

Many Swedish social workers also use systems theory, as practitioners do at Framnäs, and make full use of the networks of individuals who use the services of social work agencies. The Crisis Unit at Botkyrka and the Network House at Älvsjö, agencies that are both part of the European Union-Canada Exchange Project, are fine examples of this in practice.

Another exciting example of the use of networks can be found in Kista, an area on the outskirts of Stockholm that is home primarily to immigrants. I visited the Child Protection Unit there and spoke with the supervisor. He described to me the use of Family Group Conferencing in decision-making in child protection cases. I found this so fascinating that I will describe its workings below.

The investigation process when a report comes in about a child from the Kista district is similar to that utilised in Nova Scotia. Beyond this point, the similarities end. In Kista, two social workers take the case to the supervisor who decides whether the outcome could be decided through a Family Group Conference (FGC). The social workers then describe the process to the family involved. If they agree to take part, the supervisor contacts an FGC co-ordinator who he or she feels would be suitable for the family.

There are twelve FGC co-ordinators in Kista. Half are of white Swedish descent; the others are from visible minority ethnic groups. They come from all walks of life and do all kinds of work. They are chosen by the community and have no affiliation to the social services office. The co-ordinators' responsibility is to co-ordinate the FGC.

A written agreement is drawn up between the co-ordinator, the family and the social services office. The agreement states that all of the signatories are concerned about the child. It also presents some open-ended questions that must be answered during the FGC. The questions are chosen through negotiation between the social workers and the family concerned. The 'family' can include members of the extended family.

A meeting takes place where the family and social workers decide who shall come to the FGC. These people can be family, friends, or professionals involved with the family. The co-ordinator then visits the proposed guests, explains the process and invites them to the meeting.

The actual meeting takes place in a neutral location. The first part is an information session. The professionals make their case, stating why they are worried about the child in question and give their reasons for calling the meeting. Everyone has a chance to speak, and then the professionals and the co-ordinator leave the room.

In the second part of the FGC meeting, the family, including the child that is being considered, and their (non-professional) support people meet. Their task at this point is to answer the questions agreed earlier. The co-ordinator and professionals remain in another room and are available for clarifying matters, informing people about potential resources and helping to resolve any major conflicts.

All the questions must be answered and those answers must be agreed upon by all people participating in part two of the meeting. For each solution offered, someone has to agree to take responsibility for seeing it through. An agreement must also be made as to what to do if the plan fails. Those involved must chose their next meeting time as well.

The final part of the meeting involves the return of the social workers who must agree to the solutions proposed as long as they do not endanger the child. If the solution involves unusually large sums of money, social workers will have to consult a supervisor and return with an answer.

The supervisor I spoke with told me that research has shown that families participating in FGC tend to draw upon their own resources and networks when creating solutions. They tend to place a child, who must leave his or her home, with a family member rather than in a foster home with strangers. In traditional child protection work, the social workers also tend to draw upon their own networks, but these are largely comprised of professionals. The research also shows that the success and failure rates of the proposed solutions from both FGC and traditional practices are about the same but family satisfaction is much higher with the use of FGC (Tommy, Kista CPU).

While I am aware that a model similar to this is often used in First Nations communities where family members and elders gather to make decisions about the 'best interest' of a child from their community, I would like to see this model used in all parts of Canada. It is a clear example of professionals relinquishing some of the power that they have over clients in child protection cases.

Also my work within child welfare in Sweden provided a couple of very interesting programmes and facilities for youth from which, I think Canadians could learn. One of these is the concept of a reception centre for youth. Every *Kommun* has one. Young people pay a small membership fee per year. The fee is waived if the child cannot afford to pay for it. At these centres they can talk to counsellors about the issues facing youths: relationships, sexuality, and other matters. These reception centres also offer education on reproductive health, and have a nurse on hand who can give medical check ups and dispense contraception. The youths are ensured confidentiality.

The other facility revolves around youths and drugs. It is called Maria Ungdom and is run jointly by Stockholm city and the *länstning*. It is a centre that counsels youths involved in drug abuse and their families. It believes in early intervention. If young people are found wandering the street under the influence of alcohol or some other drug, they are brought to Maria Ungdom where they can sleep it off. A counsellor stays with them through the night to counsel them and to ensure that no complications occur due to the drugs in the youth's body. Parents are called and counselling is offered to the family, which they can accept or reject.

Maria Ungdom also offers drug testing, long term detoxification and treatment for youths, and a family treatment unit. It believes in catching a potential drug problem before it gets too big. The majority of cases that the counsellors at Maria Ungdom engage with are young people who have just begun to experiment with alcohol or other drugs.

Another concept, not specifically related to child welfare, that I think would be useful in Canada is that of supervision. All social work agencies in Sweden bring in a supervisor, from outside the agency, for a few hours once a week or once every couple of weeks to consider issues arising from their work. The supervisor can be a social worker or a psychologist and is bound to the same rules of confidentiality as the agency workers.

The agency social workers describe ethical dilemmas or situations that are not progressing well. The supervisor may offer a fresh perspective and bring some new insight to the situation. The workers are not tied to any advice the supervisor gives and can pick and chose which ideas are helpful and which are not. I think that this practice could be useful in Canadian social work agencies. Sometimes it is possible to learn much from situations in which one is not closely involved.

Conclusion

This paper has provided a very small glimpse into the wealth of information and ideas to which I was exposed during my four months in Sweden. The experience is one for which I am very grateful. It has contributed greatly to my personal growth as well as to my development as a social worker. It has opened my mind to some new ideas that I hope will positively influence my practice in the field.

The experience has also caused me look at the Canadian system in a fresh light. I am now more able to see what is good within it having gained some knowledge of another similar system. The Swedish system like the Canadian one has both good points and bad and I think that people can learn something from each of them.

5 Not so Familiar: The Case of 'H'

MELANIE MYLES

Introduction

Experiential learning is often cited as one of the most effective methods of learning. Experience leads to an understanding that cannot be gained though simply reading or listening to others. My experience as an exchange student within the *EU-Canada Exchange Project* has proved to be rewarding both professionally and personally and I have gained new insights into the value of sharing information, ideas and experiences. Experience adds a whole new dimension to a subject and allows a student the opportunity to integrate information, thought, and feelings. In this chapter, I will reflect upon the exchange and what I have learned.

I was chosen along with another student to complete my field placement in Southampton, England. Southampton is located on the country's southern coast. It is a city dominated by an impressive harbour and has a long-standing seafaring heritage. Southampton is a large, sprawling city, with a population of about 200,000 plus those living in the extensive surrounding environs. The city itself is divided into numerous districts each of which has its own sense of community.

In this chapter, I reflect upon my experiences on a children and families placement, using the work I undertook with a particular client as its basis.

Working with Children in a Social Services Department

I was placed with the Child Protection Enquiry Team in Southampton. Southampton Social Services has three area offices, but only one office has a Child Protection Enquiry Team. The three regions of social services are East, West and Central. The Child Protection Enquiry Team is located in a part of the city known as Shirley. The Enquiry Team is responsible for all child protection referrals throughout the whole of Southampton. The Enquiry Team handles the initial investigation of a case before it is either closed, or moved to another team.

The Enquiry Team's responsibility for the co-ordination of all child protection enquiries is prescribed under section 47 of the Children Act (1989). The Children Act (1989) is a comprehensive piece of legislation that deals with all issues surrounding the care and protection of children. The Children Act (1989) is a piece of legislation that applies to the whole country. Section 47 of the Children's Act is comparable to section 22 of the Nova Scotia Children and Family Services Act (1991). Section 47 of the Children Act (1989, p 228) outlines the local authority's 'duty to investigate'. Where a local authority:

(a) is informed that a child which lives, or is found in their area
    (i)   is the subject of an emergency protection order; or
    (ii)   is in police protection; or
(b) has reasonable cause to suspect that a child who lives, or is found in their area is suffering, or is likely to suffer, significant harm.

In these circumstances:

'the authority shall make, or cause to be made, such enquiries as they consider necessary to enable them to decide whether they should take any action to safeguard or promote the child's welfare' (Children Act, 1989).

There was some discussion with the social workers from the Enquiry Team regarding the differences between the two pieces of legislation. They seemed to feel that the philosophy and the beliefs supported by the legislation were similar but commented on how Nova Scotia's Section 22 is much more explicit, whereas Section 47 in the UK leaves more room for individual professional interpretation. It was interesting to note that no one was sure which approach would prove to be more beneficial to clients.

The responsibility for incoming child protection referrals fell to those workers on the duty desk. The Enquiry Team operated a rotating duty system, where all team members took turns to spend scheduled days 'on duty'. Two workers were on duty each day, with two others acting as backup. The social workers on duty were responsible for managing all current and pending investigations as well as any new referrals or case developments. I had the opportunity during my placement to work on the duty desk under the supervision of an Enquiry Team social worker.

In the office where I worked, there was another team of social workers known as the Assessment Team. This team was often differentiated from the Enquiry Team by their mandate of working with 'children in need', as opposed to the Enquiry Team's mandate of working with 'children at risk'. In many cases, this Team often worked with adolescents and offered forms of intervention and preventative work with families and young people.

It did not appear to me that child protection practice in England was significantly different from that in Canada. During my final presentation, I shared some of the research generated by the EU-Canada Project on the critical issues facing Nova Scotian workers in child welfare (Gilroy, 1999, 2000). The child protection workers in Southampton really responded to the issues that were raised by the research and identified a number of these as being personally relevant to them in their own practice.

This experience served to illustrate many differences between the two countries, but it also was illustrative of the commonality of experience. The most significant difference identified was the legislation and social policies governing their work with children and families. Beyond this difference and a series of similarities occasioned by culture and region, the child protection workers on the Enquiry Team reported many of the same concerns as workers in Nova Scotia.

The structural barriers that individual clients and workers face in Nova Scotia are also evident in Southampton. The realities of high caseloads, shrinking resources, public pressure, and structural inequalities seemed to transcend the differences that existed between the two teams. Child protection work in England deals with the effects of poverty and child protection staff work primarily with women. People experience racism and other forms of oppression and social workers search to find ways of working in an anti-oppressive manner within a field that yields such startling power imbalances.

My placement with the Child Protection Enquiry Team was a diverse and rewarding experience. I had the opportunity to carry a small caseload and to engage in direct work with families. I completed assessments, engaged in supportive counselling, and completed life story work. I also had the opportunity to visit other agencies and professionals that work closely with child protection staff and provide services to children and families.

These visits to other professionals allowed me to appreciate the scope of services to children and families in Southampton. In many ways, the system seemed much more comprehensive than that prevailing in Nova Scotia. In Southampton, there is tremendous co-operation between all of the professionals involved in the lives of children such as school nurses, education welfare officers, health visitors and general practitioners.

Participating in a Child Protection Conference

The comprehensive nature of services to children and families was often most evident at child protection conferences. A child protection conference brings the family together with a range of child protection professionals. The conference is held within eight days of an allegation being reported to social services and is charged with deciding whether a child(ren)'s name(s) should be placed on the child protection register.

A senior manager from social services chairs the conference that is attended by the family and their support person(s), the social worker and representatives from health, education, probation and the police. In addition, other professionals who know the family, for example, family centre workers may also be asked to attend. I think it is important to note that despite my commending the presence of all these professionals, it could also be experienced as very overwhelming and intimidating for the family concerned.

As a student, I had the opportunity to attend meetings, interviews, and child protection conferences as an observer. I believe this gave me additional insights into what an overpowering experience that something such as a child protection conference can be. It was very frightening for me to enter a large room and see a table full of professionals before me and I thought, 'If I feel this way, how do the parents feel?' I also felt that it was wrong for me to be there as an observer. The family would always be asked if they minded my presence, but I believe that the imbalance of power between the family and the child protection staff would leave the family in a position where they might feel unable to say 'no'.

In many ways, feeling uncomfortable was a common experience for me in that I was always interested in taking advantage of opportunities to learn something new, but I was sometimes upset about what I was seeing and became critical of the impact of what I witnessed upon women and their families.

I carried four cases under supervision during my placement at the agency but also had the opportunity to work with other team members on their cases and to observe interviews, home visits and child protection conferences. Throughout my placement, my practice teacher and all of the other social workers were more than willing to involve me in their work and share advice and experiences.

Working with 'H'

One of the main cases that I worked on from the beginning of the placement was with a young woman whom I will call 'H'. 'H' was 16 years old when I first met with her. 'H' self-referred to the child protection enquiry team alleging physical abuse by her father. 'H' was already known to the child protection enquiry team because of her past involvement with a man who was soliciting young women into the sex industry.

'H' was afraid to return home. She feared further violence from her father if she was to return home and she had no other friends or family that she could live with. My work with 'H' consisted of securing safe accommodation, attempting to reconcile issues with her family, and helping her to obtain financial assistance. The issue of safety was further complicated by a pending court case against the man who solicited 'H' into prostitution and pornography. 'H's co-operation with the police had left her vulnerable to threats from the accused man and other young women.

The most significant issue that arose out of this case was 'H's age. As she was 16 years old, she was not considered a child. My practice teacher informed me that if I had not been on placement at the agency, 'H' would have simply been referred to a number of community youth agencies. In my role as a student social worker, I had the flexibility of a small caseload and therefore had time to devote to working with 'H'. 'H' may have been referred to the Assessment Team, but given the Team's circumstances and the large caseloads carried by its social workers, they are also likely to have referred her to other community agencies.

My practice with 'H' was also influenced by the belief that all work with children and families should be premised upon working in partnership with them. This concept is an explicitly stated element of the Children Act (1989). However, this aspect proved challenging at times, as 'H' wanted no contact with her family of origin. She agreed that I could keep in touch with her family, and I was able to do this through meetings and over the phone.

Given 'H's age and vulnerability, I had hoped that some sort of acceptable reconciliation could be made, if not with her whole family, at least with some of its members. 'H' accepted the fact that her parents were concerned for her well-being, but she was not ready for direct contact with any members of her family. By the time I finished working with her, 'H' was working towards re-establishing a relationship with her mother.

It is hard to imagine how my practice with 'H' could have been different if I were to be working with her in Canada. The issue of youth services is of growing concern in Nova Scotia as well. Often, it is a case of not having the resources to support the provisions of the relevant legislation. I know that it was partly my status as a student in the UK that allowed me to work as closely as I did with 'H'.

I also feel that many of the other challenges that I faced in my work with 'H' would also be relevant in Nova Scotia. In this context, it is difficult to imagine that my practice would have been significantly different. The challenge of finding suitable accommodation for 'H' would most likely have been replicated in Halifax given the lack of appropriate housing options for young people living in Nova Scotia. The cuts in social spending in Nova Scotia are also mirrored in Southampton and made accessing services challenging and waiting lists a reality.

Despite the differences of setting, legislation and country, my work with 'H' covered familiar territory. Although I was based in a statutory agency in the UK instead of a voluntary agency in Canada, I found I could transfer the knowledge and skills acquired elsewhere to the situation at hand. This increased my feelings of confidence while at the same time highlighting the many new things I had to learn.

Attempting this comparative analysis has highlighted for me what has been one of the biggest challenges of my participation in the *European Union-Canada Exchange Project*. It was frustrating to not always have the knowledge of my own system and what it was like to have actually worked in the child protection services in Nova Scotia. It was often the elements of daily practice that I found that social workers in the UK were interested in hearing about. Often, I did not have the answers. Upon reflection, I realise that it was unrealistic to expect that I would know everything about the system in Nova Scotia. But it was nonetheless, frustrating at times as I asked myself, 'Is this the same at home?'

The other challenge that I would identify is an experience that would have existed even if I had completed my field placement in Canada. This challenge was the reconciliation of my education with my practice. Throughout our social work training we are usually surrounded by other students who most often share our beliefs and are learning the same theories. Such an environment is almost 'safe' in a way, but it does not always reflect reality. It was interesting for me to work closely with so many social workers of diverse backgrounds and observe the realities of everyday practice.

Conclusions

The exchange with Southampton allowed me the opportunity to work abroad and experience so many new things. It was also an opportunity for me to practice social work in a different country over a significant period of time, something that I have not had the opportunity to do before. This placement challenged me to reconcile my education with the realities of social work practice and allowed me to develop a sense of my own personal approach to practice. I also have a greater sense of the wealth of information and experience that is to be found if we simply reach out to others and consistently seek to improve our own practice.

6 Supporting Families through Multi-Level Interventions

HELENA ALBERTSON

I have been fortunate to do my placement at Family Service of Support in Nova Scotia where I had my own caseload and the freedom to work with people with different kinds of family histories. This placement enabled me to work with families in voluntary agencies in Canada on a number of different levels and compare the forms of support on offer there with those provided in Sweden.

In the course of my reflections, what occurred to me was that all the families I was working with had some kind of abusive background. As I pondered their situations, the questions that stayed with me were many. How will I negotiate differences in agency philosophies and mandates? How are we dealing with child protection issues in Sweden compared to Canada? Is it possible to become a functional parent after having been abused as a child? How are we dealing with these issues differently in Sweden compared to Nova Scotia? I address some of these questions in this chapter as I reflect upon my learning experiences.

Background

I did my placement at the Family Service of Support (Family SOS). Regardless of whether I had been a Swedish or Canadian student, this was a very special agency to be placed at. The Family Service of Support Association was formed in 1974 because of concerns about child abuse and neglect in the Halifax and Dartmouth area of Nova Scotia. Family SOS is a non-profit organisation, the membership of which is open to any person or group that has an interest in the prevention of child abuse. Its work is based on the principle that parents can be supported in the difficult task of raising a child, and that by doing so the likelihood of the further abuse of children by their parents is reduced.

The staff who work at the Family SOS visit their clients in their homes. The focus of their activities is on teaching parents more appropriate methods of handling stress and anxiety, understanding the stages of a child's development, and gaining an appreciation of a range of ways that can be used to discipline a child.

The workers do not have the legal right to apprehend (or take into care) the children from their parents, even if they find the child's safety to be in danger. What they have to do if they have these kinds of concerns is to call the Children's Aid Society. The Children's Aid Society has the legal authority to take the child away from an unsafe environment.

The workers at the Family SOS often link parents to other community resources such as doctors, social workers, and public health nurses, psychiatrists and housing authorities. Through their contacts, a Family Preservation Worker is used to teach the parents how to advocate for themselves.

The caseload that I carried at Family SOS contained about 10 families that I had worked closely with. As a student from another country, I faced many challenges, including a struggle over the fact that I could no longer utilise my language as my strongest weapon.

The Challenge of Child Protection

It is hard to believe, but in the 1800s, protective services for children in Halifax were carried out by the Society for the Prevention of Cruelty to Animals. Since then, provincial governments in Canada have taken the primary legal responsibility for the protection of a child. The first comprehensive child welfare legislation was passed in Ontario in 1893.

Today in Canada, there are at least 12 child welfare systems, one for each province and territory. Within most provinces there are often several different organisations responsible for child welfare. Many of these are voluntary agencies such as Children's Aid Society in Halifax. However, the federal government is responsible for funding at least 50 per cent of child welfare services under the Canada Assistance Plan (1966).

In 1920, it was decided that a separate service should be established for children. Consequently, the Children's Aid Society was created in Halifax, with the main purpose of offering help to children considered to be neglected, abused or exploited. Child welfare provisions of this nature have been generally constituted as a 'poor people's social service system'. And in most Canadian provinces, Nova Scotia included, child welfare is regarded as a poor woman's social services system. A demographic feature that cannot be ignored is that the clients of child welfare agencies are poor and live in substandard housing in unsafe neighbourhoods. Many of these poor children grow into adults who feel neglected, unloved and worthless.

I did not become involved in any apprehension of a child (undertake care proceedings) during my time with Family SOS. I was fortunate to be welcomed as a social worker into the homes of the families' that I worked with. All of them considered me as offering help and support. However, I could not hide from some of the families the threat that they felt emanated from the Children's Aid Society. In my opinion, it was easier for me to be working from a private agency that had no direct powers of intervention, although I had the indirect power to apprehend a child combined with a responsibility to see that the children I worked with were living in a safe environment.

It is important to have a clear definition of what child protection really entails. When working at the Children's Aid Society, workers have to follow the structural authority emanating from the Child Welfare Act and regulations that require the Society to protect children's rights. This kind of authority should not be confused with legal authority because the court and its institutions alone can act juridically to enforce certain courses of action.

Nonetheless, for both the parents and the social workers, structural authority is real and not imaginary. Its presence is always there and cannot be underestimated. It can be used to tell neglectful and abusive parents that they must co-operate and work with the Children's Aid Society to improve childcare or else face the consequences that would include court action and the loss of their children.

Child welfare in Nova Scotia is the responsibility of the local municipal government, which decides how to organise its services, even though these are all subject to the same provincial legislation. Local authorities also have considerable freedom in choosing what services to provide. The result is a wide variation in provisions and ensuing practices between localities. In one city, families 'at risk' can be placed in an assessment centre during an investigation, in another, they are provided with different forms of social support during the process, and in a third they are simply summoned to the agency's office.

In Sweden, the first child welfare legislation was enacted in 1902. The child welfare legislation aimed to keep young people away from assumed future criminality. This Act was replaced in 1924, wherein the criteria leading to compulsory care was further extended to include small abused children. Sweden enacted a new Child and Young Persons Act in 1960. It added nothing new to the Child Welfare Act of 1924, but the emphasis changed. During this period, the field of child psychiatry grew in influence and held an arsenal of theories providing the dominant legitimation for taking children into public care.

The present child welfare legislation, The Social Services Act, was passed in 1980. According to this Act, when interventions concern children, primary consideration should be given to ensuring the 'best interests of the child'. Most placements in Sweden have this form of social support. The criteria for care without consent (involuntary care) mark the threshold for traditional child protection. The practitioner's weapon can be phrased as, 'If you agree to our proposals, you will get social support, if not, we will take coercive action'.

Child Welfare and Residential Services in Canada, Nova Scotia and Sweden

Family SOS has a Foster Care Programme that provides children with an alternative home setting on a temporary or long-term basis. The programme provides a safe home for children when biological parents are unable to provide this care. The programme recognises and addresses the cultural, racial, and linguistic heritage needs of children.

A foster home in Nova Scotia is defined as an approved family home in which a child is placed for care, supervision, and other services he or she may require. Foster parents are to provide temporary parental care for the child in an environment where the child can grow mentally, physically, emotionally, and socially, until he or she returns to the parents of birth, is adopted or remains in planned, long-term foster care.

Swedish children have been placed in foster homes ever since the 18th century. Foster care is, by law and tradition, preferred to residential care. Adoption, without the parents' consent and measures taken to 'free children for adoption' no longer occur in Sweden today.

In Nova Scotia there were 179 adoptions in 1995–1996. Of these, 73 were agency adoptions, 90 private relative adoptions, and 16 private non-relative adoptions. The primary focus of adoption services in Nova Scotia is the placement of children with special needs. Swedish child welfare workers do not promote the adoption of children in long-term foster care, even when birth parents suggest this as a course of action.

The social workers in Nova Scotia assume that infants and children in long-term foster care should be put out for adoption. The legislation promotes this view as well. For example, a young, poor, and homeless single mother who uses crack for her weekend parties will have a hard time getting her baby back once it has been put into a substitute family. The young woman will have a 12-month period to make the home environment safe and show that she is capable of taking care of her child. If she fails, the Children's Aid Society will apprehend her child and put it up for adoption.

The mother has the option of placing her child with relatives, who also have to show that they will be good parents before the authorities will place the child with them or let them adopt. But if the mother decides to go to court and fight for her child and loses, the Children's Aid will get custody of her child and will make sure that the child is adopted. As a mother she will have no idea where her child is placed, as until 1997, adoptions were 'closed' adoptions, i.e., adopted children were not given information about their birth parents, nor were birth mothers provided with details as to the whereabouts of their children.

Family SOS has maintained a voluntary adoption registry whereby adopted children as adults, adoptive parents, and birthparents can register if they want to receive information regarding the adoption. During the year of my placement, 598 inquiries were received and 80 reunions were facilitated.

Policy and legislation concerning adoption is currently being reviewed following the implementation of the Adoption Information Act that came into effect 1 January 1997. As a result, all the adoptions approved in Nova Scotia are no longer closed; and the children in open adoptions have the possibility of maintaining contact with their birthparents, even though they have been adopted outside the family network.

Definition of Child Abuse and Neglect in Canada, Nova Scotia and Sweden

The issue of what constitutes child abuse and neglect is also a contentious one. In Sweden even minor physical punishment may be sufficient reason for making a court order. To use 'spanking' as a method of parenting has been unlawful in Sweden since 1979. Sweden was the first country to have this law against all types of physical punishment, but today one can find similar laws in five other countries: Norway, Denmark, Finland, Austria and Cyprus.

According to Canadian legislation, in Nova Scotia, physical abuse is a deliberate non-accidental physical assault on a child that results in physical harm. Physical abuse can also result from excessive inappropriate discipline. Nevertheless, parents still have a right to 'spank' their children as long as no marks are left on the child. During my stay in Canada there was a considerable debate about the 'spanking' issue in the media. Many people are in favour of making spanking – including 'just spank him or her on the bum', illegal. At the agency, 'Family SOS', the policy was totally against all 'spanking' as a parenting method.

Abuse can also be emotional or psychological. Emotional abuse is difficult to define and identify in any society. According to Swedish law, mental abuse is defined as subjecting the child 'to psychological suffering through systematically degrading behaviour, terror or deprecation'. Examples of psychological abuse include disparaging comments such as repeatedly telling a child that he or she is stupid, clumsy or worthless. If a child is told often enough that he or she is no good, he or she may come to believe it and act accordingly.

The Children and Family Services Act, Nova Scotia, states that a child is in need of protective services:

> 'where the child has suffered emotional harm demonstrated by severe anxiety, depression, withdrawal, self-destructive or aggressive behaviour, and the child's parent or guardian does not provide, or refuses or is unavailable to consent to the treatment'.

Child neglect, according to the Children and Family Services Act, Nova Scotia is a chronic and serious omission by the parent or guardian resulting in physical harm to the child. It does not include emotional harm. The neglect must have already caused the harm and cannot be presumed to cause physical harm in the future.

Sexual abuse in both Canada and Sweden is a generic term used to describe a range of sexual behaviours perpetuated by an older person towards a child (under 16 years in Nova Scotia and under 15 years in Sweden). An older person is generally defined as someone five years older than the victim. The abuse can occur inside or outside the family. According to the statistics that I have come across most of the cases of sexual abuse are perpetrated by someone that the victim knows, thus complicating the situation.

Case Study

Working with Amanda

I met several families that had experienced sexual abuse during the course of my work. I will describe a case where I was in no doubt that the abuse had had a bad effect on the family. I became involved in working with the family because my colleague was on sick leave and I took over her caseload during her leave period. In examining this case, I describe how difficult it is to be a parent and bring up children, when you can't really trust the authorities to be on your side.

The mother, Amanda (fictitious name), is 21 years old and had been sexually abused during her childhood while living in a foster home. Today, she lives with her boyfriend, who I will call Tony, the father of her two children, Jon 18 months and Sara 7 months. Amanda had gone through a difficult period when I met her for the first time. She had been involved with Family SOS for over a year. The family was living in a neighbourhood where the government pays most of the rent. Those living in the buildings that belong to the government pay a percentage of the rent from their income.

When I visited, I found the environment somewhat charming. The houses were located on a hill and were painted in different colours. Amanda and Tony's house also had a small back yard. The house was not very big and did not have much furniture, but it was clean and the children had a lot of toys to play with.

Amanda said by way of explanation, 'I did not have any toys when I was a kid, so I make sure my children will have a lot'. Amanda did not talk much at my first visit in their home, and it was really hard for me to get an idea of what was going on in her mind. When Tony came home, she did open up a little bit and all three of us started to talk.

Family SOS was not the only agency involved with this particular family. Children's Aid and a psychologist were also involved. Tony and Amanda told me that Children's Aid had taken their son Jon into foster-care 15 months earlier. They never understood why. They are presently fighting to regain custody of their son. The family had been getting a lot of support from the various agencies working with them and they said that for the moment, they were allowed to keep Jon from Monday to Friday.

In my opinion, Amanda had a hard time expressing her feelings. We never talked directly about the fact that her foster parent had sexually abused her as a child. But we did talk about her fear of losing Jon and that she had a hard time dealing with all the professionals that were involved in their life. Amanda said, 'I have such a difficulty trusting them, sometimes it feels like they are all against us'.

Amanda was going every second week to see a psychologist. I do not think that Amanda really thought that it helped her, but the psychologist thought that she was making progress and cut down her sessions accordingly.

Attending a Case Conference

Children's Aid called for a case conference. The agenda for the case conference was to see if the young parents, Tony and Amanda, were ready to get their son back. I must say that I was a bit worried about attending this case conference; as I had only met the family together for three occasions before the conference. In my opinion, the family was ready to take care of their first born child. Of course they were young and poor and had a baby girl to take care of as well, but I felt strongly that it would do more harm then good to let Jon stay in foster care. I expected the family as a whole to get support in their home.

At the case conference all the professionals gathered together – the Children's Aid workers, the psychologist, Amanda's and Tony's lawyer, the foster-family who took care of Jon, and the social worker. Not all of them were of the same opinion as I that the best thing for Jon would be to stay with his biological parents. But the case conference was interesting for me to attend.

Everyone in the room was asked what they thought about the parents and the agenda item. Amanda felt very attacked when they started to have opinions about the way she raised her children. They all agreed that she needed more help to be a better parent and that she should attend a course called 'nobody is perfect'.

Amanda thought that was a good idea, but she found it scary because she did not feel comfortable meeting new people. Some of the people in the room thought that she was unwilling to do what was necessary to get her son back and that she had a bad attitude.

I felt uncomfortable at times during the meeting and I felt constrained in expressing my opinion, but I did so anyway. I argued that it was important not only for Jon to get back home but also for his sister who was old enough to miss her brother when he was gone. I also did not approve of the idea of moving Jon back and forward.

Amanda and Tony got their son back home before I returned to Sweden. They still receive considerable support from Children's Aid and Family SOS. The foster parents also promised that they would call any time Amanda and Tony needed help with Jon. In light of this I think that the family will make a good future for themselves and their children. Amanda will hopefully be able to trust her feelings again, and be able to express them. However, it is difficult to be unaffected by one's childhood experience and the abuse she had been through will remain be an issue while she is raising her children.

I liked the idea of a case conference and it reminds me a bit of a Swedish network meeting. But I still think that it would have been easier for the parents if they had been able to bring a friend or another support person along. I found that the family was sometimes stuck in a corner with the professionals judging them.

Conclusions

I think it is very important to discuss child welfare and compare different child welfare systems. In my opinion, it is interesting to look critically not only at another country's welfare systems, but also at one's own.

During my stay in Nova Scotia, I started to be really interested in the child welfare system in both Canada and Sweden. Many questions stayed with me and I still haven't found the answer as to which system is the best, Canada's or Sweden's. But I really don't think that one can tell. I found that in Nova Scotia they have a tradition of working individually, for example, with the mother. They do not work with the whole family as we do in Sweden. I am of the view that the type of network meeting in which I have participated in Sweden, considers the position of both sides more than the case conference as exemplified by my case study in Nova Scotia. I found the case conference that I participated in unpleasant in the sense that the family was surrounded by professionals and did not have anyone, except for a lawyer on their side. According to the social worker that worked with the family in my case study, families are allowed to bring a support person to the case conference. However, it is not common for families to do that.

In my opinion, it is very important for a child to have close contact with his or her biological network, even if the child cannot stay with its parents of birth. I find it necessary for a child's positive development to know its roots. Social workers in Nova Scotia normally try to place a child who can't for one or another reason stay in its home environment, within the child's family network. I found this tradition very strong. Even when the child was put up for adoption, the child's contact with the parents of birth remained. The more open adoptions also indicate a step towards the child's right to knowledge about its biological parents and theirs and their parents' right to maintain contact with their child(ren). In the Swedish system, a child who is placed in a long term foster home can never legally be a part of the foster family. In Nova Scotia, when a child gets adopted, it gains security as a child of a new family. However, I am concerned that through this approach, the lack of attention given to the child's heritage means that it is lost.

Doing my practicum in Canada my learning experiences at Family SOS has been both extensive and extremely exciting. And I have had the freedom to try my wings in many new ways, for which I am very thankful. It was not easy all the time, but I had great support from everybody at Family SOS. What really helped me a lot were the weekly dialogues with Marika Lethman who helped me not only with my placement work but also in understanding my own feelings about what I was doing.

I must admit that working in Canada was hard for me in the beginning, especially with a new language and new social roles to learn. Nevertheless, I think that not knowing the language perfectly and being unable to use it as my strongest weapon also helped me to learn more and try new ways of doing social work. I used paper and pens to communicate.

It also made me realise more than before that it is not so easy to be a foreigner in a new country with another culture to adjust and become part of their new environment. I must say that the families I worked with did not have a problem with my accent, and soon, I did not think much of it either. One of the things that I thought was difficult in the beginning was talking to professionals on the phone. I must admit that I felt a bit insecure, because I knew how important those phone calls could be for the families I worked with and I did not want to make a fool out of myself either.

Many other people have also played an important role in my learning processes and in making my stay in Canada such a great experience. I am deeply thankful. Thank you, Joan Gilroy, Wanda Thomas Bernard, Gwen Macdonald Slipp and Marilyn Peers for your help, support and kindness and for inviting us to your homes.

Thank you, Seven Hessle, Lena Cederlund and Ingalill Westman for all the support from Sweden. I would also like to thank Nicoline Isacson and Greger Helin for their encouragement in my taking this step. And, finally, a special thanks to those involved in the Canada-European Union Project community and to my friend Lisa Roos who shared my experience.

7 Context Matters: Child Abuse in a Deprived Community

BETHANY J. SAVOY

Introduction

Poverty and deprivation provide the contexts in which many social work interventions occur. As I show below, poverty can exist in the most developed countries in the world. Moreover, poverty can have adverse impacts upon the relationships that are developed between practitioners and their clients.

I was based at the Familjecenter, Hagalund, Solna, Sweden during my international exchange period. For me to sum up four months' learning in a different country with a different social services system is difficult, especially because my learning was not only about Sweden, but also about Canada.

In this chapter, I examine work undertaken with an abused child in a Family Centre in Sweden to explore how children can be empowered in many different ways. I also consider how I might have worked with this child had the case been one that I might have encountered in my work in Canada.

Additionally, I have attempted to provide an overview of the Swedish legislation and my placement agency. At the same time, I comment upon my own learning and give some of my thoughts on the strengths and weaknesses of the systems that I saw operating in these two countries. I use a case study to better illustrate my experience within the Swedish system.

Law and Legislation

There are three main legislative acts governing social work in Sweden, all of which provide a framework for practice rather than details on specific uses of the Acts. This allows for wide interpretation by the social worker, and also by the political board that represents the *Kommun*, which determines where money will be spent in the social services.

The most important law is the Social Services Act (SSA). Section 1 of the SSA states its objective as follows:

> 'Public social services shall, on a basis of democracy and solidarity, promote people's economic and social security, equality of living conditions, and active participation in the life of the community. Social services shall be aimed at liberating and developing the innate resources of individuals and groups. Activities shall be based on respect for people's self-determination and privacy, consideration of the best interests of the child shall be specially observed' (SSA, Section 1).

This Act goes on to state what social services the municipalities are obliged to offer. These include financial aid, assistance to women who have suffered abuse, emergency social services, measures to combat substance abuse, child welfare services, services for older people, services for people with 'functional impairments' (section 21). The SSA is built on people's respect for each other as individuals, and certain rights and entitlements that each person enjoys.

The Act also gives each municipality the responsibility of providing social services. These services must have an organisational framework, but there is no indication of what this should be. The framework is determined by a committee of politicians in each municipality, and is based on financial considerations and recommendations made by social workers. Therefore, there are considerable variations in provisions amongst different municipalities in Sweden, although there are some national standards.

Certain groups, for example, older persons, must have special services provided for them in each municipality. Additionally, certain programmes such as women's shelters must be provided. But politicians have sole control over how the organisation takes shape, how the money is allocated, and how certain major decisions in individual cases are taken, for instance, in determining when it is necessary to apprehend a child or take it into care.

The other laws provide for services to particular groups of people. The first is the Care of Young Persons Act (LVU). LVU covers situations in which the parents do not agree with the social worker's opinion of what constitutes the 'best interest' for their child, and it becomes necessary to apprehend the child. The case proceeds to court where a decision is made as to where the child will be placed in the future, or whether he or she will be returned home. If the parent(s) agree(s) to the proposed plan for the child, the action is taken under the SSA instead of the LVU.

A child can also be apprehended if it is determined that the manner in which the child is living 'exposes his health or development to a palpable risk of injury through the use of addictive substances, criminal activity or some other socially degrading behaviour' (section 3).

The Care of Abusers Act (LVM) deals with treatment for people who are experiencing substance abuse problems. Initially, intervention should be a co-operative effort for planning and treatment, but if the abuser refuses to co-operate he or she can be apprehended by force if deemed to be at risk of causing harm to self or others or 'ruining his life' (section 4). This law applies to those over the age of 18. Until 18 years of age, anyone with abuse problems is treated under LVU or SSA.

All these laws share one important feature: their interpretation is to a large degree based on economic factors and the philosophies of the politicians in the municipality. The legislation is so broad that the organisation of social services in one municipality may bear little resemblance to those in neighbouring ones. My main critique of the legislation, apart from the fact that there is too much room for interpretation, is the language that is used.

In my view, the language used is patriarchal and judgmental. For although the legislation speaks of respect for individuals and self-determination, the language does not reflect these values. How professionals use language is very important, because words may impact in deleterious ways upon others, and may thwart professional attempts to be as inclusive and non-judgmental as possible.

If the Acts governing the work of social workers are not written with the same consideration, there is a risk of failing to provide services or providing less than the best services available to those requiring them.

The Familjecenter in Hagalund

My placement was based at the Familjecenter, a multi-service centre for children and families. It consisted of a prenatal clinic, a children's clinic, an open pre-school, and a social services office, all sharing a common facility, manager, and philosophy. Funding for its work is provided by both the Swedish Health and the Social Services Departments. The Familjecenter is located in the city of Solna, just outside Stockholm, in an area known as Hagalund. Hagalund has between 8,000 and 10,000 inhabitants, over half of whom are immigrants or first generation Swedes.

The area is a disadvantaged one in which there is high unemployment and long term disability. Salaries are low and many people receive financial assistance. The Familjecentre, or Family Centre, is located directly in the largest apartment complex in Hagalund, and is very heavily used by members of the community.

The Hagalund Family Centre employs one manager, one receptionist, two midwives, two nurses, two pre-school teachers, and five social workers. An additional two social workers connected to the Family Centre are located at a nearby middle school. All child welfare social work for Hagalund is conducted from this office.

The goals for the Family Centre were developed and agreed upon by the staff before it opened in 1993, and they are reviewed and amended annually by staff. These are its current goals:

- to focus on socially vulnerable children and families;
- to be located in the community and easily accessible;
- to be easy to contact;
- to become a meeting place for children and families in the area;
- to strengthen family networks;
- to support the parents' own initiatives and ideas;

- to promote good physical, mental, and social health for children and families through early intervention;
- to create a safe environment;
- to offer various group activities;
- to be a source of information and knowledge; and
- to facilitate and accrue the benefits of co-operation between professionals.

These goals are reflected in the work undertaken at Familjecenter. Here, professionals attempt to provide the best service possible to the people who live in Hagalund, and acknowledge that the people themselves are the experts as to what constitutes 'best service'. The professionals work together with the families to give every child the best chance at happiness, health and safety.

Case Study

Working with Family 'A'

I now turn my attention to Family 'A', consisting of two parents and two children. Social workers have had contact with this family since 1991. The Family Centre received the referral on this case when it initially opened as a transferral from another office.

One of its first interventions undertaken in this case consisted of the staff assisting in arranging access visits between the father and his two sons, when the parents began to live apart in 1992. Social workers had already conducted child abuse investigations into this family because the father had earlier claimed that the children were being abused by the mother and half-siblings.

However, the ensuing investigations found no evidence of abuse. The mother has asserted that she had been abused by her husband during the marriage and that he is now trying to harass her by claiming that she abuses the children. She also alleges that he threatens and demeans her in front of the children. The parents have consistently given conflicting versions of events and the social workers have found it difficult to help them come to some agreement about the children.

The father questions the mother's intellectual capacity to be a good mother. The mother has custody of the children and has asked for no help other than that of stopping her husband from harassing her. The man had a restraining order made against him for a short time. But it expired. Unfortunately, it could not be renewed without proof of further harassment.

In early 1998, the school reports to the Family Centre. It claims that the older boy, aged 9, is having behaviour problems, and is aggressive. In response, the staff have increased their contact with the family and offered further services including counselling and assessment to the mother who has declined them. The staff group continues to facilitate access visits.

In the summer of 1998, the father arrives at the office with the older boy saying that in order to resolve the situation, someone must die: the children, the father, the mother, or all of them. The father also assaults a male social worker at the Family Centre and accuses him of uttering threats, abusing the children, and having a sexual relationship with the mother.

The father is admitted by force to a mental hospital, and the son is returned to his mother. The hospital reports that the father might be dangerous to the family but he is not mentally ill, and so he cannot be detained, even though the family fears him.

The mother and children are placed in an emergency family home for their protection. Whilst they are here, the social workers will try to determine what support and services they might need. They stay there for eight months, during which time it becomes apparent that mother cannot take care of the children and work on improving her own situation at the same time.

The woman has a loving relationship with her children, but she is unable to manage daily life and set limits for them. It is evident that children's emotional development has been delayed, and they continue to have some behavioural problems. The children look to the emergency family as parents and authority figures, and their relationship with them is good.

The social workers decide to place the children in foster care until the mother is able to take more control of her life and obtain some security and protection from the father. The mother agrees with this decision and signs a voluntary agreement that is to be reviewed every six months. She retains custody of the children throughout this period, but the children are placed in foster care, two and a half hours away by car. The mother is assisted in visiting every second weekend, and the Family Centre is currently attempting to get an injunction against the father's visits with the children for at least six months.

These actions are all taken under the SSA. If the court refuses the Family Centre's request, they will initiate proceeding under the LVU to take custody of the children, in order to keep the father away from them for their protection. The mother has agreed to give up custody in order to protect the children from their father if this occurs.

This case is typical of the families that I saw at the Family Centre. However, it is more complex than most as the involvement of the social worker begins at a non-crucial point and continues as the family moves closer to a crisis. The case also illustrates a number of interesting facts about child welfare in Sweden. First, the school calls the social worker to report aggressive behaviour in one of the children, and the social worker is able to open an investigation on that information. In Canada, where the privacy of the family is very important and crisis situations are frequent, it at first seemed very strange to me that an investigation could be initiated on the basis of aggressiveness in a child.

Moreover, I noted that although the mother had declined services, the social workers remained in contact with her and checked periodically to see if she had changed her mind. Another interesting feature for me was that the relationship between the police and the social work office was not a very good one. The social workers often have trouble getting reports from the police and investigations do not take place together. In cases like this where the wife has been abused, I believe that it is very important for the social workers to be aware of police involvement, and that agencies co-operate in order to ensure safety.

Given the abuse of the mother in this situation, I think the situation would have been handled differently had it occurred in Canada. Under Section 22(2)(i) of the Family and Children's Services Act, provision is made for taking a child into protective care if:

'the child has suffered physical or emotional harm caused by being exposed to repeated domestic violence by or towards a parent or guardian of the child, and the child's parent or guardian fails or refuses to obtain services or treatment to remedy or alleviate the violence'.

As these children had been exposed to repeated domestic violence, they would have been deemed as emotionally harmed. Moreover, as the mother did not accept the services offered, Section 22(2)(i) of the Act could be applied. As a result, the children could have been placed in foster care and had visitation with the mother until she felt able to take them back again. In Sweden there are no references to child protection in a situation of abuse by, or of the adults in the home. There is also no legal provision by which the father could have been forced to stay away from the children because of threats he had made.

I was involved in this case for almost my entire placement. And there are a number of other issues which are pertinent to the case and how it was handled, but which I cannot discuss fully within the scope of this paper. The parents were both immigrants, and it was extremely difficult to find a foster home for these boys. This is often the case in Sweden and highlights shortcomings in provisions that need to be addressed.

Additionally, the case changed workers for a number of reasons. The lack of continuity also impacted on the work that was done with the family. These and other issues further complicate the case. However, my involvement made this a good learning experience for me, and highlighted the importance of being aware that all the people involved were human beings with their own strengths and needs. In both Sweden and Canada, it is easy to lose sight of this fact when dealing with such difficult and complex cases involving a great deal of paper work.

Significant Learning

It is difficult to know where to begin in talking about my learning form the exchange experience. The wide exposure to different forms of practice and variety of agencies, I was able to gain a good overall picture of the Swedish social welfare system, especially as it pertains to children and families. I also have an understanding of what it means to be an outsider, and this will be an invaluable lesson to use when working with people who have been marginalised. Because I am white, Christian, English, young, and educated, my experience of being an outsider was fairly painless. Moreover, any difficulties that I had were easily overcome with the help of friends and colleagues. But through this experience, I have learnt more about my own and others' positions of privilege.

For me, the most significant piece of learning that I acquired was the development of a new scale against which to measure social services back in Canada. The experience enabled me to step back from my taken-for-granted assumptions and to see both the positives and negatives in my own system. I have learned about its strengths, such as the dedication of its staff, the progressive nature of the Family and Children's Services Act, the Code of Ethics, and the profession's commitment to the notion of social justice and social action. And I have learned about the weaknesses of the system, such as the need for more money and resources to be put into services, the poor working relationships that often characterise work with other professionals, especially those in health care, and the failure to do more preventative work which could help eliminate some future crises.

Many of the programmes and policies that I encountered in Sweden have been very progressive. It astonishes me to see the number of options which are available to social workers when resources are less of a problem. I also admire the way in which people from many professions are encouraged to work together to provide the best service available. The money put into social services by government is much greater than the amounts allotted in Canada, and it has been refreshing for me to work in a system that appreciates the importance of the work that social workers are doing, and that to do this work properly, adequate funding is needed.

From my experience in Canada, I know how difficult it is to make decisions based on availability of money and other resources. As the global economy makes social services budgets smaller and smaller world-wide, I would encourage social workers in Sweden to advocate for the system that they have, and focus on retaining what they have worked so hard to build. It is only through making politicians aware of the importance of social work interventions that practitioners can ensure its continued quality is not sabotaged by shrinking budgets. The realities of practice when this happens have provided lessons that Canadian practitioners have had to learn only too well.

I conclude by saying that I cannot adequately express my appreciation to all the people in Sweden and in Canada who made this experience possible, and who helped me to learn so much in such a short time. Thank you, all.

8 Away from Home: Reflections from Working with Asylum Seekers in the Netherlands

RENEE MEUSE

Introduction

Students on international placements are themselves away from home. When based in social work settings, they can be called upon to work with others such as asylum seekers who also experience the loss of their usual networks and families. In reflecting upon my work with this client group, I begin to draw parallels between their coping strategies and experiences of being in unfamiliar territory and my own. In doing so, I have been able to make comparisons that have highlighted similarities and differences between us.

As a social work student who has been considering entering the field of child welfare, I am aware of the many challenges that practitioners in this field in the Canadian province of Nova Scotia face in their daily work. In thinking about it, the questions that I have asked myself are: what can we do to improve the system's effectiveness? And, what can I do in daily practice in the meantime to truly make a difference in the lives of the families that I might work with? When I heard of the international exchange programme, I saw it as a source of answers to my questions along with the possibility of using the wealth of knowledge that I had gathered during my studies of anti-oppressive practice.

There were numerous other benefits to international field placements that I could foresee. For me, these included being able to work in a different system, in a country with a different social welfare environment, and with many cultural differences. I thought that the Netherlands would be an interesting country in which to undertake such an exchange because it has a strong commitment to social welfare policy and a number of innovative approaches to social problems.

In the Netherlands, I had the privilege of working in a Centre for Young Asylum Seekers. In exploring my position as a student social worker abroad in this chapter, I provide an overview of the Dutch system for asylum seekers, a critique the current child welfare system in Nova Scotia and examine alternative feminist, anti-oppressive approaches to practice. These will provide answers to my questions regarding child welfare practice.

I begin by considering the young asylum seekers in the Centre in which I worked, and contextualise these in the larger Dutch system for asylum seekers. Finally, I focus on the tasks that I did and comment on the strengths and limitations of the Dutch approach before moving on to consider the child welfare system in Nova Scotia in the light of my new found knowledge.

Unaccompanied Minors

My placement was in a Centre for Young Asylum Seekers in the Netherlands. The young people in the Centre were known by the acronym AMA which stood for *alleenstaande minderjarige asielzoeker* in Dutch. In English, it has been translated as asylum seekers who are unaccompanied minors. What does this mean? Essentially, they are young people who are seeking asylum, or refuge in the Netherlands due to the unstable circumstances in their home country. AMAs are all under the age of 18, the age of maturity as established by the United Nations Convention on the Rights of the Child (CRC).

The AMAs receive additional attention as they have reached the Netherlands alone, i.e., they are not accompanied by family members. Most often, their own parents have been killed in their home country and this is the basis of their request for asylum. Most young people arriving in the Netherlands have not fled from a situation considered life-threatening enough to be granted refugee status according to the definition for refugee status provided by the 1951 Geneva Convention. According to an interview I conducted with an Immigration and Naturalisation Department Centre Co-ordinator on 25 June 1999, AMAs are permitted to stay and receive welfare benefits on the basis of the Dutch Alien Law which states that this course of action must be followed if a minor has no parents in their home country.

According to statistical records, 5,000 to 6,000 unaccompanied minors were expected to enter the Netherlands seeking asylum in 1999 (Aronson et al., 1998). In 1994, their geographical origins were as follows: 37 per cent from Somalia; 16 per cent from China; 9 per cent from Angola; and 8 per cent from Ethiopia. However, as the political climate in the world changes, the reasons that young people flee their countries changes and so do their demographic characteristics. Thus, those in the Centre where I worked came from a large range of countries – Angola, China, Somalia, Sierra Leone, ex-Soviet states, and Guinea. I also estimate that about 80 per cent of the AMAs were male and 20 per cent female.

I cannot speak about these young people without recalling their strength and ability to cope with the fact that they had to leave their countries and the atrocious circumstances that they had endured prior to escaping. They have faced unimaginable horrors and many of them now have to come to terms with their experiences of sexual assault, the loss of parents, the unknown whereabouts of siblings and other relatives, unlawful and unwarranted incarceration and questioning, as well as the culture shock of being in a new country so radically different from their own. Despite all the heavy issues they have to deal with, they still manage to greet everyone with a warm smile and carry on with their daily lives. They provide living proof of the strength and ability of the human spirit to adapt and filled me with resolve in facing my own adjustments in a new situation.

The COA or *Central Organ Pang Asielzoekers* in Dutch which translates into the Asylum Seekers Reception Service in English is the organisation responsible for the accommodation of asylum seekers in the Netherlands. It has three Application Centres (AC) and an AMA must report to one of these when they arrive in the Netherlands to declare that they are seeking asylum. AMAs normally stay there from 24 to 48 hours in which time they are interviewed to determine whether they will be permitted to start the asylum procedure. If permission is given, they are brought to a Relief and Investigation Centre (OC) where they stay for an average of four months.

During their stay in the OC, they are interviewed for a second time in more detail to determine whether they will receive permission to stay in the country and what type of status they may hold. A medical clinic nurse that I interviewed on 3 June 1999 claims that they also receive extensive medical attention. They are given medical exams, tested for tuberculosis, vaccinated and receive medical treatment according to their needs. They also go to school to learn the Dutch language. Their time in the OC is considered very important in that it allows AMAs time to rest and adjust to their new life. For many, this is the first time in months that they do not have to live in constant fear. Feeling safe is essential to promoting their well-being.

After approximately four months at the OC, the AMAs are transferred to their next home, where they will stay until they are 18 years old or their asylum procedure is completed. An Opbouw Foundation worker makes this decision. The Opbouw worker assumes the role of legal guardian for an AMA. The group of Opbouw workers taking on this legal duty is responsible for meeting the material needs of the AMAs; providing housing; promoting their ability to care for themselves with regards to cooking; cleaning; and learning Dutch. The Opbouw Foundation bases its work on the belief that these young people need assistance only to become self-sufficient in the Netherlands and so caters solely to these (Aronson et al., 1998). Ophouw workers also make the decision relating to where the AMAs will live after they leave the OC. Although this is their largest role, Opbouw workers will take the recommendations of other workers involved with the AMAs into account. Thus, the range of workers who intervene in the lives of the AMAs are responsible for assisting the Opbouw workers with their decision as to what type of housing is most appropriate to meeting the needs of each young person.

According to my interview with an Opbouw worker, 2 June 1999 there are several choices for where they might be placed: with relatives; in other families; or in housing set aside for them. AMAs may be placed with any family members such as an aunt or uncle who may already be in the Netherlands. The Opbouw Foundation provides housing to many AMAs. These houses are known as Opbouw houses, and usually accommodate four AMAs each. In some, a worker comes to the house for only 20 hours per week to offer AMAs support and supervision. In others, the number of hours is higher, although these are normally used for the younger AMAs. The Opbouw workers try to place AMAs with families from similar nationalities wherever they can. However, this task is very challenging as it is difficult to find families who are interested in offering suitable placements.

Adult AMAs are usually placed in other COA Centres. In the COA Centres, they are one of many, and receive virtually no one-to-one attention. These Centres are appropriate for an AMA only when he or she is considered mature enough to cope with an independent setting. Rising numbers have made sending AMAs to COA Centres common practice.

OC-Gravendeel

I worked in an OC Centre, named OC 's-Gravendeel. The Centre houses approximately 400 asylum seekers, 90 to 95 of which are AMAs. The AMAs live four per caravan, which are found in rows within the Centre. The Centre also houses many services for the asylum seekers. Some are available to all asylum seekers regardless of whether they are adults or children. Others are reserved specifically for the AMAs.

A service that is open to all is made available by the Legal Aid Office. It provides legal council regarding their asylum applications to all asylum seekers. Lawyers also assist in preparing appeals when necessary and clarifying the procedures that will be followed. A group of volunteers from the Dutch Refugee Council (VNN) also assists the asylum seekers in the specifics of these procedures. In an interview I held on 31 May 1999 with a VVN Centre Co-ordinator or VNN as they are referred to, the purpose and importance of the second interview that the Immigration and Naturalisation Department conducts was explained to me. Additionally, VVNs help the individual applicant to clarify their story. They are also present for the interview to ensure that the proceedings are just.

Another key service that is provided to all asylum seekers comes through the medical clinic. There are doctors and nurses on site as well as specialists who see patients at the Centre once a fortnight. Each asylum seeker must be medically examined and tested for tuberculosis. The AMAs are vaccinated on the same basis as all Dutch children. Any illnesses or medical problems are dealt with by the clinic or by specialists in the relevant area. An interview I conducted with a medical nurse on 3 June 1999 revealed that an AMAs' social history is expected to take into account any problems that could arise from the exceptional circumstances precipitating their arrival in the Netherlands.

The Red Cross visits the Centre on a regular basis to provide family tracing services. Asylum seekers can try to locate parents, siblings or other relatives throughout the world. There are additional services in the Centre to meet the variety of needs the asylum seekers. These include a small library with books in a variety of languages, a second-hand clothing store, fitness Centre, and a recreational Centre. As AMAs, these young people require additional services. The United Nations' CRC recognises the special rights held by children, meaning all persons under the age of 18. The Netherlands recognises that children have the right to be cared and provided for. For this reason, additional services exist specifically for the AMAs.

Consequently, there is also a school in the Centre where the AMAs go to learn about Dutch people, their society, language and culture, and some social sciences. This is thought to be essential in helping them to understand their new surroundings and become self-sufficient. Social work services are also available for individual AMAs who need assistance in dealing with the traumas that they have endured prior to reaching the Netherlands. In addition, there is a recreation room for the sole use of AMAs where they can socialise with their peers. The AMAs also spend a lot of time on the football field, playing soccer.

The AMA Team

Finally, there is the AMA-team, the group with which I worked. This group of workers see the AMAs daily and play many roles in their lives. The AMA-team sees the AMAs formally on three separate occasions at which time an AMA's ability to care for himself or herself is independently evaluated. The AMA-team's informal contact with them ranges from checking school attendance, playing a game of soccer, talking over a cup of tea or accompanying them to a doctor's appointment. The AMA-team also advocates on behalf of AMAs and is in constant contact with the other service providers who intervene in their lives.

Being a member of the AMA team, I was able to spend a lot of time with the AMAs. Besides being with them, I was able to advocate on their behalf, check on their school attendance, plan activities for them, including a group for the young women, meet with them formally, participate in team meetings, and speak with other service providers to further understand the system in which I was working. I was able to learn so much from the AMAs especially about the personal strengths that they exemplified daily.

There are a number of positive points that I identified in the way that the OC worked. First, the various needs of the AMAs were addressed by a range of service providers, each of which had their own specific responsibility. This approach assists in reducing the numbers of conflicting roles and the duplication of work. With so many workers, a multi-professional approach is beneficial because it allows the variety of workers to work together in carefully tending to the diverse needs of the AMAs so as to provide them with the best care possible. The fact that all these services are situated in the Centre means that they are accessible to the AMAs and to each other.

There are also strengths in the methods of practice adopted by the AMA-team. I considered their team approach as their biggest strength. Rather than having individual workers responsible for a specific caseload, a system which they referred to as mentorship was used.

The workers were divided into three mentor groups. Each group was responsible for specific AMAs, but only in the capacity of a mentor. A mentor would provide special attention to a particular AMA while still assisting in the care of all other AMAs. A positive feature of this approach enabled a worker to turn to the other mentors in the group for support, and also to the entire team at the daily team meetings. In addition, an AMA has some choice as to whom they feel comfortable approaching for a discussion about their lives, and could always see someone, without having to wait for their worker to come into the office as would have been the procedure had a casework approach had been used.

The power imbalance between the AMAs and the AMA-team was minimal. This enriched the interactions between them in so many ways.

The power that I speak of is the amount of authority over the AMA that the individual worker holds and the amount of control over their contacts that the AMA perceives. Within the AMA-team relationship, the imbalance is kept to a minimum by the fact that a lot of the work of the team is a result of the needs the AMAs have identified for themselves, whether that is advocacy, referral, or support. The informal walk-in atmosphere of the AMA team's office allows the AMAs to feel comfortable in approaching the team at any time. Also, the team spends much time in and around the caravans so that the AMAs have access to them in their own environment as well.

Because the AMA team has so few official tasks such as paperwork and formal evaluation interviews to perform with the AMAs, the workers can spend substantial amounts of one-to-one time with them. The workers are also very open about their work with the AMAs so that the AMAs feel a part of the process. In this environment, the closeness of the client-worker relationship and the valuing of the informal role of the workers, allows beneficial relationships to form and assist in the empowerment of the AMAs.

Another benefit of the way that the AMA-team is organised is that it is not limited to particular ways of working. So, if specific needs arise, these can be dealt with in whatever way the team sees fit. Specific plans can be developed for an individual AMA, or group activities can be organised if the need is identified.

The AMA-team follows the fundamental philosophy of COA – that of ethnic awareness and respect, something that I was familiar with from my anti-oppressive practice studies back in Canada. The AMA-team workers try to be aware of cultural norms and to respect those practising them. Translators are used whenever possible, particularly in formal settings, to allow the AMA to express him or herself in his or her maternal language. COA publishes resources for its workers, providing descriptions of cultural norms on various topics, including death and childbirth.

The method of practice at the OC and of the AMA-team also has some limitations. The majority of the AMAs have been through unimaginable circumstances in their countries, and during their journey to the Netherlands. Along with the reality that they are also adjusting as adolescents, the AMAs have much to deal with, especially now that they are rested and safe and have the time to reflect upon what they have been through. Given this reality, the likelihood that these AMAs will find it difficult to deal with their experiences is high. Unfortunately, their emotional needs are not addressed unless they request such help. In addition, the assistance that exists is limited.

Another weakness of the system is that as more and more asylum seekers enter the country, the legislation is being tightened to limit the numbers of those who are permitted to stay. An example of this is that authorities now require asylum seekers to provide identification papers and any other documentation that will support their story. However, if someone is fleeing from their country, the chance that they will have time to find all the documentation that is required is minimal. Hence, their chances of being allowed to stay are low.

On the other hand, if an individual possesses all the proper documentation, the authorities often get suspicious since the story seems fabricated and their application may be turned down for this reason. The government seems to want to reduce the numbers of asylum seekers by whatever method it can, and thereby takes away from the due process.

Aside from these weaknesses, it is my opinion that the asylum seeking process in the Netherlands adequately meets the needs of those it aims to serve. The Netherlands has developed a very comprehensive system to deal with the constant influx of asylum seekers.

Away from Home: Reflections on Canadian Services for Children

Meanwhile, back in Nova Scotia, there is no equivalent system for asylum seekers. The number of people in this category is small, and this can go someway towards explaining its absence. However, we do have a large child protection system, which in some respects, is comparable to the Dutch system that I came to know. In my reflections on its provisions, I demonstrate that it is possible to learn from one system to improve the services on offer in another.

The current Nova Scotia child welfare system is similar to those found in other Canadian provinces. It is based on the Nova Scotia Children and Families Services Act (1990) which provides workers with a legal framework for child protection and adoption. The idea of the 'best interest of the child' guides its policies (Gilroy, 1999). An emphasis is placed on the demand that the least intrusive method of intervention must be used. Other important points of the Act include limiting agency involvement, using voluntary services to maintain the integrity of the family. Additionally, the ties between the child and parents must be maintained if at all possible. Placing children in care is deemed a matter of last resort.

While this Act may be considered progressive, social workers in Nova Scotia feel that it has bureaucratised their interventions and in the process taken away much of their authority in deciding how they work with families (Gilroy, 1999). Social workers feel that the courts now hold the power as they have become much more dominant in the child protection process. The practitioners have taken more of a case manager role and lost much of their ability to define for themselves how to work with the families who come to them for help. Some social workers feel that this context has made it very difficult to practice from a framework of social justice in which the family's needs would govern the working relationship.

The current system serves to identify unacceptable behaviour amongst parents and children and attempts to change it on an individual level (Callahan, 1993a). This individualised way of practising is evident in the way that individual clients are assigned to individual workers. The policy of confidentiality further isolates clients within the system by hindering their chances of meeting and thereby supporting each other. Social workers are also isolated by their methods of working. They must deal with cases on their own and receive little support in doing their work. When they do, it is always after the fact (Callahan, 1993b). By keeping the work very individualised, practitioners and clients often fail to see the larger structures that influence their lives in disadvantaging ways.

Some Thoughts on Reshaping the Child Protection System in Nova Scotia

My experience in the Netherlands has sharpened my ability to look critically at the way in which child welfare workers in Canada operate and consider alternative ways of moving forward with changing its more oppressive elements. In my view, the work of child protection workers in

Nova Scotia can be reframed by feminism. Feminist thinking has taken many shapes, but all its beliefs are based on the notion that patriarchy exists in all structures of society and that feminism serves to decode patriarchy. That is, it exposes how a patriarchal system maintains gender norms in society and oppresses women. In contrast, feminists intend to promote equality between all individuals (Mullaly, 1993).

The well-known feminist saying that 'the personal is political' has implications for how child welfare work might be carried out. First, it looks at private troubles and places them within a structural reality. In doing so, the political nature of the practitioner's interventions within individual cases becomes evident. In the current system, the state sets standards regarding how children must be cared for and intervenes when the parents do not meet these standards (Kitchen, 1995).

If I widen my thinking, I can see that the parents that social workers encounter lack the material resources necessary for providing for their children as the state expects. However, through its policies of intervening on an individual basis, the state protects children from their parents but not from the societal forces that impact negatively on their families and impede their being able to care for them.

The feminist adage also assists in de-pathologising clients (Mullaly, 1993). The individual client is now seen as having strengths that arise from their capacity to deal with the structural realities they live in rather than as someone who has personal problems. By reframing the situation in this way, the clients can see themselves in a more positive manner and can reduce the self-blame for their predicament that they may be feeling.

The de-pathologising of clients is very important in addressing the needs of the majority of people who come into contact with child welfare agencies as they are from oppressed groups, including poor people, minority groups and single mothers (Hegar and Hunzeker, 1988). These individuals are likely to go along with being held personally responsible for all that happens to them when they feel personally attacked, their capabilities questioned and the reality that they live within – poverty and discrimination, is not considered.

Another influence of feminist thinking is making visible the experience of women, who tend to be the majority of clients and service providers. Mothers, foster mothers, childcare workers and protection workers are all unpaid or poorly paid, making their work invisible in society (Wharf, 1993b). Child welfare tends not to recognise the work that is done by these women. Their status in society is worthy of greater recognition because the work that they do is linked to the well-being of children (Callahan, 1993). But this acknowledgment is not given because women in Canadian society are disadvantaged through the patriarchal structures and discourses that define their position as women.

However, women's experiences of disadvantage are not all the same. Although they share a common experience of womanhood, this also differs according to ethnicity, economic status, parental and marital status, sexual orientation, and ability. Women who care for children are more likely to be disadvantaged (Callahan, 1993a). More single mothers live in poverty than was previously the case. The high price for childcare impoverishes many women and is a reason for underemployment and unemployment amongst them.

Living within these realities, means that the more disadvantaged the mother or caregiver is, the more disadvantaged the child (Callahan, 1993a). There are two predominant ways in which children are more 'at risk' due to the disadvantaged situation of their caregiver. First, children are more likely to live in poverty and suffer from its results. Second, children are also under a greater risk of violence and sexual abuse since their mother cannot protect them from likely abusers. Child welfare services ignore the disadvantages that women face in situations of neglect and abuse because they do not consider the poverty and lack of resources that the women face.

The child protection workers, who are also predominantly women, are also affected by patriarchy. The majority of the work done by workers and the skills that are attributed to them such as counselling and comforting others are largely invisible and not valued as they are seen as women's natural talents (Callahan, 1993a). Meanwhile, child protection workers are expected to take on roles of prosecutor of the offender, defender of the child and judge of the parents' abilities. While these roles may demand knowledge and skills not associated with what they do, they also do not allow them to fully use those that they have. Workers, like their clients, are affected by oppressive social relations.

As we can see, although women are the majority of those involved in child welfare, they and their concerns are invisible. Child welfare services ignore the reality of poverty and the reasons for it (Callahan, 1993a). The agency may also worsen the situation through its actions. For example, by becoming involved in cases of wife abuse on the basis that the mother is unable to protect her children against the violence she experiences, the agency is ignoring the reality that she is powerless as well and that a crucial issue in her situation is the lack of resources that would enable her to leave that particular environment.

With such an analysis, I can see that there is much to be done to adequately serve the families who are in need of assistance. Fortunately, there are approaches that can assist individual workers to practice more effectively in responding to structural constraints (Mullaly, 1993). One such method – partnership, focuses on how a social worker relates to a client. In it, the client becomes a partner in the relationship with the right to make decisions regarding the situation. The social worker would share casenotes with the client, and the client would have the right to object or make suggestions regarding their contents.

Clients are also involved in decisions that affect them and provide feedback on the services that they receive. In addition, there are other simple ways of reducing the social distance between the client and worker such as disclosing things about his or her own life when appropriate, dressing casually, providing the rationale for the techniques used, visiting clients at home, using first names, speaking clearly, paying attention to body language and sharing his or her personal limits and biases. It is also important to provide the client with information regarding the agency and their rights as a client. Within such an approach, the client feels that the social worker is there to help them. This relationship emphasises the service function of the agency and de-emphasises its control function, thereby empowering the client.

Empowerment is important for clients in that it helps strengthen their capacities to deal with their lives. Social workers do not empower clients directly, but provide the climate, relationship, resources and procedural means through which the client can grow personally (Mullaly, 1993). The social worker must remember that the person they are working with is the expert regarding his or her own situation. But the practitioner has to have a knowledge base that encompasses the realities of poverty, racism, heterosexism, and sexism so that they can contextualise the realities of the clients' lives. The social workers may be able to help name what the client is living through, but it is important to remember that clients know their realities best and that their views must be kept uppermost in their minds.

An indispensable tool in forming a collaborative relationship between the client and worker is consciousness-raising (Mullaly, 1993). This involves reformulating the circumstances of the client by focusing on the social conditions in which they live. The social worker helps the client understand the social structure that shapes his or her life and reframes his or her responsibilities within this.

The bulk of the blame is shifted away from the individual and placed on societal attitudes and structures. The social worker must be empathetic to truly understand the reality of the clients as they feel it. Such a change in thinking may take time and the worker must allow for this (Hegar and Hunzeker, 1988). The clients must reconstruct and reorient themselves with the new information that is made available to them and rethink their outlook after a long time of internalising their oppression.

It is also helpful for clients to feel that there are other people who are dealing with similar issues (Mullaly, 1993). One way of achieving this is by providing clients with information and facts that demonstrate that others are facing similar problems. Another possibility is to connect them with others in like circumstances. Not only does this help them let go of their guilt and self-blame, but others can become a source of mutual support. And, a group that promotes social change can be developed as a result of their interactions with one another. A social worker can take the lead in getting a formal mutual aid group off the ground, or he or she can support user-led ones (Hegar and Hunzeker, 1988). These groups are especially beneficial if they meet regularly and have an open membership so that individuals can enter or leave the group as they need.

Some critics may believe that reconstructing the way that clients see their lives may be a positive intervention, without being conducive to changing clients' abilities to parent. However, research has shown that people do not become better parents from parenting courses, but from redefining their outlook of what they expect of themselves (Hegar and Hunzeker, 1988). Child protection workers must base their practice on the assumptions that all people and environments have usable strengths, which they can use to improve their lives (DeJong and Miller, 1995).

All environments contain resources and a way to identify these is to look at how the client has survived to date. A client can be motivated to change by focusing on these strengths as they realise that they have always found ways of managing their lives. The client and worker must work together to uncover these strengths. By collaboratively identifying client strengths, the client will be able to feel more confident and become empowered. Through recognising the positive aspects of the client's life, the blame and guild felt may be removed. As Mullaly puts it:

> 'The task, rather than working on personal change and accommodation to society, is to engage people as producers and participants in comprehending and acting on their contextual environment' (Mullaly, 1993, p. 172).

The worker has to carefully negotiate their relationship with a client to ensure that the client can exercise as much power as possible over the decisions regarding their lives and that they can identify the more positive aspects of themselves and their surroundings.

Apart from their interactions with clients, there are other specific actions that the social worker can undertake to promote structural change in the agency and the legislation that governs it. The social worker can challenge oppressive policies and procedures, for example, by refusing to apprehend children in a case where the mother is unable to protect the child from an abusive partner and demanding instead, that resources be made available to them (Callahan, 1993a). Such instances can be used to raise awareness of the links between child welfare and poverty, violence and powerlessness within the agency and broader society. The public, by expressing its voice and the woman's movement can be used to raise awareness at a community level.

A worker can also try to identify like-minded people within the agency and the community to encourage alliances that promote change on a collective level. Such alliances should include individuals from all levels within the agency (Callahan, 1993a). This approach can encompass all viewpoints and encourage people in the higher echelons of the agency to create opportunities for change. Gaining the support of individuals outside the agency is also important in such a change process so that clients, concerned community members and other organisations can also add their voices to the proceedings.

Although these suggestions can improve the relationship between clients and workers, they are still working from within an oppressive system. Several authors have made suggestions regarding the creation of an alternative child welfare system that would better serve the needs of clients. Based on our analysis to date, it is evident that women and children must be a priority of any child welfare system (Callahan, 1993a). The experience of women must be central when considering what services are appropriate and women must also be at the centre of the change process.

It is impossible to say that there is one best system. As our understanding of poverty, oppression, and abuse develops, the type of services that will be considered acceptable will also change. Also, each community has its own specific needs and resources, which must be taken into consideration when developing a new child welfare system.

In conjunction with feminist beliefs, new organisations that are developed should be without a divisive ordering of positions in the workforce, that is, without either horizontal or vertical hierarchies and structures of inequality (Callahan, 1993a). Workers, clients, board members, and others would be involved at all levels in the policy-making and management of the services. Changes would also have to occur at all levels – policy, legislation and agency structures to promote positive client-worker relationships (Wharf, 1993b). Wharf (1993b) also suggests that a larger governmental ministry should be created to encompass all services concerning the well-being of children, including day care, health, and education.

In this alternative child welfare structure, the needs and the realities of children and women must be at the forefront of developments. Their needs may differ and at times oppose each other. However, such contradictions must be acknowledged and work should proceed so as not to pit the interests of one against the other (Dominelli and McLeod, 1989; Callahan, 1993a). To allow possible contradictions to exist, each individual must be able to define their own circumstances and needs so that these can be addressed.

One way of changing child welfare policy would be to reformulate the mission for the work done by agencies (Callahan, 1993a). Such a mission would focus on the relationship between the client and worker and the development of a positive analysis of the problems encountered and a common vision for change. The development of such a mission has to include all concerned citizens, clients, workers, policy makers and community members (Cassidy in Wharf, 1993a). Such an approach is also beneficial because it increases the awareness of child welfare issues in the community.

The likelihood of success is also increased because those who must live with the outcomes are involved in the process. By involving everyone in developing the mission of an agency, such goals can also be achieved more readily. A study in the United States revealed that the key factor in reducing out-of-home placements for children was the philosophy of a service that emphasised the dignity and worth of the clients as well as having a match between the needs of clients and the services provided (Wharf, 1993b).

Reformulating the mission of an agency may not be enough to make an agency adequately serve the needs of a community. It is also possible that a community may want to assume the powers essential to providing child welfare services and develop an organisation independent from the provincial government (Callahan, 1993a). In creating a decentralised service, the level of bureaucracy could be reduced, thereby increasing its potential to be more welcoming to clients (Cassidy in Wharf, 1993a).

A community could also create a service that supplements the current child welfare system by focusing on the needs identified by the community. The new organisation would consider the status of women and the care of children in developing advocacy and other services. This type of community governance would be overseen by a locally constituted board of directors and the provincial government would provide the funds and legislation that would govern the agency. This structure could ensure that the clients' fundamental rights of citizenship are protected.

At the local level, it has also been suggested that the services currently provided by child welfare agencies be shared amongst agencies to minimise existing conflicts in the roles played by child welfare workers (Callahan, 1993a). As I pointed out, the relationship between the AMA's and AMA-team in the Netherlands benefits greatly from such a separation of services into a multi-professional team and the creation of an almost egalitarian working relationship between them.

In child protection, the mandate of child apprehension could be separated from those offered by voluntary agencies. The child welfare agency could then become a source of support and resources for families. Meanwhile, an alternative organisation, perhaps the police or the crown attorney's office, could deal with criminal charges related to abuse and neglect. Another part of this new system would be removing the crime of neglect from the child welfare statutes and reframing it as a resource issue. Voluntary care orders would be kept as an option for parents but apprehensions would become the responsibility of the criminal justice system.

The services and resources available would be based on a system of self-help to better serve the needs of clients (Callahan, 1993a). Workers would be able to develop a team approach to their work, perhaps like the one found in the AMA-team in the Netherlands, while still maintaining the confidentiality of clients where appropriate.

These suggestions may seem unrealistic. However, I have identified several of the benefits of following such a course of action. Clients are more willing to seek help if the threat of apprehension is not directly present in the work done with them (Callahan, 1993a). In dealing with issues through the use of resources and voluntary care agreements, the courts are avoided as disempowering and invasive structures. Clients are more likely to achieve and maintain control of their situation when voluntary care agreements are used. Social workers would be less isolated and this would help them provide a better service.

Finally, such a system is consistent with feminist beliefs. Critics might argue that in transferring the responsibility of criminal abuse investigations to the criminal court system, clients would suffer since this system lacks the compassion that child welfare workers hold. Those obligated to deal with cases of abuse and extreme cases of neglect could hire social workers in their department to fulfil these tasks. Moreover, through an improved child welfare system, the assumption is that the number of those that would have to be referred to the courts would be reduced.

These suggestions also include the creation of additional organisations and the need to make changes in other structures. An advisory council regarding child welfare could be created to allow all citizens to learn about the reality of child welfare and the related topics of poverty and violence (Wharf, 1993a). This council could review policy and practice and develop proposals for change. Advocacy groups such as client rights groups could be developed to provide a voice and support for those involved with child protection.

As I have tried to argue, the problem of inadequate responses to meeting children's welfare does not only exist within the agencies, but also in society. Caregivers are not valued for the work they do, as is evidenced by the low wages or lack of pay for those performing these tasks. In not recognising the value of their work, society is showing its lack of interest in the children that it cares for (Wharf, 1993b). If the wages of foster mothers, day care workers, homemakers and child welfare workers, were to be raised substantially, the recognition of their work making a valuable contribution to children's well-being and in turn the valuing of children would be clearer.

For example, it would be possible to provide a wage to parents for the care of their children (Wharf, 1993b). This idea may seem a little extreme, but the state pays workers in other societal roles more appropriately for their work without objection, so why not include those working in child welfare? Historically, society has accepted the state's involvement in what were previously deemed parental responsibilities, e.g., the education and health of children, recreation and public assistance.

Making provisions for a parental wage would help make parenting a public issue and ensure that the work is valued, given that paying for services is the traditional way of ascribing worth to work in Canadian society. A parental wage would also help improve the situation of single parent families and low income families. For in eliminating poverty, a number of neglect cases would be prevented. A parental wage should not become another method of asserting the state's control over parents. Rather, the emphasis should be on the state helping parents with the care of their children and assisting them in the performance of this task.

Alongside the benefits of a parental wage, a comprehensive system of resources and the possibility of voluntary care agreements provided for by a child welfare system, the number of criminal abuse cases are likely to decrease and would make the idea of removing investigations from child welfare system feasible.

Such a system of support rather than investigation would make the current structure of child welfare much more accessible for those who require assistance as their first consideration and would not be based on the fear of losing their children if they ask for help (Strega et al., 2000). Also, by returning power to the clients, they are more able to feel in control of their situation and take action to improve it. Additionally, social workers must be valued for their work and be given adequate space in which to do their work. My experience in the Netherlands provided me with the opportunity to work in a positive environment where my relationships with those with whom I worked were positive and, I believe, empowering to all of us.

Conclusions

The ideas may seem radical and unrealistic now, but major change in the system is possible. This has been proved by steps taken to empower other oppressed groups. For example, the returning of control of child welfare services to the Mi'kmaq in Nova Scotia as well as other First Nation groups across Canada. Such action would have been unthinkable 20 years ago. But as the endeavours of First Nations people have demonstrated, ideas can become reality if people and their communities firmly back them.

As a result of my experiences in the Netherlands and my knowledge about what changes have already been possible in Canada, I conclude on an optimistic note. Canadians can improve the present child welfare system in ways that would better serve the needs of parents and children.

9 Learning about Child Welfare in Nova Scotia

ANDY MARKLAND

Introduction

Working with clients provides excellent opportunities for learning about other people, social systems, and the self. In this chapter, I discuss my involvement with 'Jane', a 19 year old African Canadian single mother of three with whom I worked during my placement with the intake unit of a child protection agency in Halifax, Nova Scotia. Working with Jane enriched my life and contributed immensely to my learning experiences. I left England to undertake this work as part of a European–Canadian social work student exchange programme. I begin by outlining the child welfare system in Nova Scotia as I understand it and then move on to consider the work that I did with Jane. I conclude by considering alternatives ways of delivering services to vulnerable clients. All identifying names and places in this case study have been changed to respect the anonymity of the client, her social set and the agency with which I worked.

Canadian Welfare and Child Protection System

Welfare services in Canada are mandated by provincial legislature. Hence, the service, its remit and quality varies enormously around the country. Government cuts to expenditures on welfare services and the sheer remoteness of some communities also contribute to variable levels of provision. Social services in the Northern Territories of Canada, for example, are responsible for some settlements that are not accessible by road. Social workers in this region fly into communities on Royal

Canadian Mounted Police helicopters for one or two days a week and perform social work across all its areas of responsibility – child protection, adult services, income assistance and other activities.

The Taskforce on the Child as Citizen (1978) pointed to inequalities in the child protection services between provinces. Rural areas tend to be where indigenous Indian, or First Nations, reserves are located and Nova Scotia's Children and Family Services Act 1990 (hereafter referred to as CFSA) has sections aimed at providing services specifically for the Indian communities.

These are authorised under Section 35(3) which requires social workers to refer children who are, or who they suspect are Indian, to the Mi'kmaq Children and Family Services Agency. The Mi'kmaq are the indigenous First Nations community local to Nova Scotia. However, as Johnson and Barnhorst (1991, p. 118) note, First Nations children, along with children from other lower income families are disproportionately over-represented in the child protection system. This could be due to the differing and higher expectations about their behaviour by the courts and social workers.

Johnson and Barnhorst (1991, p. 232) also claim that in a 'perfect world', children in need would be aided by the extended family. The high numbers of poor children in the system indicates that the extended family is unable to act as the alternative carer of choice in many instances. This leads me to the assumption that there are un-negotiated social and political factors at play in the equation to reduce the number of children in state care and in determining the balance between society's minimum standards and those anticipated in individual cultures and communities.

Nova Scotian legislation in child protection prioritises the investigation of abuse and few resources are leftover for prevention and only a minimum remains for therapeutic help for the abused (Sarago 1993). The Task Force on the Child as Citizen (1978) has called for government cuts to child protection services, and has led to government neglect of children. Canada's federal government was Liberal at the time, but it had been heavily influenced by the political changes that had occurred during the 1980s and had been fuelled by the Conservative government that came into power in 1984 (Gustavsson and Segal, 1990, p. 6).

Similar neo-liberal influences have been evident in Britain since the shift to conservatism in 1979 following the election of Margaret Thatcher as leader of the Tory Party. Either of these two countries could have chosen to increase taxes rather than reduce public services, but both governments chose the latter option and targeted amongst other provisions, welfare services.

Gustavsson and Segal (1990, p. 6) point to what they call a 'crisis of legitimisation' where people's expectations have been challenged and changed by the forces of hard-line government action. Britain's 'Beveridge Report' and Canada's 'Green Book Proposal' have framed the post-war reconstruction of their country respectively and have led its peoples to expect their government to provide for their welfare needs.

The 1980s saw radical changes to these expectations as both Canadian and British governments called for reduced centralisation and increased individualism and self-reliance. Those who were not self-reliant were labelled 'deviant' and in need of 'realignment' (Mulally, 1997, p. 120). Jenson (1989, p. 9) argues that Canada did not follow this monumental shift as far as Britain and the United States. Nonetheless, the changes it implemented resulted in increased waiting periods for unemployment benefits, a reduction in the duration of benefits payable to claimants, decreased funding for women's and First Nations groups, and cutting monies for social housing.

Between 1980 and 1995 the poverty rate for all persons in Canada rose from 15.3 per cent to 17.4 per cent. But for families, the rise was from 9.4 per cent to 12.6 per cent and amongst children, it went up from 14.9 per cent to 20.5 per cent (National Council on Welfare, 1997). These policies have led to the formation of soup kitchens, food banks and clothing banks staffed by volunteer groups and religious organisations (Gustavsson and Segal, 1994, p. 9) and today, these provide everyday forms of support for poor people. Canada continues to protect low-income earners by having in place a minimum wage in each province.

Minimum wages are approximately 47 per cent less than the Low Income Cut-off Point (LICO), which is the measure by which Canada determines poverty lines. For example, the minimum wage in Nova Scotia (based on a single parent earner working thirty five hours per week for fifty two weeks a year) is currently $5.50 per hour (approximately £2.20 in Britain). Statistics Canada suggests that the necessary hourly rate for Nova Scotia to meet the LICO requirements should be $10.51 (HRDC Labour Division, 1996). The rate of child poverty in Nova Scotia has risen from 15.7 per cent in 1989 to 23.5 per cent in 1996 (Campaign 2000, 1998).

In Britain, the Children Act, 1989 was designed to meet identified failings in the previous child welfare legislation and to highlight the importance of inter-professional working in reducing professional territorialism. One of the provisions of this Act was the formation of Area Child Protection Committees, which sought to bring together all the players involved in child protection to co-ordinate training, policymaking and protocols.

Pringle (1998, pp. 34-35) has said that social services are required by law to quantify the abuse that has happened before being able to launch an investigation and that the Children Act, 1989 gives little emphasis to prevention. Pringle (1998) also claims that the shift from treatment and preventative services to the 'identification of dangerousness', promoted by the Children Act exacerbates bureaucratic forms of working, ghettoises child abuse and limits inappropriate parenting to a "small band of people from the lower classes who are unable to function adequately (Pringle, 1998, p. 36). In this paper, I intend to show that the deviance model that is applied to poor and disempowered people is an inadequate explanation for their dysfunctionality. A wider view that encompasses societal values and the organisation of its social relations also needs to be taken on board.

Section 2(1) of the CFSA states that its purpose is to 'protect children from harm, promote the integrity of the family and assure the best interests of children'. It places a duty on all persons, whether professionals or lay members of the public, to report suspicions of child abuse (Section 24(2)). The Act also comprehensively defines abuse as a child being in need of protective services (Section 24(1) in Section 22(2)). Section 22(2) deals with a 'child in need of protective services' and has fourteen sub-sections, each of which is worded to include within the definition both the actual physical or emotional abuse, sexual abuse or neglect and the 'substantial risk' inherent in any of these.

An example of the latter would be where a child protection agency receives information that leads them to 'reasonably believe' that domestic violence is going on in a home. This would highlight a possible, though not actual, risk that a child in that home is suffering from emotional abuse including that caused by being witness to physical and/or verbal altercation. Section 22(2)(i) gives the local authority the right to conduct an investigation into the matter.

Section 13(1) authorises 'services to promote the integrity of the family' and provides that services be offered to 'promote the principle of using the least intrusive means of intervention' with families. These services may include financial, day-care, parenting and homemaking skills and substance abuse negotiations (Section 13(2)). However, nothing within these sections provides for preventative provisions, that is, offering children protective services *before* an allegation has been made and *before* an inappropriate act can occur.

Working with Jane

My involvement with Jane and her family was quite accidental. On my first day on placement, and as a part of my induction, I accompanied one of the workers on a home visit to Jane's apartment. En-route, the worker offered me the background to the case: At that time, Jane had two boys, aged one and a half and two and a half years old. Their father Tyler, was not on the scene, but was in Jane's life. He had three other children by another woman, his other girlfriend. These three other children were currently under the permanent care and custody of the agency and up for adoption. Tyler had a long criminal history involving violent crime, drug dealing, theft and substance misuse. Like Jane, he himself had had extensive involvement with the child protection services as a child as he had been physically abused and neglected.

Jane had been referred to the agency by her family doctor six weeks before I met her, regarding a concern about a lack of post-natal and other medical care for the children. The worker had been working with Jane to get this rectified and intended on this day to be saying 'goodbye' as she was closing the file.

Upon arrival at the apartment we noted serious concerns regarding the well-being of the children. The apartment was filthy with faeces and urine on the floors and in buckets around the home. There was rotting food strewn across the kitchen floor. The only furniture was one mattress on the sitting room floor and a cot in one of the bedrooms. Jane told us that her other furniture had been repossessed due to non-payment of loans.

There were worn and bare electrical cables trailing across the floors. The toilet plumbing system was blocked and the bowl was over-flowing with faeces. It seemed that the bath was being used as a toilet, as were the floors of the apartment. In addition, there was little edible food in the cupboards and refrigerator. Jane admitted that she and the children lived on take-out burgers and chicken. The children were not wearing diapers, which Jane explained with, 'they don't like wearing them'.

The children were crawling unhindered amongst the filth and Jane was seemingly surprised when we challenged her over the conditions. When I pointed out to her that the children could contact all manner of diseases from crawling through faeces and urine and putting their fingers in their mouths, Jane responded that she 'didn't let them put their fingers in their mouths'. During this visit, we also learned that Jane was six and a half months pregnant, again by Tyler.

As per agency protocol, we returned to the office to seek supervisory consultation, having told Jane that we would be back later that day. The consultation quantified for us that what we had seen constituted 'substantial risk' to the children under the CFSA, Section 22(2)(b) outlining physical harm and Section 22(2)(j) physical harm and serious neglect. This gave us grounds to return to Jane's apartment and explain to her that we felt she was providing neither an adequate level of hygiene for the children nor making adequate arrangements for their health and nutritional needs or those of the baby that she was carrying.

Jane was furious at this definition of her situation and denied that the home was unfit for human habitation. She claimed that she was caring for her children alone and was doing the best she could with no help, no support, and little money. Jane was on family benefit and with family credit (or family allowance) this gave her a monthly income of around $1200 (around £500). She also stated, 'You guys should have been around when I was a kid, then you'd really have seen abuse and neglect'.

This highlighted to me how feelings of helplessness and anger over her own childhood had affected her as an adult and as a mother. However, at that crisis moment, our concerns were primarily for the children and we advised Jane that we would work with her to sort her problems out. But the children had to take priority 'there and then'. Jane was advised that the children would not be staying in the apartment until it had been cleaned up and she was requested to suggest a relative with whom they could stay for at least the next few days.

Jane had contact with her mother, an aunt and two sisters, but she claimed that none of them was able to care for the children. So we offered her the chance of placing them in agency care voluntarily. Jane was totally unable to see why we felt a need to have the children removed and so she refused this offer. Consequently, we had to apprehend the children involuntarily and they were placed in a foster home, which is where they continue to remain five months later.

Despite our endeavours that afternoon, we were unable to ascertain why Jane had ended up in this situation. There must have been some trigger to her current inability to cope. She had not been like this during any previous visit by my co-worker. The next day we set about trying to establish what the likely causes might be. It transpired that Jane had suffered a serious breakdown in her relationship with her mother after she had tackled her about having been physically abused as a child by her stepfather – her mother's ex-husband. Although her mother had played a large role in the upbringing of her grandchildren, this help was terminated after this conflict erupted with her daughter.

It was evident from the condition of the house that Jane simply did not know about hygiene, budgeting, or nutrition. We also had to appreciate that as a 19 year old girl, Jane wanted to be out partying and buying clothes and other things which her existence as a single mother, struggling on welfare, would not allow. She was, I felt, mourning the loss of herself.

Also as an abused child herself, it was likely that she also suffered from a lowered self-esteem, depression, behavioural extremes and impulsiveness as an adult (Youngblood and Belsky, 1990, p. 85). Also, I was struck for the first time by the replication of similar problems through generations of families and was concerned that this could replicate itself again in the children.

Prior to meeting Jane, when my co-worker was giving me the details of her history in the car, I was acutely aware that alongside a case-history, I was also being given some prejudicial information regarding both her and Tyler. As a person, I am not immune to judgmentalism. Ridding myself of 20-plus years of exposure to the attitude-forming mechanisms that prevail in the wider society does not happen simply because I have the capacity to analyse and form my own value systems. I needed to be aware of the possible danger of my subconsciously passing negative judgements on someone that I had yet to meet.

Knowing that Tyler had had three other children that had been taken away by my agency could pose barriers to my need and desire to constantly ask the question *'Why had this happened?'* 20-plus years of conditioning has prompted me to rate someone like Tyler as irresponsible, sexually immature and deviant. I needed to ensure that I looked for a reason other than a deficit understanding of his way of life. The influences that he had been exposed to have shaped him to be how he is today. Strapps (1991, p. 142) found in a study of 385 university students that significantly more children who were physically punished engaged in both violent crime and property crime in their adolescence.

Single Parenting

Johnson and Barnhorst (1991, p. 105) have highlighted how the past thirty years have seen massive changes in patterns of family behaviour and to the growing acceptance of unmarried mothers. This has occurred alongside a shift in public attitude toward self-determination, self-reliance and an expectation that people take individual responsibility for their behaviour. Murray (1994, p. 48) thinks that single mothers are 'harmful' and that public welfare is a means of supporting 'deviance' such as bearing children without having the means to support them. He considers that with the wider acceptance of abortion and the availability of contraception, mothers and not the state should be made fully responsible for their babies. Hence, measures such as the contemporary 'Wisconsin model' (*Detroit News* 15/9/96) of welfare-to-work reform in the USA are applauded in New Right thinking.

Introduced in the fall of 1995, the Wisconsin model sought to initiate a wholesale revolution of the welfare system in the state of Wisconsin. It required all able-bodied adults to work, or enter training for work in exchange for benefits. Measures put in place to facilitate these initiatives included social workers working with clients to identify and negotiate barriers to working such as childcare and substance abuse problems. It was a system that theoretically aimed to tackle the real issues.

However, reality appears somewhat different. Although initial results looked good, a study by the University of Wisconsin-Milwaukee in 1997 has shown that among other things, one in six families had left welfare by September 1996 and were earning wages in excess of the poverty line, but this figure had dropped to one family in twelve by March 1997. Also, 65 per cent of single parents who attained work in 1996 were no longer employed by March 1997.

The question that such results prompt me to ask becomes, 'Is there anything in place to help people in Jane's and Tyler's position to become self-reliant and begin to participate in society, other than individual responsibility?'

France and Germany take a different approach toward families than do Britain and Canada. Families in these two countries are seen as social institutions and society takes steps to give *families* protection and not just individual players (Hantrais and Letablier, 1996, pp. 26-27). Cannan (1996) concludes that in France, 'the family' is seen as a social institution in itself and that through assessment, training, contracts and goals, social workers in that country work at getting people who are on the edge of society, *integrated* into the mainstream. In other words, French social policy and thinking is geared to incorporating people into the broader societal structures.

It may be that if the radical changes to welfare made in Wisconsin had included a wider view of the causes of the difficulties that poor people face rather than simply draw upon the deviance model, and merely target the presenting problem, more suitable responses might have been developed.

One of the striking points I observed from my placement in child protection in Nova Scotia was the high number of today's parents in the system who had been yesterday's children in it. A cycle of abuse and neglect that replicates itself is evident to me. Research backs up this view in that it has shown that teenage mothers who drop out of high school have only a 1 in 100 chance of getting off welfare (Harris 1991). Children from single-parent families are twice as likely to drop out of high school and two and a half times as likely to become teenage mothers themselves (McLanahan, 1994, p. 6). The Wisconsin model and others like it that preceded it, could be significant in reducing family involvement with child protection agencies across generations, if a wider view of the problem could be included within them.

Wider Social Structures can Contribute to Dysfunctionality in Families

Both Jane and Tyler fit in with the cycle of being involved with child protection agencies across several generations. A review of agency files showed that both had endured abuse and neglect as children. I was able to speak with workers in my agency who had been working with Jane and Tyler's two families a few years earlier.

On reflection, I am not sure of how much benefit their interventions had produced. The overall sense I got from my colleagues was one of resignation: 'Oh well, it's only to be expected with his or her history'. It was almost as though the agency expected abused and neglected children to turn up on the system again as the abusing and neglecting parents.

Mulally (1997, p. 120) states that in North America the prevalent social work intervention is that of the 'order perspective', i.e., one in which behaviour must be modified through counselling and rehabilitation. This approach assumes that the client is deviant and is consistent with the neo-conservatism of North American approaches to welfare. He also claims that the emphasis during and after the investigation is consistent with the neo-conservative approaches to welfare. In other words, leave families to govern themselves and utilise state intervention only when absolutely necessary. He illustrates similarities between the neo-conservative influences of North American welfare and the liberal characteristics of the prevailing political climate in Canada.

He views Canada as a liberal-capitalist society where liberal characteristics such as major personal reform and limited social reform equate to the conservative values still entrenched within the thinking of the country's political elite (Mulally, 1997, p. 60). Thus, here too, a neo-conservatism that views people in receipt of welfare services as 'lax, immoral and irresponsible' prevails. Its adherents also assert that clients have missed their chances in life through their own failings.

Marchak (1987, pp. 42-43) highlights the interference in the political process by private business as a key consideration in Canadian social policy developments. This trend was evident in my work with Jane and impacted on the possibilities open to me. For example, I had to solicit counselling services for her from the private sector and had to apply to an in-house funding approval panel for authorisation to do so. I had been more familiar with looking to the state as provider in my previous work in the United Kingdom.

Working within the child protection system posed other problems for my view of the world. Jane was defined as a 'problem' by the agency because she was a black, unemployed and uneducated single-parent mother. The end result of such labelling was to confirm that she could not provide adequately for her children's nutrition, hygiene and health needs. This situation is complicated by views that filter across the border from the United States.

Liberal critics in the United States use the term 'single mother' as a codeword for a *'black welfare mom'* and utilise this perception of the 'problem' to enable contemporary society to shift attention away from the social causes of the 'problems' encountered by single-parent women such as lowered educational standards, increasing racism and fewer employment opportunities (McLanahan, 1994). Thus, people like Jane easily become scapegoats for social ills. I would prefer to frame Jane's problems as being the result of the racist practices that also prevail in Canada.

As a black woman, Jane has had fewer opportunities to education and employment than other women in her position. This problem was further aggravated by her mother also being a black woman with few opportunities. Her life under the constant worry of poverty had also impacted upon Jane's upbringing.

Additionally, the patriarchal social context that Jane lived within did not help her either. For example, Jane did not understand why Tyler should share responsibility for the children and work to alleviate her current predicament. She had been socialised to believe that it is her sole duty to raise her children and did not want to deviate from the expectations this placed upon her. I would prefer to tackle these wider contributing factors to her problems rather than focus on re-aligning their manifestations. But, as I demonstrate in my discussion of the issues later, tackling the outward shows of Jane's inappropriate parenting abilities on their own does not guarantee ongoing success. It simply deals with the immediate crisis.

Young (1990, p. 139) claims that oppression is found in structures such as education, health care, and in the production and distribution of social resources. However, these sources are legitimised to the extent that the oppression that occurs protects an oppressing dominant group. And so, liberal views dictate that the causes of dysfunctionality are sought within families, while society seeks to maintain the status quo by promoting a two tier system with those labelled 'deviant' being those on the bottom tier.

As Young (1994, p. 41) says, 'social workers should seek to challenge oppression whilst working with the individual'. Hasenfeld (1987, p. 487) points out, that 'the major role of social work should be to empower people to make choices and gain control over their environment'. Jane could see nothing wrong with the structure of her environment. What was wrong in her eyes was that she didn't have enough money to live on, not that she was unable to earn enough money.

Listening to Jane

After the children were taken away from Jane, my co-worker and I set about arranging for her parenting skill education, budgeting lessons and counselling for her past abuse and current status as a victim. We ensured that all her access visits with the boys which were determined by us were scrutinised by a family aid worker who would report to us on each interaction Jane made with her sons. We made the appointments for Jane to get pre-natal medical care. We also saw to the medical needs of the boys.

But what we were doing was taking over her life and running it along the same lines as the social system had run it before. We worked from *within* the system and we did nothing about the facets of that system that disempowered and oppressed her such as racism, patriarchy, classism and other reduced opportunities that Jane has encountered in life. As Galper (1975, p. 46) has said:

'agencies and services are organised so that they support or reinforce conformity, among clients and workers, to the very institutions and values that generate the problems to which the services were addressed in the first place'.

Jane had what Longres (1986, p. 413) terms 'false consciousness' in that she understood her problems in a way that promoted the interests of the dominant group in society. She did not, for example, define the problem as her unhygienic flat. Although she acknowledged the lack of hygiene, she considered the problem being that *I* was a dominant character in her life because I had powers vested in me as a child protection worker. On the stand in court during one of her appearances over the apprehension, Jane explained to the judge that we as agency workers should have told her *before* we apprehended the boys not to have Tyler around her apartment. 'So, how was I to know that you guys wanted him out of my life?' she asked.

Here we see Jane framing the problem of having an abusive partner in a way that upholds the values of the dominant group represented by the agency workers and not in a way that rationalises the abuse to herself. In other words, Jane was not involved in her 'remedy'. We did everything for her and expected her to go along with whatever we said. Naturally, she would do this and her performance was used by us as a measure of her success. But, how can we rely on her 'doing what we tell her to' as a measure of her behaviour? What real choices does she have?

In the circumstances Jane is living within, she *is* going to say all the right things and do all we ask. She has no option, if she wants her children back. We beat her into submission and formed her to our liking. We did not empower her or give her the opportunities in life that she has been denied. More than that, we took over her life and made her be what *the system* tells social workers that clients should be like.

My Department's mandate was to negotiate the presenting critical issues and lay the foundations for future work that would be developed when the case was transferred to one of the long-term teams. Child protection workers wear two hats – those of sanctioner and enabler. In my opinion, my co-worker and I did a lot of the sanctioning of Jane, both formally and informally. We removed the children, but I believe this was the correct course of action because the situation for them was dire.

But now, looking back at the situation, I find the amount of informal sanctioning that we did unacceptable. We told Jane that Tyler was 'no good' and in a valid effort to get her to appreciate that she was a victim and that she had a right to be treated better; we indirectly put across to her that she was *wrong*. We should have worked more with Jane on exploring her victim status from *her* own understanding and assisted her to realise that what Tyler was doing was bad for her, not that *we* thought he was bad for her.

Jane was very much alone in all of this disruption to her life. In the United Kingdom, however, she would have had at her disposal a Family Centre to go to as a part of the attempts made at 'remedying' her situation. Family Centres are statutory provisions operated by local authority Social Service Departments via the Children Act, 1989. Their purpose is to offer occupational and recreational activity, advice, guidance and counselling to recipients of child welfare services. I believe that this service would have a positive effect on disempowered clients like Jane because at a Family Centre, she would have been with other people who were in the same position as her. In their midst, she would have been able to identify and grow with the services offered instead of just being a passive acceptor of the services provided.

At another court hearing, Jane informed the judge that Tyler had *only* given her a 'good' beating. He had beaten her because she had 'shamed him' in front of his friends. Jane believed that she deserved a 'good' beating because of her own actions. During this beating she had been holding her youngest child. But she went on to explain that Tyler would have been guilty of giving her a 'bad' beating if he had physically hurt the baby. Jane did not appreciate the emotional effect of violence on the child. But in her view, as he had not physically harmed the baby, Tyler had only given her a 'good' beating. Although Jane had laid charges against Tyler for assaulting her, the week following this appearance, she attended the youth court with him. Tyler received a $250 fine (approximately £100). Jane told me afterwards that he could easily get this money together from his other girlfriend for whom Tyler acted as a pimp.

On average, 100 women in Canada are murdered each year by their partners. One in six women report violence from a partner and one in five of these sustain physical injury (Family Violence Unit, 1999). Spousal violence or abuse covers behaviours such as verbal aggression, degradation, confinement, threats, emotional abuse, fear, intimidation and physical violence. Jane had suffered all these at the hands of Tyler. For me, the question remained, 'Why did she still maintain a relationship with him?'

To find an answer, I examined patriarchal relations. Jane had been brought up witnessing aggression waged against herself, her mother and her siblings by a dominant male (her stepfather). In addition, we discovered that Jane's aunt who had been raised as her sister had been sexually abused by the stepfather and that the family knew this whilst it was going on. Child protection workers had been involved with the family many times during Jane's childhood. But, as Jane put it, such behaviour 'was a secret that you don't talk about'. I believe that it was this upbringing and social relationships that had led her to accept that women can be mistreated and that there was little that could be done to prevent it.

My co-worker and I arranged counselling to address Jane's status as a victim, and over the course of time, we hoped that a positive effect would be achieved. But, during our crisis involvement with Jane, we reinforced the here and now, dealing with her acceptance of being a victim through our mandate of dealing with the crisis of protecting the children rather than negotiating the range of issues surrounding the family.

I do not for one moment; consider that my co-worker, the agency or I were insensitive to Jane and her social set, or, that we wielded the 'hammer of our power' over them. I do think, however, that as a part of a larger system, we were constrained in what we could do. Madge and Attridge (1996, p. 36) have pointed to the mass of written protocols and guidance that child protection workers in England and Wales have to guide their every move and assert that this is because the service has been hammered by media representations of scandals and child abuse.

They argue that practitioners work in fear and that his has led to a lowering of personal social work in child protection cases as the need to tackle the presenting issues of child abuse takes precedence. Hallet (1995) considers child welfare in England to be driven by the judicial system rather than the welfare professions. Pringle (1998, p. 37) claims that child protection social workers seem to have become judicial assistants.

This is very much how I felt working within the Canadian system. My desire to work on a wider field to incorporate the total influences upon *'Jane who neglects her kids'* was over-shadowed by a structural requirement to ensure the immediate safety of the boys and to work at *correcting* Jane's behaviour for their eventual return to her care.

As in Britain, with the purchaser-provider split, social workers in Canada are being increasingly separated from the services they *'put in'* to negotiate identified needs (Parton, 1997, pp. 214-216). Ife (1996) offers as a critique of social work practice in contemporary society that under 'neo-conservative economic rationalism' new social expectations have devastating effects on social work practice and argues that the emphasis is now on 'logical analysis of data and *not* values'. In other words, the objective rules the subjective.

Liability is a further big issue that Canadian child protection workers face. The fear of liability has a significant effect on the practice of core social work values (Rees and Rodley, 1995, p. 15). I felt very much the contradiction of whether I am organisationally required to reflect my social work values or the values of neo-conservative society, constrained as I was in my every move and decision by protocols and guidance. Belsky and Vondra (1989) have pointed out that parenting is influenced by more than just the home and emotional environment. The macro-environment also plays a large part. This was evident with Jane whose chaotic parenting was borne from more than just an inability to keep a clean and orderly home.

Conclusions

My co-worker and I were involved with Jane and her family for around ten weeks. At the point of transfer I was asked by the receiving worker if I would like to stay involved with the case because I understood the wider issues impacting upon her problems. I declined after discussion with my colleagues because I believed that long-term intervention with Jane was merely going to continue addressing the surface issues and not tackle the structural ones. Hence, I could see no point in staying involved. It is not that individual workers *would not* tackle wider matters; it was that the structure that they worked within gave no room for doing so. I also felt that I had been so instrumental in the nasty side of social work such as the apprehension of the children and invasion of her privacy, that I felt that at that point the bulk of the intrusive work had been completed. And, it would be easier for Jane to start a-fresh with a new face and to build a relationship that would not be tainted by the intrusion of past events.

I have, however, visited Jane once with her new worker and as a means of boosting her self-esteem, conversed regarding the changes that I noted she has made between my two visits. Jane has come a long way. The boys are still in agency care, but she is now at the point where she has them stay over at weekends unsupervised apart from ad-hoc drop-ins by the out-of-hours emergency duty team. She has been allowed to keep the baby when she was born, again with strict supervision. She says things now like, 'I know why you guys had to take my kids'.

But she also cannot understand why she cannot yet have them back because her apartment is now clean. She also says, 'I've got Tyler out of my life like *you* guys wanted'. For me, these statements highlight the serious deficiencies of child protection work. We base our evaluation of Jane's progress on the physical removal of Tyler and not any emotional removal of him. She talks today of loving Tyler, but appreciates that she cannot see him or 'child protection will come and get the kids'. I do not see this as a healthy resolution of her situation.

It is likely that Jane will get the boys back within two months. The long-term worker and supervision by the out-of-hours team would continue for a few months longer afterwards. The possibility, therefore, exists that by the end of this year, Jane and her family will be alone again. It is my concern that by that time that Jane will be able to budget and see to the health needs of the children, she will still be a 20 year old black woman, living in poverty on welfare, disempowered to make positive changes in her life and still holding an emotional attachment to a man who society has conditioned her to believe is dominant over her as a woman.

Child protection has protected the children for now, but it has done nothing to negotiate the wider reasons for the children needing protection in the first place. My experience of child protection in Canada suggests that it is not good social work practice. It is inappropriate to live in fear of getting that 'knock on the door' again sometime and that the upshot of it will be losing the children – like Jane.

Ife (1996) has said that current changes in economics, politics and the social environment are in opposition to the values of the social work profession. I believe that social work of any description cannot merely look at the presenting issues. It must take account of the impact of wider environmental and structural inequalities on the lives of clients. Additionally, social work must be political and understand racism, the effects of capitalism on clients, economics, and the dramatic changes made to the structure of society over the past two decades by political decision-makers and be given, by the system, a license to negotiate these with clients.

10 Impressions from an English Exchange Student in Canada

PHIL BECK

Being Part of an European Union-Canada Exchange Programme

I undertook a placement in Victoria, Canada as part of an exchange programme with Eliot Smith, a fellow student on my first year MSc/Diploma in Social Work (DipSW) course. This was the first assessed placement and lasted 50 days. The European Union-Canada Exchange Programme linked Southampton University with the University of Stockholm (Sweden), a university in Holland and three universities in Canada. Through the co-ordinated efforts of Lena Dominelli from the University of Southampton and David Turner and Walene Whitaker from the University of Victoria, Eliot and I had placements arranged with the Ministry of Children and Families in British Columbia's capital city, Victoria.

Placement Outline

Our placements were statutory sector ones within the Protective Family Services Team (city office) in the municipality of Greater Victoria. This Team constituted one of the three integrated child protection services that the Ministry of Children and Families (MCF) provide. The team had two types of client groups:

- family service clients (those cases where the child resides with family members); and
- child service clients (those children who were in the care of the MCF).

The team took its referrals mainly from the intake teams who were responsible for child protection enquiry and investigation. Those investigations that warranted further input from MCF would be transferred for further assessment and where required, short and long-term intervention work. The focus of all interventions was on people aged from birth to 18 years of age and, wherever possible, the family member connected with those children and young people.

The Student's Role

As students, Eliot and I were linked to experienced practice teachers who were two of the seven social workers on the Protective Family Services Team. The workers' caseloads were divided into geographical sectors of the Greater Victoria city municipality and were overseen by the team leader, Riley Hern. Through our practice teachers, Eliot and I were attached to separate areas within the city. Each of these had very different communities, socio-economic trends and geographical locations to work within.

The ethos around which the Team's social work practice centred was that of community-based service delivery in providing and integrating child protection services. This focused social work intervention through neighbourhood house projects, community support services and voluntary sector programmes.

Each placement was arranged to expose each of us to this model of social work intervention, through the casework and geographical area allocated to each of us by the team leader and the practice teachers.

All social work intervention carried out within the MCF occurs under the directions laid out in the Child, Family and Community Service Act. The Act requires anyone who has reason to believe that a child may be abused, neglected, or in need of protection to report to the Director of the MCF or a delegated social worker.

The social worker's role may include:

• providing or arranging the provision of support services to the family
• supervising the child's care in the home, or

- protecting the child through removal from the family and placement with relatives, a foster family or specialised residential resources (not available in Victoria).

As students, each of us was expected to actively participate in fulfilling all the requirements placed upon a designated MCF social worker within reason and under the supervision and guidance of the practice teacher. Each of us was able to use all the members of the team for support and advice. However, decisions on our cases were made following consultation and discussion with the relevant practice teacher and/or the team leader.

My Placement Experience

I was based with Claire Miller who was the case holder for the largest geographical area on the Team. Claire was responsible for several community neighbourhoods, which were predominantly white middle-class suburban areas with low levels of unemployment. The challenges inherent in working in these neighbourhoods were exemplified by the hostility shown towards any kind of social worker involvement around child protection issues because this was considered an infringement on their private lives. The local population were largely tax-paying, educated working people who saw their role in relation to the MCF as exercising their right to advocate for services for themselves.

The focus on community-centred interventions was generally considered of little relevance in these neighbourhoods because individuals felt that their financial status enabled them to provide sufficient childcare support for themselves. The absence of a community spirit and collective neighbourhood interest posed significant difficulties in getting accurate and representative information as to the welfare and protection of the children living in these areas. Although mandatory reporting of suspected child abuse exists in law, reporting in this community was practically non-existent. The social workers' right to intervene in these neighbourhoods was regularly challenged by residents and many practitioners had to defend strongly their involvement in private lives personally.

Although community facilities were available and were very well-resourced, their users were unrepresentative of the people the Centre was meant to attract and support. Sadly, when I tried to link families with their local community resources, feedback from parents was often very negative. They claimed to feel either unwelcome or that their presence and need for services was over-emphasised by those working at the Centre. My experience of James Bay, a well-resourced and the longest established centre in the city, was that of a clinical style, purpose-driven environment that was for those who knew their place and why they were at the Centre. This approach flies almost directly in the face of the spirit of community ownership where those least empowered to help themselves are welcomed and actively assisted to get the support they need to protect and parent their children fully.

On two separate occasions, I visited the James Bay Community Centre in the same week. The first time, I dressed formally in a shirt and tie with a briefcase. I was welcomed by the receptionist and not questioned as to the purpose of my visit. The second time, I went dressed in casuals, and was immediately approached by staff asking who I was, why I was there, and had I made an appointment to see anyone. The second visit highlighted for me the very real experiences that many families in need face when trying to access what was their local community resource and the barriers the Centre inadvertently had put up against the people it was intended to help.

The role of my practice teacher was to be very flexible in trying to meet the needs of children and families living in what I experienced as non-community-oriented neighbourhoods. This location seemed to me to be the primary area where the Team's model of intervention could not be applied easily. As a placement student, I found that I was constantly questioning the way in which resources were allocated directly to families who had the means to provide for themselves, often over families who did not.

This was largely a result of needy families not having the community support that would help them to acquire these resources because the local people did not recognise and value the benefits of community-based resources and how these might offer support to both well-off and poor people. The frustrations my practice teacher felt in carrying out her duties as a child protection worker became clear to me when I began the difficult job of trying to match community resources with the needs of the families and children that I worked with.

These neighbourhoods perpetuated the false view that there were no children in need of protection from abuse or neglect in these areas. These opinions compounded the already complex process of engaging with families who had come to the attention of the MCF. Shame and secrecy surrounded their involvement with child protection social workers. These perceptions resulted in an automatic labelling of those receiving any social work intervention as unfit parents and upheld the community's negative image that these people, who usually tended to be young single mothers, did not deserve to have children.

I believe that challenging the stereotypical images and oppression of the less fortunate members living in these neighbourhoods could only be addressed in face-to-face discussions with individuals who expressed these views rather than dealing with the issue across the community as a whole.

From working in these parts of Victoria, I gained the impression that the all-powerful minority was there to represent their personal views over and above those of other members of their own communities. The political influence that key neighbourhood figures held in relation to privileging their access to services highlighted for me the injustice that many of the clients that I worked with felt in not getting the services that they and their children needed because they were not valued members of local society.

Like many others in statutory social work placements, I felt that the opportunities afforded to students to do direct one-to-one work with children and their families was increasingly becoming a peripheral luxury for the Team's social workers. This was largely due to the ever increasing caseloads of 25 to 30 cases that each of the workers had to manage, often leaving them in a position to do little more than co-ordinate packages of interventions that were based on reactive risk-reduction policies. The luxury that I had as a student to uphold good practice in working directly with families on an almost daily basis made me fully aware of the increasingly distant relationship that social work practitioners are now having to develop with the people they are designated to assist.

For me, the work I did with families in providing support through accessing resources and one-to-one involvement was about trying to interpret if and how community-based service provision worked in Victoria. If such a thing as a community exists, I feel I have learned that there is a need for social workers to be accepted as a useful and support-enabling member of that community. Professionals have to learn how to work with local people and develop the services necessary for protecting the children within the community.

While there should remain a focus on the protection of children and vulnerable young people, it seems to me that the era of government agencies dictating to society how protection and intervention operates is increasingly becoming out of touch with local realities. Professionals acting on behalf of the state can no longer claim with confidence that they represent the fragmented and increasingly diverse nature of local communities that range from the indigenous First Nations peoples to the large and varied ones composed of immigrants from overseas.

Conclusions

By having the opportunity to develop and broaden my social work experience in a culture both similar to my own and at the same time unknown to me in Victoria, I have been able to actively challenge my own prejudices in relation to how people should be treated. I also acknowledge the need to constantly strive for good practice in the face of bureaucratic controls and dwindling resources. In being given the temporary mantel of student social worker, I now have a fuller understanding of the responsibilities and pressures Family Protective Services practitioners face in striving daily to meet the needs of society's most vulnerable people – children.

11 Reflecting on a Practice Placement in India

CHRISTINE BENNETT

Introduction

'An international practicum to fulfill my 4th year Social Work degree practicum requirement! What a great idea', I said to myself, very naively. I really did not know what I was getting into, but was ready and willing for a challenge. Now that the experience is over, I want to share my reflections with others in the hopes that they can capitalise on my learning and thereby enhance their own experiences.

I am a 34-year-old Canadian; white, heterosexual, female, divorced, with no children. When the University of Victoria offered international placements, I jumped at the opportunity. I love to travel, and have gone overseas many times before, but always as a tourist. I always felt, that as a tourist, I did not get a real appreciation of the people, their culture, and their experiences.

I was hoping that by working with the local community I could connect with the population and really begin to understand a different way of life. I had no idea I would learn as much as I did through what proved to be an amazing experience.

Setting up the contacts was relatively easy, thanks to e-mail. The University of Victoria's (UVic) practicum co-ordinator, Walene Whitaker, suggested a College in India, where a former UVic student had worked previously in community development. I was welcomed, over the e-mail, and told that I would be taking part in the College's community development programme, only to arrive and find that this was not possible!

Apparently their programme was having a range of internal problems. So, the director had to put all his efforts into sorting out his programme.

He also felt that the students on this course could not accommodate an international student at this time. And he did not want me to begin my placement without their support.

Persistence paid off for me, I toured the College's satellite programmes and found a great placement. I had to be very clear at this point regarding my expectations. The College director really thought that I should just tour about, visit different places and get an overview of everything before I made a decision about where to stay for my placement.

They were a bit surprised when I toured 3 places in one week and picked a placement so quickly. The agencies that I visited were separated by great distances and required a lot of difficult bus travel. It seems to me that their sense of time is very different from mine, and I had to be very assertive in this matter if I were to meet my objectives. I was not in India to be a tourist; I was there to work. I could become a tourist after my practicum obligations were fulfilled, but not during my contracted placement time.

The placement I chose was situated in Southern India with 5 Roman Catholic nuns who were running a community development programme for local women. The programme had a staff of approximately 25 community workers. I went out with the staff everyday, and participated in the daily activities that the women undertook in the self-help groups. I lived in the convent for the entire time I was on placement, and I could write a paper just on that experience alone.

I was born Roman Catholic but am not a practicing member of a congregation. The nuns were very accepting of my inadequate religious knowledge. They made it clear that my participation in the religious aspect of the convent life was entirely voluntarily. However, the members of staff were less tolerant about my choices in this regard and found ways of expressing their views.

One morning I slept in, and the fact that I missed mass was quite a topic of discussion amongst them. I had to make it clear to all of them that I had missed mass by mistake, and not by choice. They accepted this, but afterwards I always had a wake-up call by one member of staff, to ensure I did not miss the services. I was tolerant and respectful of their religious practices, and this played a major part in my being accepted into their community.

Prior Expectations of the Placement

I wrote down the following points before I journeyed to India to begin my placement:

What am I scared of?

- Not being 'accepted' as a helper. Being seen as an outsider. That no one will talk to me and I will not be able to help in whatever capacity I am placed in. I am willing to learn the culture, the language, but are my clients willing to accept help from a white foreigner? As I am not able to be as helpful as local professionals, is it ethically wrong for me to be placed in a helping capacity in these placements?
- Language barriers
- Cultural barriers
- Communication barriers. Will I really be able to communicate with the people I meet? Will I understand their needs, wants, feelings, thoughts, not only from a language viewpoint, but from a cultural viewpoint as well? What skills will I need to overcome these barriers? Will honesty, a non-judgemental attitude, an interpreter, knowledge of local agencies and services, knowledge of religious obstacles, traditions and etiquette be enough?

Now that I have completed my placement, it is interesting to reflect back on my fears. And yes, some came true. My biggest fear was the inability to communicate and this turned out to be the biggest challenge I faced. I really had to look for other ways of communicating and learning.

I remember the first e-mail I wrote to Walene in an absolute panic, asking her if it was OK if I taught English to the children. I thought that would be the only thing that I was capable of offering those I sought to help. I was very lucky to have found a community development project where I could work alongside the staff, who knew some English. I then had to revamp my goals and objectives to suit this type of placement, that is, of moving from individual counselling to a community development focus.

Some fears turned out to be false. I was accepted into the agency and community wholeheartedly. All the people I met were curious about me, my background, my family, just like I was curious about them. So many times the staff would tell me that the women in our self-help groups wished they knew more English, so they could talk with me.

I was right when I predicted what skills I would need for the placement – honesty, a non-judgemental attitude, an interpreter, knowledge of local agencies and services, knowledge of religious barriers, traditions and etiquette. I worked on these skills continually, and was lucky enough to have the resources to do so.

One Sister had a library with many books about India and she let me read as much as I could. The staff gave me language lessons and helped me to translate and interpret their language into English. These were not perfect translations and interpretations, but they were good enough for me to gain a general idea about what was going on most of the time.

Areas of Major Learning

Below, I identify the major areas that provided me with my most important learning experiences.

Cultural awareness

I was exposed to a totally different culture, traditions, celebrations, food, etiquette, behaviour, religion and so on. Throughout my stay I had to practice open-mindedness and tolerance to these differences. A non-judgemental attitude was key in building rapport with my co-workers and clients.

Community Development

I have participated in a community development programme that uses an economic model of self-help groups to empower women. This exposure is new to me, and will open up new doors for me in terms of interest and career. I am eager to seek out employment opportunities in this area and hope to find agencies willing to use my service in Canada or abroad. I now have an international linkage and was offered a job teaching at the India College if ever I get my MSW.

Self-Reflection

Sitting under my mosquito net at night and journaling has given me the opportunity to reflect inwardly, something that I am 'too busy' to do at home. I have had to process many thoughts and feelings by myself. This process has been very good in terms of personal development. I'm not saying that I have all the answers, but I am at least asking questions of myself. Many of my questions are ethical dilemmas, for example, is it right for a white Canadian to work in rural India? The course offered by UVic dealing with ethical dilemmas, was one of my favourite, and now I see why, I continually seek answers to these types of questions.

Gender Issues

I was able to really feel and understand the differences between the male and female in the lower classes of poor rural poor of India. In a broader sense, I also became aware of the conflicting roles between the genders and the status of women. In Canada, women fight for equality, and in some places in India they fight for their lives. I saw a visible patriarchal society and understand more of the oppressive elements associated with this. I have a greater understanding of the traditional role of women, and the struggle for balance between the many roles a woman plays in her life – daughter, friend, neighbour, worker, wife, mother.

International Relations

The India College and the Sisters running the community development project have asked me to link them with UVic. They are eager for further dialogue in terms of exchange programmes or more students going on placement. The India College put together a one-month workshop for an American University. The American students were taught classes (in English) on subjects ranging from the poor in developing countries to community development initiatives. This is just one example; the potential and possibilities are numerous.

Group Dynamics

The self-help groups have 20 female members, and the staff member has to be a good communicator and practice conflict resolution. The largest groups I have worked with before I went to India had around 5 members, so it was a great experience to deal with much larger groups of people.

Illiteracy

I felt the frustration of illiteracy, and this was a great learning experience. The Indian State language is written with Arabic script, so I could not read, write or speak! I felt what many immigrants to Canada must feel – the frustration of communication barriers. I spoke with little English words and used sign language a lot.

I did this to such an extent that when I spoke to my family in Canada they laughed at my chopped sentences. I had forgotten how to verbalise in complete sentences. I became language starved and I found I craved anything English. I smiled at white tourists like they were my long lost friends. They did not smile back! All I wanted was to talk, but I guess they were not as communication starved as I felt.

Being a Visible Minority

I felt at first hand what it is like to be a visible minority. Next to language barriers, this was the thing I liked least about the placement experience. I was so tired at being stared at by people that I bought an umbrella to hide under. I had to leave a couple of restaurants because people would stop eating and stare at me. The worst though, was when adults would drag their kids over and make them touch me. The kids would cry and I could do nothing but stand there and cringe. I did not know enough of their language to ask the parents to stop. This was a major learning experience and I pray that I never make someone feel like I felt.

Language Barriers

The lack of language through which to communicate was, I think, the hardest challenge for me. The frustration of communication took me to the brink of tears sometimes. I am the type of social worker who loves fieldwork and direct contact with the clients. Before I left, I imagined myself counselling the Indian women and really getting to know them. Unfortunately, most of the Indian clients I dealt with had little education, which meant that they spoke little English.

I really questioned whether I could practice 'Social Work' when I couldn't communicate on a personal level with the clients. I had to change my expectations and goals to reflect other learning opportunities, like cultural awareness, exposure and community development study.

I was able to communicate more with the staff, and I felt lucky to have been placed in an agency where I was allowed to accompany a staff member at all times. A key drawback of this is the extra responsibility my lack of local language skills placed on the staff who had to try and translate for me.

During group meetings tending to my needs would have placed a further burden on the staff, so I always waited until after the meeting to get the translation. Some staff knew more English than others. So over time, communication became easier once I knew what words they understood. Key words for these exchanges were *problem, no problem, like, not like,* and the famous *OK.* You'd be amazed how far these phrases got me.

If I had the chance to do it over again, I would hire a translator. Although it was too late in my placement for me to do it, I learned that local Indian graduates with a Masters of Social Work (MSW) would have been happy to be hired as translators for $Cdn150 a month. This would have solved many problems for me, and I wish I had inquired about this option before I had started my work. Everything would have been easier for me, from interacting with the clients to catching buses to eating in restaurants.

Having a MSW person with me would also have satisfied UVic's requirement of having a MSW supervisor involved in my practicum. I would have arranged payment to go through UVic, because ethically I do not think it is appropriate for a student to directly pay her own supervisor or translator. This might have carried the danger of biasing my evaluation, and, therefore, it is my view that engaging in this practice would certainly not be appropriate.

Instead, to fulfill the evaluation requirement, I had to arrange meetings between the India College and the convent which was 5 hours away by bus or train in order to have my mid-term and final evaluation papers completed. This was a time consuming event, and hard to schedule between the two agencies. I had to be very assertive with the deadlines, because otherwise, evaluating my work was not a high priority for either institution.

Ambassador and Diplomat

I represented UVic, Canada, and all things associated with being the colour of my skin. I was 'on display' at all times and really felt the pressure and responsibility to behave respectfully and appropriately.

Diplomacy, I feel, means knowing when to bite your tongue and when to express your opinion. For example, I watched, in horror, a cement brick operation that employed local women from the self-help groups. The agency staff were all enthusiastic about these projects because these women would be earning a great wage.

With tears welling in my eyes I had to bite my tongue; can't they see the blisters on the woman's hands because they have no gloves? Can't they smell the sweat of the women clothed in full-length heavy dresses? Can't they see the crushed toes in the open toed sandals the women wore when carrying the concrete bricks? I guess others may have handled this differently than I, perhaps stepping out, voicing an opinion, advocating for better working conditions for the women. Me, I remained silent and I struggled with the question, 'Do I, as an outsider and a student, have the right to say anything?'

On the same subject, the first agency I toured in my quest for a practice placement was in a very remote location. No guesthouses or hotels existed; I was given the priest's room at the rectory. A local man brought food, cooked by his wife, to me, everyday. At night, this man slept in my front porch to 'protect' me.

I liked the people and the work there, but decided not to do my placement there because of the burden I would be placing on the priest and the local man. Had I taken up the offer, the priest would have had to sleep in another rectory, half an hours' drive away. And, in my opinion, the local man should be protecting his own family at night, not me.

Well, my decision caused some commotion at the India College. Apparently I was 'wrong' in thinking I was being an inconvenience. They believed that I did not understand this part of their culture correctly. I was told that in Indian culture, the servant type of work is part of their culture and as for the priest, well, if he did not like it, he could tell me himself. I struggled with this viewpoint. Just because culturally something is acceptable, does this mean that I have to accept it?

Finally, my own feeling of being a burden to these people won, and I went elsewhere, to the convent, where I did not feel like a burden. I participated in the chores, the cooking and the cleaning, like all the other staff did. This helped me feel acceptance, something so important for me. I would have never felt like part of the rural community when I had a servant attending to my needs.

My last challenge at diplomacy came at the end of my practicum. For the India College I had to submit a paper on the subject, *Empowerment of Women in India*. My first draft was rejected; I was told I had focused on too many issues facing the poor of India, and this was too stereotypical and depressing. I was told to focus on the accomplishments of the middle and upper class women of India. I was very frustrated when I explained that I found this difficult to do, having just spent 2 months in the slums of India working with impoverished people. We finally settled on a general paper on women empowerment, and this was thankfully acceptable.

Concluding Reflections

On a very personal basis, I learned that I could meet the challenge of doing an international exchange. I had travelled extensively before, so I was prepared for the trials and tribulations of being a Third World country, or so I thought. The placement experience was much harder than any travel I have done.

When travelling, I am on vacation. I am a tourist. If I don't like the room I am staying in, I have the option of choosing another touristy type of accommodation. I can roam from tourist attraction to tourist attraction and when I get bored, I just move on.

In contrast, the placement experience I had was not a 'touristy' experience. I lived, worked and breathed the community development project the entire time. For the 2 months that I was on placement I was without a single day off to call my own. I was touched and moved by people in a country very different from mine.

I lived in a convent and was exposed to the Catholic religion and then went outside and worked with Hindu, Christians and Muslims within the same self-help groups. The emotional roller coaster never seemed to stop for a rest. It was really hard going, and I am a better person for sticking this through to the end. I feel stronger, more confident and definitely more empowered and enriched because of this experience.

The people I met and the staff I worked with were truly great people, and I am honoured that I had the opportunity to meet them all. I am thankful that we are continuing our friendship and contact through letters. And, I hope that one day, I will be able to return and work with them again.

PART II

SUPPORTING STUDENTS ON INTERNATIONAL EXCHANGES – VIEWS FROM PRACTICE

12 Tutoring Overseas and Home Students

KISH BHATTI-SINCLAIR

Introduction

Surviving an overseas placement provides both challenges and opportunities. Many new issues come to the fore, but the chance of exploring them in new ways is also present, as are encounters with new issues and dilemmas.

In this chapter, I intend to explore how these are faced by students who experience and tutors who organise social work placements in overseas countries. I also explore the organisational systems and structures which need to be in place to receive students at the relevant universities and social work agencies. I discuss these within the context of the current debates on welfare in the United Kingdom and the globalisation of social work education which is leading to increased demands on social workers to address the needs of individuals and communities crossing international borders.

I base this chapter on my experiences as tutor to three students undertaking student exchanges in practice placements. Two of these were overseas students in the UK and one was a British student in Canada who participated in the European Union–Canada, *Child Abuse, Protection and Welfare Project*. Funded by the European Union and Canadian government, this Project supported students and staff in organised visits and exchanges.

The process involved me in one visit to an overseas university and conferences, some face-to-face contact with the relevant personnel, and meetings with colleagues who came from overseas to Southampton as part of the Project.

I also use feedback from the students and social workers to inform what I say in this chapter. And so responses to the issues and dilemmas encountered includes perspectives from the following key players: university representatives, students, practice teachers and tutors. The primary areas I cover are: the motivation of those involved; economic considerations; the globalisation of teaching and learning methods; support systems; and practical arrangements to maximise success.

From my work on this Project, I have concluded that background knowledge and experience played a critical role in understanding the roles and responsibilities of the relevant staff and demonstrated greater commitment to the proposed aims and objectives of the European Union-Canada Project. Personal contact with teachers from the overseas universities enabled me to visualise the campus and its surrounding areas and enabled me to pass on information to the student who gained knowledge based on a first-hand experience.

I also concluded that the knowledge and skills, which are currently used by key players need to be enhanced to incorporate a comprehensive understanding of globalisation and its impact on social work education. This would encourage the deconstruction of commonalities and differences across countries, particularly in relation to intangible issues such as structural and institutional power and how it impacts on work with service users. In the United Kingdom, research has indicated that individual and organisational values need to be examined in detail as they play a significant role in the content of the student's learning (Brown and Bourne, 1998).

Social Work Education in the United Kingdom

The rapid development of globalised economic systems during the 1970s and 1980s eased the movement of money, goods and trade across national borders, leading to major changes in employment practices in the United Kingdom and to increases in part-time low paid work and poverty. The imperative to provide universal welfare as advocated by post Second World War reformists such as Beveridge (Jordon, 1998), diminished as demands for services grew and successive governments rationalised welfare to promote greater efficiency, cost-effectiveness and a rationing of services.

This impacted adversely on social work service users and practitioners within the UK and at the beginning of the 21st century, only the most needy people receive state support and aid. Jordon (1998) suggests that public services in modern-day Britain appear to have a single aim – to select and assist the 'most needy' (Jordon, 1998, p. 100) through the application of means testing and other resource-led approaches.

An increase in global thinking is seen as necessary within the modernisation and rationalisation of welfare in the UK despite the fact that 'human needs remain essentially local and personal' (Ife, 2000, p. 55). The imperative for efficiency and effectiveness has also impacted on the training needs of the social care workforce in Britain, most particularly, the 80 per cent who are currently untrained. In future, all social workers and social care staff will be regulated, registered and deregistered through the recently established General Social Care Council (Department of Health, 2001).

As a result, employers in the public and private sectors are being compelled to provide backing and support to employees wishing to qualify in readiness for registration. The effects on social work education are direct. As training for social care staff has not been set at degree level, their increasing demand for training is likely to lead to fewer courses delivering educational services at degree or postgraduate level. This will in turn reduce their availability for staff who will wish to qualify with a degree.

Social work education that is currently based in universities is expensive. In future, a high percentage of basic social care training will be provided primarily in the workplace and assessed by practitioners and practice teachers who may have been engaged in training university students in the past. The emphasis will be on the development of skills and increasing technical competence. The more intangible aspects of training such assessment of the individual's capacity to understand the needs of the service user within a broader public service and political context are unlikely to be addressed substantially within this framework.

Currently, university-based social work students in the UK are largely assessed on personal and professional ideologies and values. In addition to these, practice in accordance with ethical principles is promoted and strictly adhered to. Although the General Social Care Council will require that social care staff follow a professional code of practice, there is no imperative to ensure that the principles are explored to a significant extent and assessed in basic social care training.

Historically, social work has aimed to respond to the personal needs of service users and reflective practice includes an evaluation of the impact of the professional persona on service delivery. Those who enter the profession currently are motivated by its strong value base and appreciate the opportunity to examine personal ideology and philosophy in relation to practice.

The effects of globalisation filter through to social work courses in a number of ways. First, the increase in harmonisation (Williams, et al, 1998) within the European Union is likely to challenge national policy on standards of education provided within the UK both positively and negatively. There is an expectation that social workers will readily cross internal borders within the European Union and work anywhere in Europe, holding qualifications, which are recognised and accepted by all member states.

However, in the UK, the legislative backdrop is country specific and the partnership arrangements which allow the students to be placed within a social work agency (statutory and non-statutory) for 50 per cent of the course. These are usually located within the geographical region that surrounds a particular university.

Two important elements of social work courses in the UK are to make active links to theory and reflect on practice. Both skills are largely demonstrated and assessed within agencies striving to respond to the particular needs of their local neighbourhoods and communities. Therefore, law and policy in practice is bound by interpretation and works differently in relation to its context.

Students in the United Kingdom are currently offered generic, comprehensive academic teaching informed by national and international research which increases understanding of the knowledge, skills and values needed to be a social worker. Within this framework, the role of the social work educator is to:

'explore the evolving practical knowledge of students in order to assist them in the process of developing, understanding, articulating and utilising practical knowledge' (Gould and Harris, 1996).

The Impact of Globalisation on Social Work Education

Students, therefore, undertake an education, which is globally inspired (politically and academically) but locally delivered and experienced.

However, if the word 'overseas' were placed before the term 'students' in the quote given above, those involved in practice experience may need to have greater comprehension of the personal concerns and teaching and learning needs effecting those individuals in greater detail. This has resource implications in relation to staff time, more funds than are currently available for travel across countries and training and development needs.

Second, globalisation privileges the economically powerful, and within the UK, the gap between rich and poor is growing as publicly funded welfare is given less priority. The poor are being exploited more, but are less able to influence market forces or those in positions of power. From these inequalities, I conclude that to provide international educational opportunities, it is essential that the organisations and individuals involved understand the issues I have discussed above and work to ensure that inequalities and power differentials are addressed.

Third, those with resources are able to have easy access to information, technology and telecommunications and, therefore, globalisation has the ability to undermine and destabilise society:

'Electronic communications and rapid transportation are critical technologies for the development of these transnational practices. Their 'instant' character may have raised the possibility of a general cultural shift in a globalised direction' (Waters, 1995, p. 37).

Glastonbury and LaMendola (1992, p. 73) suggest that those with a greatest stake in the increase in global communication, such as multinational companies, are playing a greater role in 'setting our cultural, social and political values'.

Fourth, the language of commerce and telecommunication is English and therefore, globalisation privileges those who can speak and write English.Communication in the form of the printed word is increasingly becoming central to national identity whilst illiteracy remains common and widespread (During, 1995, p. 126).

Fifth, communication is increasingly based on transmission through computer and television. Consequently, information remains in the hands of those with ready access to such resources. As the Western world is more able to utilise these facilities, their law and policy is given more air space and, thereby becomes privileged. This is advantaging those who understand and can relate to technology. It also favours those who are able to adapt and change personally and professionally, and/or challenge social work cultures and identities that are circumscribed by national boundaries.

Sixth, although nations are increasingly becoming dependent upon each other and moving away from the nation state (Khan and Dominelli, p. 99, 2000), there is an increase in insularity through the competency-based approach (Hayes, 1996), accountability (Slater, 1996) and on reflection 'in' and 'on' practice within national boundaries (Gould and Harris, 1996).

Finally, the likely effects of globalisation on students are many. Principally, however, it is clear that only those who are economically strong can access international opportunities because education (overseas or otherwise) is becoming increasingly expensive. Communication skills are becoming increasingly critical and so whether English is their original language or not, students need to be fluent in both verbal and written forms.

They need to able to relate to law, policy and regulation of host countries and transfer practice experience to home countries and sell their educational experiences to prospective employers. As the imperative to achieve economic security increases, students are not clear whether overseas experience is necessarily useful to prospective employers who wish to capitalise on experience which is relevant and applicable to the national context.

The Requirements of International Exchanges

Clearly, the key players involved in the organisation of overseas practice opportunities are driven by a number of factors, which may be parallel, collective or individualised. In the UK, the universities are by far the most powerful contributors. Depending on the individuals who represent them, universities can make a qualitative difference to the educational experiences of the students and the practice teachers who provide the learning opportunities in workplace training.

Although individuals may embark on facilitating international exchanges for altruistic reasons, universities are increasingly driven by market forces. Thus, they promote an international image to increase student numbers and attract research grants funded by cross-country institutions for projects examining global concerns.

Those actively involved in setting up and delivering educational opportunities to overseas participants carry the responsibility of looking after their needs. This role is fulfilled primarily by the representatives of the receiving universities and the social services or social care organisations. Both parties have a unique contribution to make to the students' learning processes and have to take each other's particular viewpoints, obligation and commitments into account. The student is also likely to hold strong opinions on issues such as personal and professional needs. Their views also have to be considered and acted upon.

The Key Players in International Exchanges

My experience in international exchanges, suggests that each party has a significant and equal part to play in the organisation and co-ordination of practice placement which is based overseas. However, a significant difference between them is that although the representatives of both the receiving university and the social services organisation are likely to be acting for institutions which have clearly defined aims and objectives and are resourced by public funds, the power relations between them are unequal.

In these circumstances, the structural power inherent within the role of the tutor and the practice teacher must not be underestimated. Indeed, trying to work together requires that they address the implications of this specifically. Nonetheless, both the tutor and practice teacher have more power at their disposal than the student because their positions are bolstered by institutional forms of power.

The student, in comparison, is able to exercise limited power, even though she or he has a great deal of institutional support from the home university. It is likely that she or he will experience an overseas placement disengaged and isolated from domestic comforts, country, family, friends, environment and everyday routines.

The University Representative

It is clear that prime responsibility for the student's experience lies firmly with the person who manages the course or holds ultimate responsibility for the student. The work, however, is often handed down to a representative of the course management who is likely to have a commitment as a project grant-holder. The drive to ensure success is, therefore, with the person with knowledge of the background and design of the project.

The universities involved in the European Union-Canada Project were supportive of students and wished to promote their opportunity to experience social work across international borders. This may also facilitate academic and practice links and foster the image of social work education as an international and post-modern discipline (Bisman et al., 2000).

The notion of modernisation is central to the drive behind many such initiatives as pressures grow for social work practitioners and academics to assess and use marketplace principles and strategies within public services (Khan and Dominelli, 2000; Salustowicz, 2000). Experience of overseas social work may enable students from the UK, for example, to gain greater experience of welfare funded either privately by users or through a mixed economy of care.

As British welfare is predominantly funded by public bodies (Bisman et al., 2000), social work education has long been criticised for providing limited opportunities for UK home students to gain additional skills that might enable them to function competently within organisations which require management expertise in budgeting, rationalisation and prioritisation in those agencies which provide services outside the welfare state.

The role of the university representative within this scenario is to ensure that the student gains useful experience which not only meets personal and professional developmental needs but also the requirements of the relevant social work course. It is in the interest of the university representative to ensure that the full range of organisational resources and planning skills are used to ensure that the student's educational experience is organised well. The universities' reputations as players on the field of international social work are at risk if students' training is defined as being poor or inadequate.

The Student

The rationale offered by students who have opted for social work practice placements in countries far from home have included: the desire to experience life in other countries, an idea that is endorsed by media and other multi-national influences; the bid to formulate a well-rounded professional identity as a global citizen; and the aspiration to develop and grow as individuals.

In the UK, this latter aim has been widely promoted by the teaching and learning imperatives of the former Central Council for Social Work Education and Training (CCETSWa, 1995). In addition, within the brief to form comprehensive professional identities, students are increasingly becoming aware of the need to develop knowledge, values and skills which equip them to work with groups such as asylum seekers and refugees and others who cross international borders.

The Tutor

Most social work academics are encouraged by their employing universities to develop international links (Salustowicz, 2000) and readily communicate with colleagues through use of the World Wide Web and the Internet (Hick, 1999). This is supported by the notion of applying nationally bound social work theories (Langan and Day, 1992), previously developed and used with individuals within local communities and neighbourhoods, to work with service users cross international borders. There is also an imperative to regularly publish material based on such experiences and to seek and gain on-going funding to maintain international links.

The Practice Teacher

In the UK, practice teachers are trained, regulated and registered through a national statutory accreditation body. Many have seen the drive to professionalise social work not only as an important aspect of maintaining standards and quality of work with service users, but also of ensuring that they are actively engaged with new initiatives and developments within higher education.

Practice teachers provide 50 per cent of professional training to qualifying social work students in the United Kingdom (CCETSW, 1995b) and are, therefore, concerned that learning opportunities provided within the workplace take into account leading edge academic scholarship and research.

Requirements of a Successful Placement or Practicum

The organisations and the key players need to ensure that a number of measures are in place in order to ensure success. This requires attention to practical details but also a focus on common understandings and country-based differences. Experience suggests that defining commonalities is as important as clarifying differences.

The demands on social work education across the globe includes an imperative to: address: welfare delivery linked closely to national priorities on spending; cuts in welfare; increases in public concern at provision aimed at the undeserving; focusing on individual responsibility; and responding to a growing privatisation and greater poverty. The majority of social workers have a commitment to universal and core social work values and principles of adult learning, including the importance of experiences which broaden knowledge, skills and values.

Students arriving from overseas universities need to have an opportunity to understand the origins of welfare within the host country. They also require teaching on the rationale for development; nationally focused and locally implemented laws, policies and procedures and an examination of values, which are understood universally, but applied locally. In addition, students may wish to compare issues across countries such as an increase in insularity through competency-based approaches; a rise in the culture of accountability and the threats to the notion of the reflective and critical practitioner.

This suggests that those who provide the teaching and learning environment need to have an up-to-date knowledge base in order to deliver teaching and learning of high quality. The Internet provides a useful means by which to acquire and pass on such information to students. The UK government websites provide policy documents, which are readily available to students and tutors, but less available to practice teachers who do not always have access to such facilities.

Other tools needed to ensure success include a well-developed communication system between students and their universities; clear procedural guidance on health and safety; library and computing facilities which are easily accessible; catering, housing services and the advance issuing of student cards.

I have found that overseas students seek experiences which are linked to building confidence and life skills, therefore, information on locality, city, neighbourhood, transport, leisure, tourist attractions are very important as is the provision by host universities of materials such as maps, and public transport timetables prior to arrival. These may now be accessed on the web in some countries.

Ideally, tutors and practice teachers working on international exchange placements need to have first hand knowledge of the student's home university in order to guide overseas students in an informed way and offer feedback on developments or improvements in their work.

Overseas students, like others on practice placements, are placed within a social work or care workplace and, therefore, a well-formed agreement, which includes commitment from management, is important. The receiving university needs to ensure that the information for agencies and practice teachers includes statutory requirements such as course regulations, curriculum details, health and safety issues and access to administrative and clerical systems.

Student selection systems must ensure that individuals have the ability to function well in unfamiliar surroundings; settle and respond quickly to change; relate to and enjoy the cultures of other people; and able to form relationships with others different from them. Professional skills include literacy in the relevant languages; ability to transfer skills across borders; knowledge of law and regulations which are nationally specific and aimed at groups or individual service users and/or related sectors such as housing, health and equal opportunities.

Student learning is underpinned by social work, sociological, psychological and other relevant theories. However, many of these are bound by national or (sometimes) continental concerns, and so students should be open to thinking about these differently. Student knowledge and understanding is likely to vary. And so, the practice teacher who takes an overseas student is required to relate theory to practice and examine issues such as the organisation's history, resource base, legal and procedural framework, political considerations and demographic context. At the same time, the practice teacher should have to capacity to link these new elements to the understandings, knowledge and skills that the students bring with them.

Assessment of Students

There is some variation in the way that each social work course assesses students in the UK, despite the national requirements then provided by the Central Council for Training and Education in Social Work and now by the General Social Care Council. The differences among courses is frequently present in the use of different pro-formas applied by each one of them and the quantity of evidence that each institution requires from the student.

Countries such as Canada are not bound by state national (or federal) requirements because education issues fall under provincial jurisdiction, although the Canadian Association of Schools of Social Work (CASSW) lays down the guidelines for course accreditation on a national basis. Consequently, it is likely that assessment procedures and systems will vary from course to course, making the planning and preparation process more difficult for those sending students overseas to manage.

To avoid undue anxiety, a first step for the student's home university is to send the relevant documentation to the receiving university tutors for consideration prior to the arrival of the students. At the same time, the receiving university's own curriculum materials and assessment procedures should be exchanged with the exchange student and tutor.

The methods of assessment used in each university can then be discussed and the appropriate briefing of those who will undertake these assessments can take place. Additionally, the overseas students should be prepared for the differences in language, emphasis, structure and technique that they may encounter.

Bourne and Allen (1996) suggest that assessing students within supervision is an 'interactional process'. However, it depends on the 'validation of those subject to it' and this in turn is subject to the handing over of power from the supervisor to the person being supervised. Being well prepared for this task is essential to a smooth experience. As Bourne and Allen claim:

> 'The wise supervisor is aware that this gives considerable power potentially to supervisees and takes this into account in their behaviour as a supervisor' (Bourne and Allen, 1996, p. 36).

Assessing students is a complex process and one which needs additional attention when students from another country are being judged. The basis for judgment needs deconstruction and re-formation to take into account individual needs which may be based on culture, religion, language, income and ability.

Conclusion

International exchanges involving student placements require a great deal of thought, pre-planning and preparation. If insufficient attention is being given to global imperatives, changes in educational patterns and national context are likely to lead to a poor experience for all those involved. Globalisation is leading to a greater congruity in educational experiences as a result of the impact of market forces on policy and practice.

Another common outcome brought about by globalisation that is evident across the globe is the reduction of government financing for universal welfare provisions. Although surface differences between countries are likely to be apparent to those from overseas, it is important for those involved to discuss common factors as well as to share the differences they envisage during their supervision sessions. Within the nations of the West, these are likely to be political and economic rather than societal or cultural.

The pressure on the key players in the provision of social work education to actively contribute to international exchanges is growing in parallel with other demands, whilst there is no overt commitment to additional longer-term resources or funds to make these exchanges possible. Even within this scenario, however, the gains from short-term involvement are considerable. For example, my experience enabled me to develop skills and knowledge that are not only important for work with overseas students and universities, but also with those at home. The same expertise continues to contribute to work beyond the local arena, such as that within the regional and national context.

13 Preparing and Supporting Students for International Exchanges: The Challenges of Linking Theory and Practice

SHEILA SAMMON, WALENE WHITAKER and
CONSTANCE BARLOW

Introduction

International social work field placements are a potentially powerful learning tool which offers opportunities for students to confront different views of human behaviour, learn different systems of social welfare, and see different ways to remediate social problems (Healy, 2001). As social work field placements move into the global forum, emerging professional research is now addressing issues such as evaluation equivalencies, establishment of reliable international partners, the process of student selection, and provision of student support (Barlow and Whittaker, 2002; Bolea et al., 1999; Dubois and Ntetu, 2000; Tesoriero and Rajaratnam, 2001).

A continuum of formal and informal models exist for international field placements (Lyons and Ramanthan, 1999). On one end are models that rely on formal links established between schools of social work and allied professionals that are usually financially supported by government and university sources. An example is ERASMUS, a European Union initiative that supported reciprocity in social work field placements between partner academic institutions in the European Union states (Healy, 2001). A common less formal model is based on contacts amongst schools in different countries with schools balancing numerous arrangements. Informal arrangements often are not funded but arise from personal contacts abroad who have agreed to offer field instruction to students (Barlow and Whittaker, 2002). What follows is a description of the *Canada-European Union Project, Child Abuse, Protection and Welfare*, from the perspective of the Canadian partners responsible for arranging practicum placements. Specific issues addressed are partnership-building, preparation and support of students in international field placements and demands on the host communities.

The Canada-European Project provided a formal model of exchanges that included the European partners: University of Southhampton (United Kingdom), the Hogeschool West-Brabant (the Netherlands), the University of Stockholm (Sweden); and three Canadian universities: the University of Victoria (British Columbia), Dalhousie University (Nova Scotia), McMasters University (Ontario). It united the institutions into a consortium whose overall aim was, through the maximisation of local community resources, to internationalise the training of social workers in child welfare. The Project's main goal was to contribute to transatlantic and international understandings of child welfare including child abuse and neglect, protection of children and the overall well-being of families. Specific Project activities consisted of exchanging graduate and undergraduate social work students between Canada and Europe for practicum placements, sponsoring educational seminars on child welfare in Canada and Europe, developing curricula in child welfare, advancing knowledge and theory on child welfare in an international context, and undertaking research projects.

The Project provided financial support of approximately, $1,500 Canadian dollars to each student. These funds, while they did not cover all student expenditures, were a great enabler, allowing students with strained financial resources to compete for the opportunity to complete a field placement in another culture and country. Yet, it was typically young students with limited financial and familial responsibilities that applied, and were able to go abroad. In all, seven students from each of the three Schools of Social Work in Canada, 21 students in all, completed a three-month child welfare placement at European field agencies. Also, 21 students from the European universities completed a three month child welfare placement in Canada. Additionally, there were two unassessed pilot placements and one placement that was terminated shortly after beginning.

Developing the Partnership

Finding Common Ground

After the Project was approved, a preliminary planning meeting designed to map out a strategy for the international exchanges, was held in Southampton, England. It was attended by faculty and field education co-ordinators from each school, as well as potential agency supervisors from Stockholm and Southampton. At this meeting the seeds of trust and respect were sown as all united around the common goal of creating quality field placement experiences. An element of goodwill was evident from all partners that, looking back, ultimately offered the greatest indirect support for students. The face-to-face meeting left us feeling comfortable to frankly discuss and problem-solve emerging placement issues and was the beginning of partnerships that were characterised by integrity and a commitment to students. Subsequently, the relationships solidified and were strengthened by e-mail and telephone conversations.

While engaged in the business 'of making the Project work', we discussed ways of enhancing involvement of participating universities, faculty and students, and the professional social work community. To this end, we agreed to hold a conference in conjunction with the annual business meeting that would offer a forum for discussion on international child welfare issues. In all, five conferences were held, one in each of the European schools, and two in the Canadian ones – MacMaster and Victoria.

Linking Theory and Practice

We all came from slightly different theoretical stances, but we were also very similar, were hand-picked, really, by the project leaders for our theoretical approaches and common values. So, there was an expectation that the students would not experience much dissonance between home and overseas placements. Canada and England, Holland, and Sweden by and large have similar outlooks and worldviews, a belief in human rights and the rights of children. It wasn't that much of a jump or shift in values for the students, although we in our ethnocentricity not see the differences.

Establishing Equivalencies

Particular challenges presented by this field education project were related to issues of cross-national consistency of student learning opportunities, harmonisation of requirements, development of modularised teaching materials, regularising the credit-rating systems already in place at the receiving institutions and preparation of students to work within each country's specific legislation.

To date, a uniform set of international social work educational and certification standards has not been developed (Hockenstad et al., 1992). Garber (1997) noted that international standard setting remains a distant goal that must begin with comprehensive information about programmes, educators and students. The collection of this data has already been initiated under the auspices of the International Association of Schools of Social Work (IASSW) in its World Census of Social Work Education, and is available on its website at: <http://www.iassw.soton.ac.uk>.

In their review of international field education programmes, Skolnik et al., (1999) found considerable variation in the number of required field placement hours and the nature of the field experience. For instance, in some countries, field assignments consisted of observational visits and short rotations among field agencies, while field placements in other countries were intense semester-long placements at one agency. They also found most countries in their survey offered field placement opportunities in child welfare agencies.

Our experience was consistent with the literature in that the field education programmes, of the Project partners, was highly variable, and consequently a decision was made to maintain the field placement standards of the home university and direct tuition fees to the home institution. As a result, the tedious task of determining equivalencies was circumvented. Prior to the arrival of students, particular university field programme information, field manuals, and evaluation forms were sent to the host country co-ordinators for distribution to the placement agencies.

For the European partners, this meant becoming familiar with three diverse Canadian field placement programmes since the Canadian universities were located in three different provinces with three different child welfare jurisdictions and legislations. Although accredited by the same body, the Canadian Association of Schools of Social Work, each Canadian university had differing evaluation formats and practicum policies. Concomitantly, the Canadian field co-ordinators were called upon to interpret, to local field agencies, three different sets of requirements for European students.

Field Agency Partners

In keeping with the goal of maximising community participation, local child welfare agencies were invited to commit to the Project for three years. These agencies provided the practicum placements for the students, such that each year the same agencies (sometimes with differing direct supervisors) hosted the students from abroad. They were also asked to assist in preparing students to go overseas, and agency staff became part of planning and advisory committees to the Project. They became regular conference participants who met to exchange views with agency representatives from other jurisdictions. The regular contact between university based field co-ordinators and the agency field instructors or practice teachers who were working with the students on a daily basis led to the development of a strong cross-national partnership that was crucial to trust-building and that ultimately enhanced the level of support offered to the students.

The Students

Selection process

To maximise success, priority was given to senior undergraduate students who demonstrated academic excellence and received positive evaluations in their preliminary field placements. However, performance evaluations made during the initial field placement were not automatically considered relevant for local placement decisions. Social work field education literature reports that the student qualities most desired by field instructors are honesty, maturity, and a strong desire to help others (Royse et al., 1999).

Bolea, et al., (1999) reported that international field placement agencies also valued these qualities. Additionally, those taking overseas students expected them to be adaptable, willing to challenge their beliefs and/or perceptions, and be open to cultural difference. For us to enhance the probability of selecting primarily those students who exhibited the aforementioned qualities, we used structured interviews as an adjunct screening mechanism.

In the interviews, students were asked to respond to some typical scenarios that they might encounter when they reached their new abode. These included examples such as arriving in the host country and finding no one there to meet them, trying to use a phone when currency and procedures are unfamiliar, and learning how to use the public transportation system. They were also asked to respond to the following questions:

- Why do you want to go abroad?
- What languages do you speak? What steps will you take to learn the language and understand the culture of the host country?
- How much travelling have you done? Have you ever moved to a place where you knew no one?
- Describe a time when you were travelling alone and got into difficulty. How did you handle the situation and what did you learn?
- What are your hopes for this experience? What do you want to learn?
- What are your greatest fears?
- How will you describe Canadian Child Welfare to your new colleagues?
- How will you prepare for this experience?
- What do you need from us to make this experience what you want it to be? What is your wish list of possible placements? And, tell us more about your interest in this area.

Considerations Prior to Departure

Clarkson (1990), reflecting on her years of work with international social work students studying in Great Britain, made several recommendations for placing students overseas. First, prior to their placement abroad, she suggested that students completed preliminary course work in their own country because knowledge of the home country's social welfare system served as both the basis for comparison between countries and background to adequately represent the home country. She noted that without such a background, students were more likely to be imbued with theories that may be culturally and economically inappropriate for their home country. Also, she observed that the student-field instructor relationship was likely to be enhanced if students arrived in their host country with basic knowledge of the host country's social administration, social problems, social policies and commonly practised social work methodologies.

Therefore, an essential component of our pre-placement orientation was the enhancement of student knowledge of their country, their home university and the Canadian social welfare system – a tall order when one considers the diversity of Canada's geography, culture and social service delivery system. There were false starts. The assumption that students would be experienced and knowledgeable in these areas was erroneous. In reality, their ability to articulate knowledge was limited. Therefore, an intense, short course on Child Welfare in Canada was offered. It consisted of lectures, guest speakers and discussion of a selection of articles that they subsequently took abroad.

Initially, we assumed that students would benefit by going abroad in pairs or in threes because they would be available to assist each other with the unfamiliar. Clarkson (1991) noted the importance of partners. 'I think it is wrong for an overseas student to be the only foreign student on a course' (Clarkson, 1991, p. 355). However, we found that the student partnerships that were formed were in some cases fraught with difficulties because students who went in pairs did not necessarily know each other well and were often not fully committed to establishing and nurturing a relationship with one another. For example, a pair of Canadian students who went abroad rarely communicated with one another because one of the students took her partner and that dyad was not interested in being joined by a third person. Therefore, we concluded that when students travelled in pairs or triads, expectations of mutual support must be clearly articulated and become part of their contract with the school and with each other.

The following recommendations about student preparation are based on student feedback and our observations.

- Students completing field placement abroad need to be reminded that during their extended stay in the host country they will likely experience periods of intense loneliness and homesickness. International field placements students are not tourists but rather reflective learners who are expected to be open to new experiences.
- Students completing placements in pairs should discuss, prior to departure, how they intend to support each other.
- Students should establish e-mail contact with their field agency, prior to departure as this serves to ease their anxiety and offers a medium to negotiate the finer details of the field placement.
- It is essential that the host university assists students in finding accommodation and in arranging for airport transport upon their arrival. Students also need explicit directions to the host agency and the university. They also require the office and home phone numbers of their agency contact and a back-up name and number.

Language

The issue of language skills is an important consideration in the development of field placements (Bolea, et al, 1999; Dubois and Ntetu, 2000). Typically, students selected for the project lacked fluency in the language of their host country. However, this was not seen as an overwhelming barrier since English was a language spoken by many European professionals. Alternately, although European students who came to Canada believed their language skills were insufficient, by and large, they reported having little difficulty making themselves understood. Nevertheless, students were encouraged to learn the language of the host country, but few found the time to develop fluency because selection decisions were typically made the semester before departure when they were inundated with regular course work demands.

When host agencies believed language might be a barrier to success in the field placement, they developed creative learning opportunities. For instance, several students were placed with immigrants and refugees who also were learning the language. Another group of students worked with children who enjoyed teaching them their language. In one case, the children made a nightly homework 'list of words' for the social work students. Involvement in art therapy and recreation programmes became a key mechanism for relationship-building because experiences could be shared by doing rather that talking.

One student remarked:

'I have learned from silence and I have learned amidst chaos. My inability to speak Swedish has led to both frustration and learning. Observing Swedish language conversations has often left me feeling marginalised, a silent uncomprehending bystander. Yet this experience has been invaluable in teaching me about being confined to the periphery of human interaction, of being marginalised. I have had to be patient, awaiting assistance from others. By necessity, I have had to depend on strangers in a manner completely outside of my comfort zone'.

Internet

The social work professional has embraced the advantages of technology such that today, thousands of human service agencies are linked together by the World Wide Web (Estes, 1999). Information technology has been crucial in the development of international field exchanges and has had a profound effect on social work field education. E-mail communication makes possible ongoing communication between field personnel world-wide and enables development of exchanges through co-ordinated pre-placement selection, sharing of evaluation formats, negotiating learning contracts and trouble-shooting placement issues. Placements that were considered all but impossible several years ago are now proving to be excellent opportunities for enrichment for both student, faculty and field agencies.

In this project, isolation of members of the triad – the university, the host agency and the student, was reduced by electronic mail. It was also an invaluable resource for maintaining connections and supporting students, since they were requested to send in journals of their challenges and experiences regularly. Internet was usually available to students at their placement, and the growth of internet cafes enabled them to keep in touch with home, sometimes, at the beginning, this was to the detriment of making themselves available to the newness of their experience. Initially, students would read their home newspaper, chat with friends and family, and turn sometimes to the Internet for friendship. However, as they became more integrated into the host community, reliance on e-mail diminished. One student wrote:

'I feel so very removed from home now and wish I could stay here longer'.

Demands on the Home University

For Canadian field co-ordinators, involvement in the Project meant not only assisting students with complex bureaucratic procedures such as visa applications but also listening and responding to student's anxieties and concerns. Would they be met at the airport? How would they get to their placement? Where would they live? Who would help them find accommodation? What should they take? What would be the appropriate dress in the agency? What would the weather be like? Would they meet other students? Since we had been to the United Kingdom and met the field co-ordinators from the three universities we were able to address the students' questions and provide reassurance for ongoing support when they arrived in Europe with a good degree of confidence.

As time passed, we concluded that one of the attributes most needed by the students was patience. While abroad they worried: about their ability to integrate with field agency personnel, that the students at home would be learning more than them and that their learning would be compromised by language barriers and misunderstandings about the culture of their host country. Patience, a commitment to self-reflection and to personnel and professional growth were essential student qualities that served them well as they struggled to understand that, in fact, they were learning – learning about tolerance, learning about diversity, and learning about themselves both personally and professionally.

As Canadian field co-ordinators hosting the European students, we moved beyond engaging in routine placement protocols – we did more. 'More' sometimes took the form of finding a place for the students to live, picking them up at the airport, trouble-shooting when things went wrong, arranging for visiting student status at our university so they could have its privileges such as a gym membership, use of the university international office resources and access to university clubs. We also took them bicycle-shopping, explained how the public transportation system worked, and as they planned weekend excursions we offered them tourist information on the region.

Our 'more' activities were designed to create a milieu of support. However, when personal energy levels were depleting, we utilised community resources such that each successive wave of students received less in terms of personal contact from us but more in terms of connection with resources in the university and broader community. In one case, our support efforts were not enough and a student returned home after one week in Canada.

A primary resource for the visiting students was other students. However, arranging opportunities for student interaction was challenging because of differing semester schedules. For example, Canadian university semesters begin in September and end in mid-December. Universities in the UK start in October, and in Sweden the semester started in mid-August to the end of November.

Therefore, when students arrived in Canada from Sweden in mid-August, Canadian students would still be enjoying their semester break. Similarly, agencies were on a holiday schedule which meant reduced personnel and fewer opportunities to engage in direct practice. The one method of factoring in support for the arriving students that we that we found useful in overcoming this difficulty was to ask the Canadian students who would be travelling abroad to assume some responsibility for integrating their European counterparts into Canadian student life. The problem was also eased by mid-September when the local students began their field placements because they were willing to offer peer support to the European students.

Conclusions

Although we gained considerable experience for organising practicum placements from the European Union-Canada Project, as we considered embarking on future international field placements we found that the following questions continue to surface and require responses from us:

- What are the educational advantages for the students?
- How can one practice without imposing your one's cultural values?
- How can a social worker practice in an anti-oppressive manner without being culturally judgemental?
- How does one guard against a neo-colonial stance?
- What is the role of the university field co-ordinators and how do their expectations and values effect the international placement process?

Regardless of the many questions that as we have, it was a privilege to be able to ask them and for the students and agency and university personnel to be involved in a funded project which has allowed all those involved in it to experience broader horizons and come back to our home universities and share these experiences with others not fortunate enough to go overseas.

14 Managing Overseas Placements for Students

ANNE DAVIES and SALLY COSSTICK

The *Child Abuse, Protection and Welfare Project* has been an exciting and innovative project for us to be involved in as a Directorate, team and for the individual practice teachers in our midst. Our role was to provide well-planned placements that met the overseas students' needs. The positive feedback we received from all six students who were placed with us assured us that we had met our goal. We learnt a lot from the students in the course of these exchanges and we also created a positive team experience.

Reflecting upon our Involvement

The first request to take a student within this Project arrived by the usual route from the University of Southampton via the Practice Learning Manager in the Social Services Department. The first seminar of the Project was then held in Southampton in October 1997. Anne Davies, one of two Operational Service Managers for Children and Families Services, attended along with Margaret Cann, one of the social workers who was then a practice teacher in our team. She was the first practice teacher to be assigned to the Project.

Once we had an understanding of the Project, we decided to place all the students coming for placement with the Project into the Child Protection Enquiry Team. We did not know then how much we would learn from each placement to inform the ones to follow. But it proved to be valuable to provide continuity of team and practice teachers.

The City of Southampton was established as a unitary local authority in April 1997 following local government reorganisation in England. The

Child Protection Enquiry Team (CPET) that we worked within was formed as part of the restructuring of Children and Families Services in the newly created authority. Situated within a system of specialist teams, the CPET takes new referrals and carries out enquiries, often jointly with the police, into abuse or suspected abuse of children, under Children Act, 1989. The CPET holds cases through child protection conferences and for about three months after, so all the work is relatively short term and much is immediate and emergency work.

As members within a new team within a newly established unitary local authority, we were keen to develop our own links with the University of Southampton's Social Work Studies Department. The Project seemed, and has proved to be, an excellent opportunity for developing these links and to both contribute to and gain from the whole Project.

Providing placements for students is recognised as an important part of the work of the team, and at the time that we began in 1997, there were five practice teachers in the CPET. Two of these were already involved in training and had students placed with them. We believed that providing placements for the Canadian students involved in the Project would give our practice teachers a good opportunity to learn about how child care social work was developing in Britain. This was particularly so with regards to issues relating to the 'child protection versus the family support' debate, lively in Britain then and now. Additionally, we thought this experience would provide the CPET with a chance to learn about and compare social work, training, and cultural issues between the two countries.

Managing the Placements

Our team took three cohorts of two students at a time from the same University. These students did not necessarily know one another well on arrival. However, this arrangement worked well as the students always had someone else to discuss and compare their learning and any difficulties. They could also share living, social and travel experiences. For two of the three cohorts, the students shared accommodation. Accommodation was problematic for all of the students and caused them considerable anxiety. Accommodation was found with the help of individuals at Southampton University, and in one case, a member of the Social Services staff.

The CPET team is in a crowded open-plan area in an uncomfortable building. But, we were always able to provide desk space for the students next to each other within the team area, and near the practice teachers. Administrative support is always overstretched. But, again, this was provided for the students on the same basis as the rest of the team. Students are welcomed into our midst and treated as full team members during their placement. The students are expected and we prepare for them. Practical arrangements are made for their arrival and they have a carefully planned induction period. An open office culture is encouraged and is a positive aspect of the open-plan accommodation. Members of the team are always discussing their work, sharing problems, ideas and learning from one another. And the students can both contribute to and learn from this exchange.

There is a strong commitment in the Social Services Directorate and the CPET team to properly support practice teachers to carry out practice teaching, which is considered as an important part of their work. This includes guidelines for workload relief and commitment to involving them in meetings and in-service training to maintain and develop their skills. In practice, of course, this is difficult and the operational work of the team often takes over. So practice teachers are usually providing supervision and support for students as well as carrying a heavy caseload. The team commitment helps, so students can ask other members of the team for help and guidance when their own practice teacher is not available. This system has worked well throughout all the placements, despite a high level of staff turnover in the team over the past three years.

As managers, we made the decision early on, as part of our aim for continuity in the work on the Project, to use the same practice teachers. So one, Carmel Rutledge, had one student from each of the three cohorts, while Margaret Cann had one and Dawn Maxwell the next two. This, with the commitment and interest of the whole team provided some stability for the Project placements overall while ensuring that the learning opportunities were maximised.

The practice teachers ensured that the students could visit and also take work from other teams and units in the Directorate, particularly because of the narrow specialist base of the CPET team. However, most of the students' experience was within the team. In it, there are always good opportunities for joint work on complex cases, giving the opportunity for the students to work with different social workers to broaden their learning. For the practice teachers and managers there was the added opportunity to contribute to the Project more broadly and to the learning and debate about social work and child welfare in different countries.

We attended the students' presentations about the child welfare system in their home province and their learning within the Project exchange, and with the first two students, gave a short presentation to the Director of Social Services and to the Chair of the Social Policy Committee for Southampton City. These provided opportunities to promote the positive experience of the Project for the students and us.

Sally, with another colleague from the Directorate, Leigh Clark, attended the Project Conference, *Developing Child Welfare Curriculum Across Borders* in Victoria, Canada in May 1999. Sally delivered a paper outlining child welfare provision in Britain, and also a workshop on the abuse of children through prostitution. Leigh gave a workshop on the issues around abuse in residential childcare. In March 2000, Sally, Leigh and Dawn Maxwell, practice teachers for two of the overseas exchange students from Canada, attended the last conference of the Project, entitled, *Breaking Boundaries*, in Breda, Holland. Sally and Dawn gave a workshop on children and domestic violence at it. We chose workshop subjects topical and controversial in Britain in order to share dilemmas and learn from those in other countries. Through this, we found that the same issues often arise.

At each of these conferences, we were able to take part in Project meetings to discuss, review and plan the next state of the Project. We were also able to meet with colleagues from the universities in Canada where our exchange students had come from, as well as other practice teachers and managers from placements, and university teachers and practitioners from the other European universities involved. These gave an understanding of the Project as a whole, and an opportunity to share our experience and learn from others.

Problems, Issues, Learning

The problems for the students were mostly practical, because they had to find accommodation on arrival in an unknown city. The first two arrived and suffered alone. One of them almost turned back before finding suitable accommodation. The second two pairs were well supported by a colleague from the University. And learning from the experiences of the first two, we ensured between us that they were met at the airport and properly supported.

The students struggled with Southampton's inadequate public transport system, making their way around a large and unfamiliar city to reach work and then their clients, but they seemed to cope remarkably well with this.

There were some problems with the links with the University, particularly when overseas students arrived during vacation periods and when it took time to identify a tutor. The practice teachers worked hard with the students and the two universities (their home and the receiving one) to clarify placement and assessment expectations. This was a new piece of work for them as expectations are well-known and clear from our local universities, but it was important to reduce the anxieties of the overseas students on arrival and to ensure that the placement would meet their needs.

The requirements of the Canadian universities varied, both for the placements and for the assessment reports. But, these were generally less in terms of practice experience and detailed competencies than those of the local universities. This was a help to the practice teachers in a situation where the learning was so much broader. The Canadian students would apparently expect less work for which they took individual responsibility, and their learning needs could quite comfortably be met within the placement. This meant that they were able to enjoy the learning opportunities provided by their work, and to focus on learning the legal and policy frameworks, local practice and resources, without too much anxiety about meeting the requirements of the assessment.

The fact that these were assessed placements within their own course, not just for observation, was an important aspect of the Project and could have been more problematic. It is an area where the experience gained by having the same team and practice teachers involved was valuable. It must be said that all six students were exceptionally able and committed, well ready for the experiences we would expect to provide and assess for final placement students.

Our feedback indicated that all the students benefited from, and enjoyed, their placements with the CPET team. This in turn was positive for the team, practice teachers and managers involved. The learning was continual, both about how to provide these rather different placements, and about the specific approaches to practice.

There were many things we could learn from the students and from the Canadian systems and laws. These had much in common with British law, and certainly, the same dilemmas about the conflicts between child protection intervention and the preventative, family support approach. Specific comparisons were interesting. British Columbia's law was modelled on the Children Act, but in practice was making heavy use of court intervention, following a critical inquiry into a child death. In Britain, the aim has been to 'refocus' since research told us that this is not the most effective way of protecting children. Britain's Children Act includes the requirement to ensure that the cultural and ethnic diversities of children and their families are taken into account, but Canadian law goes further it seems in trying to redress some of the inequalities suffered by the indigenous population, the First Nations peoples. This was well understood and promoted by both the students and people that we met in Canada.

Conclusions

We do believe that our original decision to aim for continuity in providing these placements worked well for all those involved, and particularly meant that we developed both links and learning over the three years of the Project. It did limit the number of staff in this Directorate gaining the direct benefit of the students' presence in our team and maybe the other opportunities we have described. We have strengthened our close and positive links with the University of Southampton through this Project. Given these, we hope that the Directorate will be able to be involved in other international projects in the future, to continue to broaden our views, knowledge and experience of social work theory and practice.

15 Network Collaboration within Swedish Child Welfare

SVEN HESSLE

Introduction

Every term around 300 students at the Department of Social Work at Stockholm University are doing some part of their undergraduate study in a field placement. Placements are a curriculum requirement of the seven-term academic study programme that alternates between theory and practice. The emphasis on practice occurs during the third and the sixth terms, where the students undertake some weeks close to social work practice in an organisation with a trained supervisor. During the sixth term the students remain in practice for 15 weeks, and there are specific guidelines that both students and supervisors have to follow.

To ensure that the special training needs of the students are met and to cover all different levels and areas of social work, the social work personnel within the Department have to collaborate with hundreds of different organisations. Their endeavours should guarantee that there are enough supervisors and organisations covering the: various kinds of agencies – state, county, community, co-operative, private, religious, and voluntary; different target groups for social work intervention such as preschool children, school children, adolescents, parents, families, older people, and disabled people; and different sectors to be covered, like maternal care, social assistance, psychiatry, school, criminal justice, alcohol or drug treatment, milieu therapy, and ageing.

Most of the organisations involved in training the Department's students are directing their attention to social work with children and families. To select among these organisations a few to receive students coming from another country (in this case, Canada) is not an easy task because of language and cultural obstacles. Another challenge is that Canada is not used to sending students abroad to undertake parts of their academic training. In Europe, we have years of experience of sending students across borders to different schools of social work. In the case of European Union–Canada Project, the *Child Welfare and Child Protection Project*, we decided to apply three criteria for the selection of training settings for the students coming from abroad:

• Best practice.
• Different parts of the child welfare.
• Different kinds of organisation.

Of great importance to us was that we could choose the settings that were publicly known to provide high quality child welfare services, care and treatment that could show for our guests from Canada the very best of Swedish child welfare. Of equal concern was that we could select organisations that covered different parts of the child welfare sector, and to demonstrate from a holistic and pedagogic point of view, how the Swedish social work and its welfare provisions are actually practised within child welfare. I elaborate this argument later in the chapter. Finally, we wanted to include representatives from different kinds of organisations to allow for comparisons to be made amongst the different training settings. Our final choice of six training settings for the Canadian students is presented below.

This has resulted in a network of different partners that was initially formed to support Swedish participation in the European Union-Canada Project. This collaboration has been successful, both as a supporting network for the undergraduate students in practice placements as well as in developing a holistic view of praxis with the child in context with the presence of different expertise representing different perspectives and positions on diverse levels of intervention in child welfare. Additionally, I will discuss the development of the Swedish child welfare – levels, target groups and measures with points of departure in a model represented as Table 15.1. The training settings that we selected will be placed in the model as Table 15.2.

In this chapter, I will also describe how profitable this Project has become for the network of child welfare organisations in Swedish child welfare. The collaboration between the selected training settings has been a necessary continuing structure of supporting everyday child welfare work for the participating actors. We still meet on a regularly basis to exchange knowledge within the field and support the services, care and treatment of children and families in the different parts of the child welfare sector in Stockholm.

A Short Presentation of the Child Welfare Organisations

The Department of Social Work at Stockholm University has worked to deliver the Project objectives in collaboration with the following agencies:

- Älvsjö Community Development Project
- Hagalund Family Centre
- Botkyrka Crises Centre
- Svalnäs School and Family Treatment Centre
- Framnäs School and Therapy Centre
- Children's Village at Skå.

These are a mixture of public and private agencies and are described in greater detail below.

The *Älvsjö Community Development Project* is an open and voluntary organisation which is run by the community and targets families with children under 18. Its basic ambition is preventive work and it offers support, advice, counselling, information and resources free of charge to families, while their network is made available to the different organisations that are connected to children and young people in the local community. The team that is responsible for the programme is located in the middle of the community in a house called 'The Network House'. The staff consists of nine different kinds of professionals who work in teams: family therapists or pedagogues, child pedagogues, field social workers, network therapists, a youth counsellor and a speech therapist.

The basic idea is to consider the child within its whole contextual environment by developing co-operation with parents and significant people around the child. The methods used are permeated by social network thinking, systemic family theory as well as cognitive solution-oriented models of intervention. By building a network of the organisations within the local community that are involved in different activities for children and young people, the team is able to give supervision, advice and support to the personnel that meet the children on a daily basis. The personnel then in turn become more able to give relevant advice and recommendations to the families (Helin and Isacson, 1999).

The *Hagalund Family Centre* is run by the community in Hagalund, a municipality in greater Stockholm. It offers preventive services in co-operation with other organisations in the same locality. The Centre targets all children up to 12 years of age and their families in this multi-ethnic area. The Centre includes in the same localities a maternal care unit, a child health care unit, a pre-school and a social services centre. The family centre is a meeting place for the families with children in the neighbourhood. It aims to strengthen family networks; support parental initiatives; promote health prevention through early interventions; and provide activities that can involve different groups in safety. The social services centre has the authority to intervene in families with 'high-risk' children for protection purposes in accordance with the provisions contained in the Swedish child welfare legislation.

The *Botkyrka Crises Centre* is run by the community but focuses on child welfare investigations and social networking in a multi-ethnic neighbourhood. It is an independent division of the local community social authority. This resource provides support free of charge to citizens and personnel within its catchment area which contains the highest proportion of ethnic minorities in greater Stockholm. The Centre is well-known for being the first unit in Sweden to develop social network methods in the community child welfare sector. Five family-network therapists and an assistant are included in its staff complement. Networking with the appropriate people when children are 'at risk' or in a 'high risk' situation is central to their way of working. Different social network methods are used to handle traumatic experiences, violence within the family, and parents in conflict over custody. The Centre also supports child welfare officers by using networking methods for investigative purposes.

Svalnäs School and Family Treatment Centre is a private enterprise with psychologists, approved social workers and teachers who own the facilities. It operates through a system of rotating leadership and shared responsibility. Each member of staff has had comprehensive training in a different psychotherapeutic specialisation. Like Framnäs, this Centre was a part of Stockholm County which the personnel took over a few years ago.

This Centre receives young children with heavy psychosocial school problems for treatment in institutional day-care setting. The child's environment is taken into account in every aspect of the treatment provided. The team might work using family therapy with a focus on the child, and apply different network methods in the child's home and school environments. Like Framnäs, this Centre also undertakes supervision, consultation and training of personnel in social and psychiatric services. Individual, pair and family therapy is also offered on a private (fee-paying) basis.

The *Framnäs School and Therapy Centre* is an enterprise owned by the people who work in it. The Centre started its independent activities in 1991 after having been a part of Stockholm County for many years. There are 15 members of staff, including teachers, therapists, a manager, a cook and an administrator. The chair position is rotated regularly. All staff receive the same salary. They become owners of Framnäs during the period of their employment by holding a share in the company. When staff terminate their employment at the Centre, they give up their share in the company.

Framnäs operates a partly institutional and partly community-based model that aims to demonstrate how services to teenagers with difficult school problems can be provided in a combined educational and day-care treatment. It prioritises working within a co-operative relationship that uses the family and its networks as a crucial ingredient for successful intervention.

Framnäs targets young children with very serious behaviour problems and heavy school problems where the local community has tried all its other resources without success. The children are offered special pedagogic interventions with day-care treatment in institutional environment. Its main emphasis is on helping parents to become a resource in supporting their child to overcome behavioural and learning problems. Milieu therapy, special pedagogy, and family therapy are basic instruments in the Framnäs setting. Framnäs also undertakes preventive work with supervision, and the training of personnel within different sectors, including child welfare and private family counselling (Hessle, 2000, pp. 65–78).

The *Children's Village at Skå* is also run by the community. Here, the entire family goes into long-term care and treatment in a residential village setting on the outskirts of Stockholm. The Children's Village at Skå provides a residential care setting for psychosocial vulnerable families with 'high risk' children under the authority of Stockholm municipality.

The Children's Village at Skä is basically composed by staff families and client families living side by side as neighbours, forming a village in the outskirts of Stockholm. Through the basic ideas of milieu therapy, the work with the families is organised as a 'training society', where children and parents can train to develop new relationships and their capacity to live an every day life in the Village.

Its ultimate aim is to return people to every day life in their normal community settings. The staff is composed of social workers, psychologists, social pedagogues, pre-school teachers, school teachers with their families. There are 13 'client families' accepted for living in the Village. When all the families are included, the Village has around one hundred inhabitants. The staff has the assignment of supporting and empowering the families to develop according to their personal resources.

The Village provides the families with all the normal institutional requirements, including pre-school, school, employment possibilities and leisure-time activities. Preserving the link to the family's ordinary local community is an important part of the treatment. This might mean creating new networks for the family, establishing networks with personnel in child health care, pre-school facilities, school, and amongst different kinds of pedagogues and child welfare officers in the family's neighbourhood of origin.

Swedish Child Welfare: Its Levels, Target Groups and Measures

A very brief overview of the Swedish child welfare sector is presented in Figure 1 below. A more comprehensive description can be found in Hessle and Vinnerljung (2000).

Table 15.1:   **Levels, Target Groups and Measures within Swedish Child Welfare**

Level	Target Group	Measure
Prevention	Children at risk: general	General preventive, Information, Counselling, Self help groups, Sector collaboration
Investigation	Children at risk: specific	Investigation, eventually resulting in supportive psycho-social work at home or public care
Supportive psycho-social work at home	High risk children	Contact person/family, Family therapy, Family building, At-home-pedagogy
Public care	High risk children	Placement of child, parent or family: Voluntary or compulsory

Source: Adapted from Hessle and Vinnerljung (2000)

In Sweden, the main actors in child welfare are professional social workers, most of them employed in social service agencies, run by the local governments. The municipalities in Sweden have a long and strong tradition of self-determination. This means that the levels of social services and their organisation might vary considerably between municipalities in Sweden. In an attempt to disentangle the decentralised Swedish child welfare and for purposes of description, the services are sorted under four categories: prevention; investigation; direct support with child in its home environment; and public care. These categories or levels for child welfare are directed to different target groups and activate diverse kinds of measures. In Table 15.1, I attempt to provide an overview of these levels, target groups and measures. A commentary which explains these follows underneath.

The level of *Prevention* in Table 15.1 is restricted to the services available to families without the families becoming individual 'cases' for the public authorities, but where child welfare personnel are involved with them on a regular basis. The main bulk of the general and group targeted preventative work is done outside the child welfare organisations, including pre-natal and post-natal maternal care, subsidised childcare. There is an array of different programmes attempting to prevent negative child development, family breakdown, placement in care and youth delinquency. These measures are basically directed to vulnerable categories of households with children 'at risk'.

Agency co-operation and intra-agency service delivery have become increasingly popular. Scores of local authorities have constructed services where maternity care, child health care, pre-schools and child welfare agencies either operate in the same locality in family centres or co-operate very closely. Self-help groups for children with alcohol or parents who misuse drugs have been organised by one-third of all local authorities. Another target group for self-help groups of this kind are children with mentally disabled parents. Support groups for refugee parents or single mothers and parent training programmes are run by some municipalities. Nearly all municipalities (85 per cent) have Youth Advisory Centres that provide advice and guidance to youth in sexual matters. Sexually transmitted disease protection and birth control are the main focus of the counselling offered by these organisations.

Investigation is a level of intervention by local authorities that is highly developed and has been debated during the past ten years. One reason for the debate is that the law is putting demands on professionals that come in contact with children and youth in the course of their work. Professionals, whether employed by public or private agencies, are required by law to report anything that may cause child welfare authorities to intervene to protect the child. Even suspicions of abuse have to be reported. Child welfare social workers must start an investigation immediately upon receiving a report of alleged abuse.

Most of the critical voices in the debate have focused on why personnel report only a minority of suspected maltreatment cases, and why so few reports result in some form of intervention by child welfare authorities. It is estimated that local authorities receive reports or applications concerning 2 per cent of all children under 18 years of age. Only a minority of these reports end up with the child being taken into public care. There are great variations in investigative procedures, mainly due to criticisms about the poor quality of investigations undertaken in the past, but also because innovative interventions that occur in the field remain unproven.

Lately, inspiration has been imported from other countries. For example, the Family Group Conference Model from New Zealand has been used in Sweden as a tool for investigation. The Framework for the Assessment of Children in Need and Their Families (DoH, 2000) that has been developed in the United Kingdom is also currently being tested in Sweden.

Direct support for the child in its home environment refers to measures that are directed towards supporting 'high risk' children, where local authorities and the law demand some kind of change to the environment of the child. This involvement does not necessarily mean that the child has to be moved to 24-hour care in foster homes, residential care or other facilities. 'Home environment' means a wider context than the family, including the extended family, neighbourhood and local community. Local authorities offer a great deal of variations in their provisions for these children.

A *contact person* is a measure that involves child welfare authorities in recruiting volunteers in the municipality to support vulnerable families with a weak social network and to complement their activities where the parental functions are missing. The volunteers receive only a small monthly fee and expense allowance for the assignment. Single mother households were originally the target group, but contact persons are nowadays used for more advanced interventions, i.e., families that have multiple problems. Official statistics show that one percent of all children aged between 0 and 18 years of age in Sweden have a contact person (Statistics Sweden, 1998).

Different forms of *social network interventions* are methods frequently used currently to activate and connect the family with their relational environment. Family treatment and family support programmes are often provided in different forms of child welfare services including in more pedagogic approaches with family pedagogues who offer advice, support and training in parental skills and give practical help on a regular basis for a family. Their interventions can last for a period of several years. Individual and family therapy for children and families are standard tools in child welfare. Special pedagogic programmes are offered to children who for different reasons cannot cope with the demands in their local school environment.

Public care for children and young people in Sweden is: foster care, residential care or homes for special supervision. Adoption as an alternative to long-term foster care, but is not presently used as a preferred form of intervention in Sweden. Only a handful of children a year are left by Swedish parents for adoption. So, childless parents have turned to international adoptions since the 1960s. Traditionally, foster care placements have been the favoured category: nine of ten placements in child welfare have usually been in foster care.

Lately, *residential care* has become nearly as frequent used as foster care. One reason for this is the small size of the residential homes: 73 per cent are designed for nine children or fewer. This makes them simulate home care more readily. Some of the residential units might be classified as 'specialist foster care' in other countries. Moreover, most of the residential institutions are used for teenagers who account for the majority of all placements.

However, placing younger children in temporary residential care together with their parents is quite common in Sweden. Among admittances to children's homes for 0 to 12 year-olds, 90 per cent involve the admission of children and parents together (Sallnäs, 2001). Homes for the special supervision of young delinquents are run by the state under the auspices of a national government agency (SiS). There are 33 homes of this kind in Sweden with room for 659 young people in care, most of them are boys (around 2/3) with an average age of 16 years (SiS, 2001).

Collaborating Networks Covering Different Levels of Child Welfare

When the main positions in child welfare as indicated in Table 15.2 are considered, it is clear that the collaborating network covers all levels in the child welfare system. Upon clearer inspection of the involvement of the participating organisations, it seems that each of them covers a wide range of levels of child welfare action.

Table 15.2:   **Levels, target groups and the collaborative network**

Level	Target group	Main Position and Levels of Action
Prevention	Children at risk: general	Älvsjö Community Development Program Botkyrka Crises Center Hagalund Family Center
Investigation	Children at risk: specific	
Direct support with child in its home environment	High risk children	Framnäs School and Therapy Center Svalnäs School and Family Treatment Center
Public care	High risk children	Children's Village at Skå

Source: Adapted from Callahan et al., (2000) and Dominelli (1999)

The Älvsjö Community Development Program is placed in first position on the Prevention level because it adopts a holistic view and has the ambition of working on all levels – macro, meso and micro. This has prompted a consequent determination to work on a consulting level, both to citizens and personnel in different organisations in the local community. Its staff specialise in connecting professionals from different local organisations for the benefit of different interventions. Most of this is true also for Botkyrka Crises Centre, but their speciality is grounded in its greater multi-ethnic context, where migrant families require a greater flexible adjustment and sensitivity to culture specific competences. The Botkyrka Centre's expertise includes specific investigation competences as it also operates as a consulting team to the child welfare authorities. The Hagalund Family Centre provides an excellent example of agency co-operation and intra-agency service delivery where maternity care, child health care, pre-schools and child welfare officers are active in the same locality. The Hagalund Centre also has the authority to make assessments when it is necessary to bring children into care.

The Framnäs School and Therapy Centre operates on a partly institutional and a partly community-based model. Its activities demonstrate how services to teenagers with difficult school problems can be provided in a combined educational and day-care treatment setting, and how working to promote relationships between the family and the network are crucial for successful interventions. The Svalnäs School and Family Treatment Centre has the same ambitions, but these also have access to different kinds of individual therapeutic provisions.

The Children's Village at Skå involves getting the whole family into long term care and treatment in a residential village setting on the outskirts of Stockholm. Using the village as a training society for multi-problem families, its practitioners apply the local community perspective both as a milieu therapy setting in the treatment village and the natural neighbourhood to establish support for families on their way back to normal everyday life.

Network Collaboration for the Benefit of Future Social Work Training and Practice

For our European Union-Canada Project, some of the best practice agencies were selected from providers in the different levels of child welfare activities and that represented different types of organisation. This heterogeneity became a resource for the students who were given a base in one of these agencies to make study visits amongst the other partners of the network and participate in the common theoretical seminars provided by the participating organisations. In this way, the students were given a holistic view of the Swedish child welfare context and the available resources within it.

Network collaboration has also been fruitful for the partners in the network in many ways. The key ones of these are outlined below. The partners in this network continue to meet on a regular basis for half a day about six times a year and have done so since the beginning of the European Union-Canada Project in 1997.

First of all, the 'vertical' model of the network including its representatives from all the different levels of child welfare target groups and interventions has given all the partners an overview of current issues within child welfare in Sweden. The resulting organic meetings of partners so far have encouraged professionals from the same level of child welfare to work together in a 'horizontal' model of networking. As a traditional way of networking, horizontal organising has a tendency to support competition between partners that are specialising in addressing the same kinds of problems amongst the same target groups. The sameness of child welfare problems seems to mitigate against a holistic view on the different levels of action. The 'vertical' model of networking in contrast can focus on current themes within child welfare that are observed from different points of view on different levels. Common themes can be shared across different perspectives within a diversity of themes. That is, special observations can be made from the approach of a specialised unit.

Secondly, the special local community perspective is always present in the network's collaborative meetings. It seems impossible to escape from it in a network collaboration of this kind. The child in its context in the widest sense of its meaning is, therefore, taken care of within an ongoing comparative analysis amongst the collaborating 'vertical' network.

Thirdly, the ongoing network collaboration also includes the university, since this project is a part of the academic social work training as praxis involving engagement with the field. Social work is one of the few social science disciplines where praxis is an integral part of the discipline. And, social work is the only university social science subject that has an imperative for action.

Social work undergraduates are doing important parts of their training and education in the field. This means searching for and using theoretical tools for understanding and acting in the complicated world of different levels of social problems. Moreover, the collected experiences direct from the field of child welfare from the different groups of competent observers, provide invaluable inputs to the university. That is how an inter-twinning of the elements contributed by the field and academy creates the true meaning of the concept of praxis.

Conclusion

International student exchanges can foster innovations in practice and promote the development of stronger links between the academy and the field. The European Union-Canada Project has been central in spurring Swedish academics and practitioners to look at their networking experiences in a new light and enabled them to come up with new forms of practice that have improved services for vulnerable children. Although this was not a deliberately planned element of our co-operation with the participating institutions in the other countries involved in this Project, it was a welcome by-product of our work together and contributed to enhancing the educational experiences of the students involved in the exchange.

16 Diversity in *the Multiversity*: An Opportunity for Co-operation among Research, Education and Practice Providers

GREGER HELIN and NICOLINE ISACSON

Introduction and General Background

Inadequate co-operation between different professionals who work with children and adolescents at risk has been a key concern of policymakers, practitioners and academics for some time. Many research reports, conferences, and seminars during the past few years have highlighted the various sources of difficulties of getting a range of authorities and organisations to realise effective methods of working together. Speculations about the reasons for the lack of co-operation cover everything from obstacles on the individual level, prestige, and personality clashes to a structural level of cultural obstacles, qualification battles, and professional hierarchies.

Another criticism of most inter-agency approaches is their inability to keep the user in focus, instead devoting too much time to internal organisation issues and ensuing conflicts. Moreover, their programmes frequently have gaps between the theoretical bases and their practical application, a tension which can exacerbate existing divisions between academics and professionals in the field.

Although our concerns emanated from our work in Sweden, our links with other professionals, practitioners, students and educators through the *European Union-Canada Exchange Project* revealed that similar tensions existed elsewhere. We hope that by writing up our own specific experience in this chapter, we will be able to contribute to the debates that others are having in this fraught area.

In Sweden, a number of research reports written during the latter part of the 1990s claimed that the public sector would require a further 500,000 employees at the beginning of the 21st century to replace those lost through changes in professional careers, retirement, and normal attrition.

Many of those now employed in education and the caring professions will, therefore, not be around when the time comes to shape a new future for their organisations. Because of this, there is a great urgency to start a process of future recruitment for the public sector, while at the same time engaging in endeavours that will break down the negative traditions that burden many inter-professional interactions.

The 'Multiversity' Pilot Project

To address this problem, a number of farsighted individuals met during a 12 month period to come up with a solution to this problem. Their efforts paid off, and an 'opportunity' was created to embark upon a 'visionary Project' – *the Multiversity*. Initiated in the fall of 1998, it continued through to December 2000.

The Multiversity is a co-ordinated effort of three branches of education and three district administrations in the municipality of Stockholm. The branches of education are the Stockholm Institute of Education (specifically the Institute's pre-school teacher's course, the recreation leaders' course, and the course for teachers of grades 1 to 7); the Department of Social Work at Stockholm University (the programme for the Bachelor of Science in Social Work); and Skarpnäck Folk High School (the programme for recreation leaders).

Participating from the municipality of Stockholm are the South Stockholm district administrations of Årsta-Enskede, Hägersten, and Älvsjö, each of which encompasses day care centres, schools, day centres for school-age children, youth centres, and the social services. Also participating in *the Multiversity Project* are other network organisations that work with children and adolescents.

To launch *the Multiversity Project,* students, teachers, and researchers from five different educational branches were invited to participate, along with practising professionals from three districts in the city of Stockholm. Together, these districts had a total of about 90,000 residents. Co-operation between childcare, school, recreation, and social services' individual and family care was included within its remit and *the Multiversity* consisted of many levels and structures.

New thoughts and ideas are expected to develop through *the 'multiversity' thinking* because this project has offered opportunities for many perspectives to meet and find answers to the concerns that have been expressed above.

Additionally, through co-operation between educators, researchers, students, and practitioners, both those in the field and in the academy are expected to be kept up to date on the progress being made through innovations in programmes that provide quality support to families with children and adolescents. Co-operation with the schools of higher education can also be seen as a recruitment source for service providers' future need for competent personnel. Another of the goals of *the Multiversity* was to counteract the territorial thinking already evident among professional groups working with families 'at risk' during the educational phase of the Project.

The Participants' Backgrounds

The rationale for *the Multiversity* has developed from topics that have been under discussion in the field, in the media, among researchers, and among the general public. A serious issue in the field has been how to prevent a situation arising where different professionals see 'children at risk' but have no common course of action for addressing the problems.

There was also a need to use the common resources for children and adolescents in a qualitatively better and more effective way. In the field training that was carried out in the Brännkyrka social district in Stockholm at the beginning of the 1990s, major shortcomings were discovered in the professionals' knowledge about other providers' tasks and obligations. There was an urgent need for them to learn to co-operate more closely and become aware of one another's strengths and weaknesses.

The key idea was that better co-ordination might counteract rivalry and prestige seeking among the professionals, behaviour which hardly benefited the families 'at risk'. By becoming more knowledgeable about the resources, possibilities, control mechanisms, and problems of the groups working in this area, it was hoped that we might achieve greater understanding and a better quality of work with children and adolescents 'at risk'.

The Department of Social Work at Stockholm University and the municipality of Stockholm have been collaborating on a development project ever since 1984. In this project, the field co-operated directly in education throughout the first five terms of the Department's study programme. Its aim had been to develop a dialogue on theory and practice between the educational community and the field. The expertise gained through this initiative was incorporated into *the Multiversity Project*.

In 1986, the Brännkyrka social district in Stockholm began to collaborate with Gothenburg University on a field programme for the Bachelor of Science in Social Work. This effort has been administered by Lasse Fryk and Bosse Forsen. Gothenburg University has since instituted its own *Multiversity* comprising its Department of Social Work and a social district in the city. Lessons from this endeavour were also brought to the attention of those involved in *the Multiversity* in Stockholm.

Meanwhile, a District Reform Programme was put into effect in the municipality of Stockholm in 1997. This reform brought together the different school programmes, youth centres, and social services' programmes under one central administration. The municipality was divided into 24 districts, each with its own district manager and district political council. Brännkyrka social district was divided up, and parts of the former network structure were parcelled out to neighbouring Älvsjö, Hägersten, and Årsta district councils.

This reorganisation brought to light the need for new expertise and common structures in the district's social service programmes for children and adolescents, and also contributed to the concerns discussed by participants in *the Multiversity Project*.

The Multiversity's Goals and Purposes

The Multiversity is a development and co-operation project to provide better quality of support when working with children and adolescents. It is also an ideas forum for educators, students, professionals, and researchers whose work is based on the United Nations Convention on the Rights of the Child. Another goal has been to teach staff to talk directly with families in difficult situations, so that confidentiality does not become an obstacle for continued help. The basic idea is to ensure that families are always included in the work that is done on their particular problems.

All actions must contribute to viewing children and adolescents holistically – in their entire social context. If a child needs attention in any of the school's remedial programmes, we should immediately consider his or her family situation. What support does the family need if the child is experiencing difficulties in school? Are other children in the family being adversely affected? What is the effect of their behaviour on the rest of their social network? How does the child spend his or her leisure time?

The aim has also been to bring about increased interaction between practice-based know-how and scientifically based knowledge. Here, experiences and issues grounded in the social services programmes constitute the foundation for theoretical knowledge, and theories from higher education can in turn be tested in the service programmes.

Students can follow the ongoing discussions on social issues, and the educational community can keep itself up-to-date on current questions. At the same time, the field gets the opportunity to use these theories and methods in its daily work. Thus, this interaction can also be used to develop knowledge among field staff.

Linking higher education to the social service programmes provided in the three city districts has made it possible to use university teachers to theorise the field's 'tacit knowledge'. At the same time, the students quickly got the opportunity to participate in the professional activities that awaited them after graduation.

The third task of research was outlined in the 1997 Higher Education Act. But it too could be linked to the service programmes by inviting researchers to contribute their knowledge to both the development and the evaluation of *the Multiversity*. They could also follow interesting service programmes in the field's many areas of activity, and thereby acquire a comprehensive picture of the life situations of children and adolescents. The researchers were also invited to participate in *the Multiversity's* various programmes and to lead interdisciplinary seminars.

The aim has also been to develop a 'network and local area methodology' by giving students in higher education insight into how social districts and municipalities function, which agencies are working with the same children and families, and what resources and opportunities these agencies have at their disposal. Their task was to consider the ways in which these groups of professionals could best co-operate to give families at risk the optimum quality of support.

Implementation

Mentor sessions

Links were established between the students, their study programmes and the three city districts. Each student was assigned to a mixed group consisting of students from his or her own study programme and from the other four study programmes. The groups met regularly throughout the whole of their education.

Representatives from each of the five professions involved in working with children and adolescents were assigned as mentors to each mixed student group. This allowed staff from the field the opportunity to meet each other and exchange experiences – an event that seldom happens otherwise.

Additionally, by using *the Multiversity* as a 'hub', practitioners from different professions could also meet. They, too, otherwise have little time and opportunity to do so. In the discussions with students and educators, the practitioners describe the range of opportunities available alongside the limitations of their work with children, the kinds of needs that exist, and what paths of development they have tried. Concrete examples of co-operation were discussed at these meetings where the students constituted an active group.

Joint lectures

Once a month, everyone involved in *the Multiversity* was invited to participate in a few days together in a programme of joint education. These days had different themes including: lectures about the new curricula; the United Nation's Convention on the Rights of the Child; recording, documentation and evaluation; questions regarding collaboration, networking and local work with children and adolescents and their families; confidentiality and the obligation to report suspected cases of child abuse to the authorities (*anmälningsskyldighet*); and information about what happens in the case of a report.

There was also extensive discussion of how clients should be received and treated, and about ways to co-operate with parents. How should we regard families and children 'at risk'? What should we take into consideration if we want to prevent these families from absenting themselves from meetings with their children's after-school day centres or day care centres? How can we help people who feel threatened by social services intervention? How can we convince them of our good intentions? How can we make better use of one another's professional expertise? How can we best work together when we suspect that children are 'at risk'?

New discussions and new dialogues arose as a result of these meetings. Suggestions were made for new activities to be undertaken in some of the projects. Even the Skandia Insurance Company and the National Swedish Police College in Stockholm have participated in lectures on the theme of collaboration, since they concurred with *the Multiversity's* comprehensive view on families and on the need for early preventive work.

Practice

Each student was assigned a trainee job in projects within *the Multiversity's* geographical area. Because the training periods for the different branches of education did not occur at the same time, students from the different branches were unable to participate directly in the programmes during their training. Instead, they were offered the opportunity to maintain contact with the field throughout their entire course in their higher education. This promoted another of our main ideas – that dialogue and linkages to the field in all courses of instruction should run like a common thread throughout the duration of a student's education.

Presentation of the programmes

Study visits, lectures, and seminars were arranged to present the programme to all of the participants. Other municipal networks and collaborators were also invited to take part and be represented. These included child health centres, maternity clinics, police, churches, school health services, and psychiatry.

The field's collaboration in advanced study assignments

The professionals invited the students to review the service programmes and make use of any information and knowledge they wished in their study assignments. The idea was that the students would also be able to discuss the material with the professionals, who could then 'sit in' when the students were examined in order to provide additional perspectives in their assessments.

Joint retreats and festive gatherings

These occasions have contributed new dimensions in the relationships that were created among the participants. New networks have been formed between the students and the professionals. Mixed work groups at the retreats discussed evaluation issues and co-operative tasks that were not always self-evident to those who have worked in the field for a long time.

The Direct Rewards of *the Multiversity*

Through *the Multiversity*, the students received a broader picture of their own profession at an earlier stage in their period of study. They had contact with those who were active participants in their future profession right from the first week of their education. Discussions about day-to-day issues were thus brought directly into their training. The students could also discuss issues concerning their future professional roles with practitioners in the field.

There was also increased interdisciplinary awareness and an understanding of others outside their own branches of education or their own professions. Through the joint lectures, the participants got a broader picture of the other branches of education and information about important theoretical knowledge from the four other professional education programmes involved in the project.

On these occasions, the most important issues and expertise from each branch focusing on families with children and adolescents were presented and considered. Thus, respect for, and expectations of, the other professions increased for all participants, new dialogues were initiated, and students and educators could discuss the new ideas to which work in the field gave rise.

As a result of this collaboration, interest in and the willingness to co-operate with other professionals have increased. We have also had many discussions about hierarchies and status in the various professions, and what relevance these aspects have for the day-to-day work. By identifying the problems, the hierarchical borderlines became more visible and in part could be more readily subjected to change.

Because the *Project* was structured as an exchange between different services, the educational programmes involved received extra resources in the form of additional lectures from professionals in the field, as well as through the sharing of resources from the other educational programmes. On the average, eight hours of 'extra lectures' per month plus two hours of mentor-led sessions were added to the students' courses. This can be compared with their regular course, which comprises seven to eight hours of teacher-led instruction per week.

Throughout the entire *Project*, the courses and the students had access to all the city districts' resources on children and adolescents. These were used by them to varying degrees. The city districts were also made accessible to researchers as a field of inquiry.

Through the District Reform of 1997, Stockholm was divided into new geographical areas. *The Multiversity* has promoted collaboration over three district administrations, and this has allowed the development of bridges of co-operation and an exchange of experience that would not have been possible without *the Multiversity*. This was a reward for which the professionals in the field were particularly grateful.

Also, for the first time, the schools of higher education involved in *the Multiversity* engaged in a dialogue with one another, and this has had its practical application in leading to collaboration among the various departments of the Stockholm Institute of Education that were involved in *the Multiversity Project*.

Furthermore, the contact between the educational programmes and educators on the one hand, and practitioners on the other, yielded a unique joint supervisor training programme for professional social workers, pre-school teachers, recreational leaders, and grade-school teachers.

Professionals who participated in the Multiversity were given the time and opportunity to theorise about their own work roles. Lectures were offered on new knowledge in their own and in others' domain of study. By meeting students, educators, and other professionals, the 'tacit knowledge' acquired in the field could be articulated.

Questions and discussions about the methods used in the day-to-day work could be formulated in theoretical terms, in some cases for the first time. These would then be discussed thoroughly by the participants. Entire days were spent in parallel seminars held by the professionals. These were greatly appreciated by students, educators, and other professionals alike.

Collaboration was attempted on many different levels (see Appendices One and Two) and the result was new dialogues and new relationships that did not exist earlier. The students otherwise usually met practitioners in their field of study only during their trainee periods, and educators and researchers only during the theory segments of their education. In *the Multiversity*, they also had opportunities to meet students and teachers from other educational fields, and to have discussions with professionals in the field, all in parallel with their theoretical training.

Difficulties

The Multiversity, as an organisation, has had to deal with difficulties on several dimensions. However, the barriers that we encountered have also offered opportunities for gaining new knowledge on the structural, general, and individual levels. And we tried to make the most of the potential for growth.

The Multiversity was not a compulsory option for the educational programmes involved. Therefore, the students could choose not to attend lectures or sessions with their mentors. This meant that some mentors felt that their contributions in *the Multiversity* were unappreciated, even though they had sometimes worked hard to be able to leave their regular workplaces. For this reason, some of the mentors chose not to attend every meeting of this *Project*.

It is difficult for teachers to leave during regular teaching hours. Substitutes are difficult to find. In some of the schools, however, being assigned as a mentor in *the Multiversity* was considered so important that the teachers were given extra time for this task. Thus, it was particularly irritating for teachers when students were absent from the mentor sessions without informing them.

Major reorganisations

Both the Department of Social Work at Stockholm University and the Stockholm Institute of Education have undergone major changes recently, and these have affected *the Multiversity*. Cutbacks in basic education have also been common during this period. The administrative districts of Årsta and Enskede were consolidated, and both have undergone financial and organisational changes. As a consequence, several administrative heads have left their posts during this period, with knock-on effects for the continuity of *the Multiversity Project*.

There has also been some difficulty in getting researchers to see the benefits of participating in *the Multiversity*. Consequently, the dialogue between researchers in different branches of education never really got underway, with the result that a comprehensive view of children and adolescents could not be discussed at the research level within the schools of higher education.

Structural problems

One such problem concerned the teachers of the grades 1 to 7 programme offered by the Stockholm Institute of Education, who were expected to conduct some of their courses at Stockholm University. As the Institute has no control of the teaching schedule, it could not dictate when students should participate in these. The Institute also had difficulty fitting segments of *the Multiversity* programme into its teaching schedule.

The Project is comprised of an extensive and complex network of people and organisations

The Multiversity Project contains many structures and a large number of participants. In effect, each activity would have needed its own project group to promote its activities, work towards gaining acceptance and following up issues within its own organisation. The work teams were isolated in promoting their tasks within the different projects. Support from directors of the social services programmes varied, and the limited time at their disposal also impacted on their participation in *the Multiversity*.

The Need for a *Multiversity* Perspective

Rapid social development requires the constant expansion of knowledge, both in the field and in education. Dialogue becomes all the more important because knowledge changes rapidly with social development and has a short shelf life. If the relationship between theory and practice is to grow, there must be a continuous dialogue built upon mutual respect and a genuine interest in the programme.

Children continue to fall into the gaps between theory and practice. Despite the research that tells us that children do not get the help they need in time, the situation still looks like it did when light was first shed on the problem in a research report in 1995. Staff who see the children first at the child health care centres and follow them up through the years do the best they can with the resources they have. But because of the lack of a dialogue and the lack of information from other authorities working with the same families, their efforts are seldom sufficient.

We need to have better knowledge of each other's resources and possibilities, and learn to use them in a better and more qualitative way. Basically, families need to feel that they are acknowledged and supported from an early stage, so that they can count on getting the kind of help that they can believe in.

In the past decade there have been appreciable cutbacks in the Swedish public sector, particularly where children with 'special needs' are concerned. Children's groups are becoming larger, and children who earlier were noticed in time and were helped to manage their daily lives now have difficulty in getting the necessary attention and resources for doing so. Decreased resources require that service programmes for children and families co-ordinate their knowledge and efforts effectively so that the children who are most 'at risk' are noticed in time, and receive the help they need.

For many years, developments in the public sector have made many parents feel they are no longer important to their children when it comes to school and recreation. To reactivate parents' own sense of responsibility, it is essential that all parents and their social networks are given greater influence in programmes directed at children and adolescents. By having more influence, parents can become aware of their responsibilities in time and take part in discussions about other interventions.

The Future of *the Multiversity*

The first phase of *the Multiversity* has now been carried out and is soon to be evaluated. Those of us who have worked on this project can see, however, that there are many reasons to develop *the Multiversity* idea on a national level.

New education programme at the Stockholm Institute of Education

A new programme for teacher education began at the Institute in the fall of 2001. All students will take 60 points in 'general education'. The programme associated with this will examine questions that are common to all categories of teachers (pre-school teachers, recreation leaders, compulsory school teachers, and high school teachers). It is thereby hoped that all the students will acquire a common basis of knowledge and understanding about each other's future professional roles.

This should enable them to become flexible, easily redeployable professionals during times of social change and shifting needs. As a result, they should be able to exchange tasks and professional areas quickly and with relative ease. Because the situation for children is seen in its entirety, it is anticipated that greater understanding will also develop between teachers, recreation instructors, and pre-school teachers.

The students will be linked to a partner area – a geographical area that including of pre-schools, day centres for school-age children, elementary schools, and in some locations, even high schools. Certain segments of the new education programme will be conducted within the partner area and designated as a programme assigned part of the training. It was also intended to give the students a broad knowledge about the local social work facilities that the families in the area and the school can use.

Knowledge-based social service

The National Swedish Board of Health and Welfare has presented, at the request of the government, a proposal for a knowledge-based social services sector. Professionals will continually update their know-how through advanced courses and by keeping in touch with current research and developments in education. The proposal put special emphasis on management training in order to highlight new topical issues in the social services arena.

The third task for higher education

This was introduced in the 1997 Higher Education Act. As a result, schools of higher education have developed their external contacts, especially with industry. Contact with the public sector is still mostly in the form of contracted courses. The third task is a Commission that is to be formulated in a dialogue with the field regarding its needs and developmental requirements. There is still much to be done here. There is a need for developing expertise in the field, which can best be kept up-to-date if a dialogue is established between the public sector and higher education.

Project-oriented work methods in education and in the field

In recent years the tendency has been towards more project-oriented work. This means that many projects run for a relatively short time, and are then replaced by new projects. Education and research should follow up all of these new projects, provide supervision, and document and evaluate them. This would minimise the risk that new projects and ideas would arise only to disappear without having any effect on future work.

Concluding Remarks

The Multiversity has been primarily a 'visionary project'. We have tested thoughts and ideas and discovered where various obstacles lie. But, we have been unable to fulfil all the goals that we had set for ourselves in their entirety. *The 'Multiversity journey'* has been stimulating and exciting, but at the same time, it has been a great challenge, and the discussions held between us were sometimes heated. Many issues have been clarified, and unclear constructions have been made more discernible. *The Project* and its aims have been judged impossible by observers who are aware of the complexity of organisations, cultures, and the participating agencies and parties. They have little faith in our being able to realise our goals, let alone generalise from them.

The Multiversity's major theme has been collaboration. The degree of co-operation amongst the participating parties, along with the dialogue and the theories to which they subscribed, were put to the test when the various cultures and professional levels diverged from one another. As a consequence, we were forced to question the degree of co-operation within the project management and organisation of *the Multiversity*. The difficulties we encountered on different levels have strengthened our belief in the need for new ways to develop and strengthen co-operation and collaboration.

It was also interesting to see that the similarities between the Swedish *Multiversity Project* and the *European Union-Canada Exchange Project* were greater than the differences between them. We have seen comparable problems and obstacles in the various countries between the educational community and practitioners. This has reinforced our belief that we have a future interest in seeking new approaches that will link together education, practice, and research in a common purpose. Our shared goal, after all, is to create better conditions for families at risk and for their children and adolescents.

In Sweden, the future of *the Multiversity* will depend on the outcome of the evaluation into its impact. Interviews with the participating parties will be among the methods used to determine its success or failure. For the good of the profession and those we work with, we hope that the results will lead to a continuation of all aspects and phases of *the Multiversity Project*. Its existence has certainly made a difference to the lives of those who have already been touched by it.

Appendix 1

Complexity in the Multiversity

Profession				
Pre-school teaching	Recreational Instruction	Teaching Grades 1 to 7	Social Work	Youth Rec. Instruction

Users				
Family Children 0 to 7 yrs.	Family Children and Young people 0 to 16 yrs.	Family Children and Young people 7 to 16 yrs.	Family Children and Young people 0 to 20 yrs.	Family Young people 7 to 20 yrs.

Educational Institution				
Stockholm Institute of Education	Stockholm Institute of Education	Stockholm Institute of Education	Stockholm Uni., Dept of Social Work	Skarpnäck Folk High School
Courses				
Pre-school teachers General	Recreation leaders	Teachers grade 1 to 7	Social workers	Recreational instructors

Research				
Researcher Education	Researcher Education	Researcher Education	Researcher Social work	Researcher Recreation

Practitioner				
Pre-school teacher	Recreation instructor	Teacher grades 1 to 7	Social worker	Youth rec. leader

The table shows how different professional education programmes can co-operate with their own professions. The Multiversity also endeavours to create opportunities for co-operation between education programmes and practitioners. For example, a student from the education programme for youth recreation leaders is given the opportunity to collaborate with a professional social worker, an educator from the pre-school teacher course, and a researcher from the grade-school teacher course.

Appendix 2

Professionals Working in Programmes for Children and Adolescents

Age of child or young person:

0yrs   6/7yrs   10yrs   16yrs   20yrs

Professional Involved:

Pre-school teacher

Recreational instructor

Elementary school teacher

Recreational leader

Graduate Social Worker

Different agencies and professional categories will work together with the child and the family during the child's lifetime. The professionals involved overlap as shown in the figure above. Thus it is necessary for professionals, educators, and students to be made aware of the expertise available in other areas, and to become more aware of the importance of co-operating with each other.

17 Developing a Child Welfare Curriculum across Borders

JULIA WALDMAN with DAVID COLOMBI

Introduction

The shrinkage of international borders in both a physical and virtual sense opens up new questions, challenges and possibilities for the development of an internationalised social work (Dominelli, 2000). The movement of people and ideas within and between countries requires those working in personal social services to understand how their work is both informed by and informs issues that spread beyond local and national limits.

This emergent perspective has implications for the education and training of social workers at both qualifying and post-qualifying levels. Programme curricula need to situate activities and influences within a global context and this in turn requires programme providers to look beyond some of their traditional and sometimes parochial approaches to innovations in teaching and learning.

This chapter explores some of the challenges encountered in developing an international social work curriculum. It focuses upon a world-wide web-based course, entitled *Child Welfare across Borders*. This course was created as part of a *European Union-Canada Exchange Project* involving six higher education institutions and a number of social work agencies linked to higher education programmes in four countries.

This chapter seeks to deconstruct the process of building and shaping a curriculum as a shared international activity, using the new technologies as the medium for both negotiations about and delivery of the curriculum. There is a focus upon:

* the key practical implications of developing a curriculum that has to fit the requirements of six institutions within four countries

- the issues raised by the process of debating and articulating the nature of contemporary policy and practice across national borders to do with professional child welfare work.

Background

A brief overview of the Project context is provided first. The development of the course was one of a number of activities that took place within an international project entitled *Child Abuse, Protection and Welfare*, funded by the European Community – Canada Programme for Co-operation in Higher Education and Training. This three-year Project ran between 1997 and 2000 and involved the social work departments from six universities and local social work agencies in Canada, England, the Netherlands and Sweden.

The primary goals of the Project were to facilitate the exchange of social work students for field placements and to build child welfare curricula within an international context. The course represented a culmination of the co-operation and shared thinking of the partners across the four countries, as well as the commitment to expanding understandings of an internationalised social work.

Although anticipated at the beginning, getting curriculum development underway proved difficult and several early initiatives yielded negligible results. The *European Union-Canada Project* had been underway for over a year before work on the curriculum development began in earnest with the appointment of Julia Waldman to ensure that this goal came to fruition. In addition to student exchanges, exchanges of research findings, publications and conferences, the curriculum development activity was seen as a means of building bridges across borders and between child welfare academics and practitioners and students.

To meet the various demands and wide scope of the work, a course writer and a programmer-website designer from the Centre for Human Service Technology at the University of Southampton in the UK were appointed on a consultancy basis to undertake the development work. The curriculum research and development activity took place over a 15-month period, until the *European Union-Canada Project* reached its end in March 2000.

The activity provided a fascinating and rich learning experience for the course writer and website designer who present their perspectives in this chapter.

Cyber Negotiations and Traditional Consultation

A feature of the curriculum development was the consultative approach that was used to accommodate the diverse views, needs and wishes of the collaborative stakeholders in the *European Union-Canada Project*. Whilst opportunities were available for direct conversation at occasional conferences held as part of the *Project*, the physical distances between the partners within and between countries meant methods for negotiating, information sharing and discussion needed to be developed that were not reliant upon face-to-face contact.

The parameters of the curriculum were extremely broad at the start of the process. It was necessary, therefore, to undertake a staged consultation exercise with Project partners to enable the course writer to move towards a refined curriculum plan from a broad initial scoping exercise.

Stage 1 – Email Questionnaire

The first stage of consultation involved an email questionnaire, the aim of which was to elicit two types of information from individual partners:

- their visionary ideas and expectations for an international curriculum
- institutional requirements and practicalities, such as the academic level, the size of the course, the student audience and technology constraints.

Whilst a somewhat one-sided approach, the time constraints of the Project were such that initial ideas needed to be collated and analysed in time for a Project Conference two months after the closing date for questionnaire replies. The questions, by necessity, needed to be open-ended and thus a large amount of text in the answers needed to be collated. The benefits of an e-mail approach immediately became apparent because text could simply be cut and pasted into a word processing programme under themed headings for analysis or sent as an attachment. The writer has subsequently used this approach in other mainstream research projects with some success.

With many organisations' internal and external communications dominated by e-mail, it is often the preferred mode of contact for many staff. The problems of low returns in postal surveys with staff groups pressured by paperwork can be helped by electronic communications. This optimism has to be tempered, however, by the reality of information overload now encountered in electronic messaging systems. As Welch (cited in Waldman, 1999) says, 'The tidal wave of the information revolution has hit us hard'.

Burkeman (2001) argues that people now find it hard to prioritise and read all their messages and as a consequence are turning away from the potential 'email burnout'. Another alarm bell rang at the first consultation stage. The questions were sent as part of the email text rather than as an attachment because not all participants were able to retrieve documents in this way. This early sign of access problems would be compounded as the Project went on.

Stage 2a – Conference Awayday

A discussion document was prepared from the replies to the questionnaire and posted out in advance of the Conference where a day had been set aside at the end to focus solely on the curriculum development project. A mixed approach to communication enabled the speed of email to be complemented by the visual and tactile impact of receipt of a paper document. Storage systems on email may mean documents are filed for reading 'later' whereas paper copies often at least encourage a quick skim read and registers with the reader a focus on the task ahead.

With the emergence of the information age it is important to gain a sense of how people use different media for communication and information sharing. The curriculum development process gave some insight into old problems of joint working, and new ones. The availability of a facility for logging receipt of emails proved helpful for being able to check which individuals had received and/or read messages, especially if replies had not been received.

Despite the advance copies of a discussion paper, it was clear that busy schedules had hindered the full reading of the text. The planned programme had to be quickly revised to accommodate the reality of people's different starting points. As in any joint venture, it was vital that all partners shared a sense of ownership about the course and for some, this meant clarifying many issues that the first consultation stage had intended to air. A significant difference emerged with regard to the potential student audience, which presented challenges for the design of an inclusive curriculum that could meet a wide range of academic standards. The strategy that was developed to address this diversity is explored further on in the chapter.

The day involved intense discussion and a small group approach was used to move prioritisation of ideas for curriculum content forward. Several members spoke English as a second or third language and this inevitably impacted on their ability to participate fully for long periods. Time spent in groups of people from the same country facilitated completion of some of the activities. In a face-to-face situation, it was more possible to be aware of people's different understandings and interpretations. With email communication such differences may remain obscured.

Stage 2b – Questionnaire for Conference Participants

Another level of consultation with fieldwork staff and students was also undertaken via a questionnaire distributed at the conference. The participants at it represented potential users of the curriculum. Approximately twenty questionnaires were received. In some ways the replies presented a dilemma because the project partners had already taken certain decisions about the direction and focus of the course. It seemed important to consider the views of the respondents, yet the wide-ranging suggestions for curriculum content meant that it was not possible to include all these in the course that was eventually prepared. Overall, with such a range of ideas and expectations it was a challenge to produce a draft curriculum outline that could meet the hopes of most interest groups.

Stage 3 – Rolling Feedback

Following the production and email distribution of a suggested curriculum outline, consideration then needed to be given to an approach for continuing communication and involvement of the key stakeholders in the draft stages. This involved questions and decisions about the use of software that had the capacity to design and edit material. The systems issues that were encountered and addressed are covered in the next section. However, the limited use of the software by key individuals during the early months of design revealed a number of communication hurdles. These were that:

- password protected access can be forbidding and exclusive
- if instructions and routes through a programme are not quick and straightforward people quickly become disengaged from participating in its use
- an editorial medium that involves access via a special programme or web-site for people with busy schedules results in its marginalisation and lack of use
- if discussion lists are not active continuously, people stop looking at them and they become redundant
- and then people resort to use of standard email for communication.

The main software that was chosen for the communication interface was not used for the course design for some of the reasons listed above. So the emphasis in ongoing communication changed to notification of requests and updates by email distribution lists. With a relatively long development period of a year it was quite difficult to sustain active interest in progress.

Reliance on 'virtual' contact was sometimes an unsettling experience as reasons for lack of responses were unknown. The ease with which emails can be sent means that it can be tempting to become a persistent messenger and there was a balance to be struck in communicating regularly but not intrusively with colleagues.

Stage 4 – Final Project Conference

The final Project conference was timely in that it provided an ideal opportunity to show and discuss the almost finished product with the Project partners. Virtual dialogue is no substitute for being with people and being able to understand their reactions and views with the help of, for example, body language, gesture and tone of voice. The impact of virtual communication on the nature of building relationships between people is so significant that it is given more attention later in this chapter in the section on ownership and continuity. As Martin (1999) says:

> 'there is no substitute for personal meetings – they appear essential for the development of trust and commitment ... . Nevertheless, modern communication technologies are clearly supporting our ability to be creative collaborators' (Martin, 1999, p. 105).

Systems Issues

In this section attention moves to the issues that arose in making decisions about the choice of virtual learning environments (VLE) to support the design and delivery of the curriculum. Creating a website for the *Child Welfare across Borders Course* started from an unpromising, but not wholly unfamiliar scenario for the Centre for Human Service Technology at the University of Southampton. For the person developing the website, the activity was one that involved a number of challenges that had to be resolved in a manner that was consistent with the Project's overall philosophy. The challenges to be addressed were:

- a virtually non-existent specification for the task to be done or guidance on expectations of it
- working with a new partner as the content provider
- moving into a new technology of HTML from the programming background of Macromedia Authorware and VisualBasic
- limited time resources available for the Project – a notional 22 programming days, with tight deadlines for completion, which provided little room for experimentation or creativity

- uncertainty at the outset about the size of the course to be developed, instead working with the course writer to create the website stage-by-stage as the resources were written
- a relatively slight published knowledge base about design of on-line course and how people learn best from them
- limited resources for purchasing or designing visual or other multimedia content
- uncertainty about the environment to be used, with an initial drive to use WebCT as an established VLE.

This list did not engender optimism, particularly as the relationship between software developers and content providers can be fraught with difficulties and conflicts over different ideas about design, functionality, structure, interactivity and suitability of content for the medium. A number of positive factors, however, substantially ameliorated some, though not all, of the negative features of this work. These were that:

- a productive working relationship quickly developed between the website designer and the course writer, unfettered by preciousness and with a mutual willingness to adapt to criticisms and suggestions
- the course writer developed ideas for the content that were informative, accessible and suited to the medium and was successful in finding relevant web-based resources
- the diagrammatic representation used by the course writer to structure each session within the course proved to be adaptable as 'visual maps' for each session on the website
- personal and CHST experience in developing electronic learning resources (or 'Courseware') such as *Interpersonal Skills* for Social Work and Nursing, *Research Methods for Social Work and Nursing* as part of the UK Higher Education Teaching and Learning Technology Programme (TLTP) proved invaluable, as did a previous role as the software developer for a multi-national European Union project on *Increasing the IMPACT of Assistive Technology*
- the worthwhile subject matter, not only in relation to child welfare, but also in bringing an international dimension accorded well with the

value base of the website designer and course writer, which brought additional personal commitment to the task

- a willingness of Centre colleagues and some project members to evaluate and give feedback on content
- the availability of technical support within the university setting and some flexibility to use some additional Centre resources for the Project and to utilise this as a learning process for skills development.

Starting Out

The design of any courseware has to address a number of inter-related pedagogical, technical and design issues of content, accessibility, structure, navigation, interactivity and user friendliness (Avison and Wood-Harper, 1990). The design stages need to consider the ways in which students may use it. Pragmatism suggests that there also needs to be a realistic awareness that they will use it in very different ways from the ones that may have been initially imagined.

While a taught course has of necessity a structured sequence in time, an electronic course is something which students can, and should, use in very different ways. Electronic learning resources that do not offer choices to the user about their use are likely to be on a short route to oblivion. There is of course nothing inherently new in this idea. Many people pick up an academic book and undertake often very rapid, preliminary assessments before deciding to read it or which sections may be of use.

One crucial difference however with dipping into web-based resources, is the absence of the tactile reality of a text that enables the potential reader to gauge the size and weight of a book even before it is picked up. In contrast, it can be extremely difficult to discern the size or metaphorical weight of this type of courseware. Web-based materials that lead the user on to the information highway exacerbate the issue. The immediacy of accessing limitless information on-line is a very different learning framework to the sort of background reading that relies on the individual undertaking physical library searches.

From a technical perspective, the key early issue was choice of environment. In addition to using HyperText Markup Language (HTML) to develop a website on the Internet, there is very wide range of Virtual Learning Environments (VLEs) to assist development of on-line courses. They offer facilities that make it relatively easy for academics to put courses on-line and also support functions such as email, chat rooms and rudimentary on-line assessment. Undertaking a proper review of VLEs would have used more than the entire resources of the project. The reality is that decisions on VLEs tend to be taken at an institutional level and that academics mostly use the system that their institution has purchased. In the case of Southampton, it was WebCT, which was also used by at least two of the partner universities.

In practice WebCT proved not to meet the needs of the project for two principle reasons:

- it required students to be registered and supported. This meant that in order to use the course, students in Sweden, the Netherlands or Canada would have to be registered on the Southampton site, requiring administrative support that was not available. The alternative of the course being separately available in WebCT in each university was considered. This would have meant, however, that the email and chat room tools would only be available to communicate locally, not internationally, thereby defeating the aims of an international course.
- WebCT is designed for ease of putting up lecturer's notes and images without knowledge of HTML. The more complex features of *Child Welfare across Borders* were more easily developed in HTML and placed directly on a web-server. The simplicity of WebCT became counter-productive and some of its specialist elements such as assessment tools were not relevant to a social work subject area that has to do with understanding complex issues rather than simple 'yes' and 'no' answers.

Experimenting with WebCT meant that in a sense critical time was lost in the development process. With the lessons learned, the decision was made to put the course on to an open website at the University of Southampton where it could be accessed not only by partner universities, but also by the outside world. The decision was also made to make the courseware available to project partners on CD-ROM for local installation on Intranets to speed access time.

Student and Institutional Diversity

Throughout the Project, it became apparent how diverse the educational institutions and their requirements of a curriculum were. Rowlings (2000), in an overview of social work education in Europe, concludes that the extent of difference is in many ways to be expected given the nature of social work itself and the 'highly contested space' (Rowlings, 2000, p. 45) that it must inhabit between the individual and the state. In addition to the debates about content that are explored in the next section, the main issues related to the student and institutional diversity that impacted on curriculum design were the size of cohorts taught by each institution and their heterogeneity.

The social work student population of the partner institutions ranged from 40 to 1600 per year group. This has a number of implications, significantly in the teaching methods appropriate to working with different group sizes. In the use of course software it suggests that large student cohorts may need either to have a very structured content or to operate as significantly independent learners.

Another issue related to size concerned the aspect of how 'big' to make the course to fit the modular or programme requirements of the different institutions. The reality of an *international* Credit Accumulation and Transfer Scheme that has a shared language of practicalities such as number of teaching hours in modules or duration of module is a long way off. Add the difficulties of translating an open-learning, open-ended resource into a taught classroom equivalent equation and the calculations get even more problematic. The dilemma was addressed in the design stages by creating a resource that was based on a fixed number of sessions, which could, if the users wished, be translated into teaching weeks. Or they could be used in a limited way by extracting or adding elements from some or all of them.

The consultation with institutional partners and within the *European Union-Canada Project* generally, elicited a picture of the different ways in which social work education and training is delivered, even within

Europe. There were very different views about the academic level at which the curriculum materials should be targeted, from post-qualification level to first year undergraduate level. At the design stage it was not clear who the eventual audience would be and this clearly was a challenge. It was not possible to resolve the dilemma by narrowing the appeal to one group because this may have made the curriculum unusable to many of the partners.

Instead, the issue was considered, as with the previous issue, as part of the structural design of the content. It was decided that core materials could be supplemented by different assignments or discussion questions set by individual user institutions or programmes that were appropriate to their particular target audience.

The linguistic and cultural diversity of the student audience and their general heterogeneity worked against the development of a curriculum that focused on country-specific contexts, as would be the norm in the development of in-house materials. The course design reflected an intention to address child welfare themes and issues that had resonance in all the countries involved but allowed for institutions to use the materials in a flexible way to suit their own needs and requirements.

Thematic Matters

A major issue raised by the curriculum development activity was to do with the focusing and refocusing of the content. This was also an area that brought into sharp relief the day-to-day differences in the way social work with children is delivered across the four countries. The first phases of consultation produced a shopping list of topics that partners wished to see covered by the curriculum. The list was extended by the questionnaire replies from conference participants, most of who were students and fieldworkers.

Even the task of creating a title that would have meaning to the relevant audiences in each country was difficult. In the end preference was given to 'child welfare' rather than 'social work with children' to reflect the different professional and structural organisation of fieldwork in the participating countries.

Inevitably, there was a sense of what constituted an ideal content and what content was realistic, given the resources available. The balance between these two possibilities had to be carefully negotiated and ultimately agreed among the partner institutions. For example, many practitioners saw a detailed exploration of the laws and procedures related to child protection in each country as something they wanted. This immediately raised issues of continuity and updating. Policies are continuously changing and there was the prospect of writing something that by the end of the development was already inaccurate. Also, although useful, a comparative perspective required an intense input from relevant experts in each country to contribute, and this facility was not immediately available.

However, many common themes did begin to emerge and it became apparent that there were issues, concerns and needs to do with child welfare that all four countries involved were grappling with, sometimes similarly, sometimes differently. For example, issues to do with accommodation and support for refugee children from Eastern Europe and parts of Africa were a high priority in both Europe and Canada. So, it became clear that a way ahead was to build a curriculum around these shared themes and that using the framework of children's rights, with a focus on the United Nations Convention of the Rights of the Child. For as Freeman (1996, p. 5) says:

'Each country has its own history and culture, and the problems they confront in complying with an international convention of this nature reflect this'.

The content that was finally included is based on a number of principles concerning both children and student learners that were agreed by the participating partners. These are described below.

Course Mission Statement

This course promotes the need for child welfare practitioners to act more effectively locally by thinking globally. The course is underpinned by a social justice perspective and the belief that children are unique, live in diverse environments, and share common rights and needs. A framework of rights will be critiqued and applied in exploring child welfare issues. The course aims to influence social work practice to effect positive change for children, young people and their families.

Course Themes

The celebration of diversity whilst acknowledging that there are values that social work academics and practitioners hold in common facilitated course development. Some core themes underpin both the content and learning style of the course. These frame the way the course has been shaped and also encompass the stance the course takes to children and child welfare. They are:

One World and Celebrating Diversity

- children and young people share similarities as well as have important differences
- children and young people have a fundamental right to social justice; therefore critiquing and understanding a human rights perspective in practice is key
- understanding child welfare in other countries can provide new ways of knowing and acting to improve social work practice in one's own country.

Connecting the Personal and the Political

- dealing with local and individual situations requires a critical perspective on the social, political and economic contexts that frame children's lives
- critiquing the dominant western or North European approaches to child welfare alerts us to the realities of patriarchal and ethnocentric systems and practices
- promoting alliances, effective and appropriate communication and partnerships as fundamental to good child welfare practice.

Power in Relationships

- building upon the strengths of children, young people, their families and communities in child welfare practice
- unpacking the multi-faceted ways in which power operates in relationships in child welfare
- seeing the individual child in a system of power relationships and societal structures.

Expectations of Student Learning

- the course uses an enquiry and action model of learning – in short this means the focus is on generating solutions and responses to problems, situations and questions independently (individually or in peer-groups) using a variety of resources including the World Wide Web
- the course takes a discursive approach – with participants and staff engaged in a critical dialogue rather than searching for and presenting the 'right' answer that requires participants to act respectfully and contribute to one another's learning
- learning is expected to take place within the paradigm of theory-practice-experience, to engage fully with situations and issues related to child welfare
- participants need to be able to understand and utilise a combination of the following:
  - theory
  - a broad subject knowledge base
  - skills and understandings gained from child welfare related practice and personal life
  - self-awareness
  - communication skills in various media and with various groups and individuals
  - basic keyboard and computer skills
- participants will plan and manage their own timetable for the course on a week-to-week basis, with appropriate support and guidance provided locally by the institution with which they are registered. As it is expected that use of the course will involve regular peer and staff

discussion and assessment, students will need to undertake course-related activities and exercises to be able to participate fully in these
- participants and staff are expected to adopt an anti-oppressive stance in their interactions between themselves and other course contacts.

Learning Outcomes for Course Participants

- to have enhanced research skills in accessing child welfare information, ideas and networks through the use of information and communications technology
- to be aware of the possibilities and limitations of the World Wide Web as a tool for advancing child welfare policy and practice
- to be more informed about child welfare policies and practices of other countries, particularly, Canada, Sweden and England
- to be able to engage in an ongoing analysis of children's rights and social justice and apply these in child welfare practice
- to be more confident in addressing local needs and issues in child welfare by comparing and using perspectives and information from other countries
- to be more aware of child welfare work as a global activity and the implications of this context, including in the use of international conventions and protocols that may be relevant
- to have a deeper respect and appreciation for cultures other than their own
- to be more critical in analysing different models of practice and policy and legislative developments.

Design Issues

Once decisions about the thematic framework of the curriculum had been agreed, these needed to be translated in to a detailed design that made the best use of the medium of delivery. Resource constraints and the necessity to make the materials accessible to people with a range of computer facilities tempered creative possibilities.

Routes

Although at the start of the curriculum project it was unclear how many sessions the *Child Welfare across Borders Course* would have, there was some idea of a logical sequence which students might choose to follow, rather than a random selection on entry points to pick from. However within each session, the 'session maps', developed by the course writer provided within each session the basis for a more flexible approach.

These combined some notion of a pathway from top left to bottom right but with branches off at different points, allowing students to take either a linear or non-linear route. One of the session maps is shown below as Figure 17.1. It gives the visual format with which students make choices about what to look at in each session. Standard box designs were used throughout the session maps for continuity. Students click on each box to go the relevant material.

Figure 17.1   Session Map for Session 3:
A Social Justice Framework

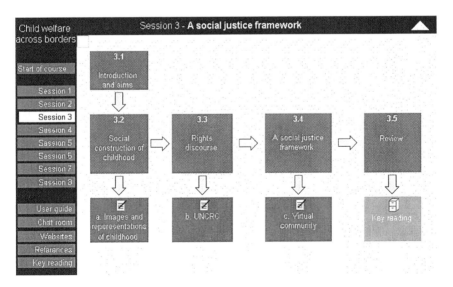

Learning Activities

The design of the course was also informed by principles of self-directed, but supported learning. It was felt that as students moved through or between different sessions they should be presented with a range of different activities, but that a number of core elements should underpin the course. These core elements consisted of:

Four core texts One book from each country involved and giving an overview of the social and policy context of child welfare in that country was chosen. These are a substantial resource in themselves.

'Virtual communities' The idea of virtual communities arose when thinking about the use of case studies and activities based on fieldwork issues. Rather than write new background material for each case, the notion of a community arose around which different themed activities could be developed. Crucially for a web-based resource, it was also felt that the communities could be presented in a visually stimulating way to enhance the look of the resource and facilitate students' engagement with the issues.

   Although it was intended to include a virtual community from each of the participating countries, local difficulties and their non-resolution before the funding period expired meant that the information needed from one participating institution based in the Netherlands did not materialise. Consequently, three communities were included from the four countries involved in the Project. Originally, these were intended to provide examples of communities of:

Locality The Canadian contribution was based on a First Nation community.

Identity The Swedish community, written by students, was based on a geographical locality.

Institution The English community was based on a children's residential unit and its design involved a young person and member of staff from a local children's unit.

Community The inclusion of refugees into an existing community, based on the experiences of asylum seekers in the Netherlands had been planned. Sadly, this proposal had to be dropped, despite sustained efforts expended in trying to facilitate its materialisation.

The communities included pictures, maps, quotes, weblinks, but without an over-reliance of technology that may exclude people with older computer facilities. Ironically, the development of the world-wide web has generated debates about its potential impact on the nature of communities (Wellman and Gulia, 1999) and there was awareness of how the selective promotion of 'community' through such a medium raises dilemmas of representation. Another consistent feature within the course was the inclusion of short reviews and tests at the end of each session. The curriculum also incorporated a ranged of participative activities, which could be linked to assessment if individual institutions wished to do so.

The other main feature of the course design that became a stronger feature as the design process went on was the use made of other web-based resources. Over the months of development, it proved difficult at times to access information and materials from project partners to include in the curriculum. A shift took place towards accessing information, from a country's child welfare policies to children's voices on their rights and needs. This seemed a logical step and also enabled the course to exemplify the ways in which the world-wide web has opened doors to a globalised knowledge bank, though one that needs to be treated with caution. The use of web resources highlighted the need for students to become critical users of the web and to be cautious of different sites' claims to authority. Ravetz (1998, p. 121) cautions against:

> 'the potential for powerful tools on the Net which are able to affect all our senses and further blur the boundary between real reality and constructed reality'.

Topics and Course Structure

The final structure of the course is summarised below:

Session 1 – Introduction to Course

Session 2 – Key Themes and Topics

Session 3 – Childhood Today. This session examines constructs of normal childhood as defined socially, culturally, legally, e.g., problematising discourses of childhood and adolescence and its impact on policy and practice; discourses of rights and social justice.

Session 4 – Poverty and Social Exclusion and Societal Abuse. This session focuses on which children are poor and some reasons for their predicament; other forms of social exclusion; local, and national and international responses to poverty.

Session 5 – Child Abuse and Exploitation. In this session, students can work on definitions of child abuse; prevalence of different forms of child abuse; and globalisation and its impact on child abuse and children's well-being.

Session 6 – Displacement and Movement of Child Populations. This session defines displacement; reasons for and the prevalence of displaced children; implications and responses – inter and intra-country, are also considered.

Session 7, 8 and 9 – Building Alliances and Innovation in Child Welfare Project. These sessions are used for students to work on their own projects. Each student plans, researches and writes their own project centred on networking to identify and critique innovative child welfare practice. Their aim is to move towards knowledge creation and sharing principles. Students post their products for others to use and read; and subject their own work to review and self- assessment, asking questions such as, 'What have I learned by doing the project?'.

Session 10 – Course Review – Towards a Globalised Child Welfare. This session reviews the course and personal learning objectives, asking the question, 'What next?' and considers ways of sustaining networks and web-based working in the future.

Ownership and Continuity

For the course writer, one of the difficulties was completing the task whilst recognising that some of the issues about ownership in the short-term and long-term remained contested. The reasons for the lack of resolution were varied. The issue of resourcing was clearly the dominant one.

The Project was a fixed-term three-year project and no monies could be requested for sustaining or developing the initiatives it started. Given the uncertain use the curriculum would have in each institution, it proved difficult to develop any longer-term partnership agreement for sustaining the management and development of the materials. Even within individual institutions, it appeared that special funds would have to be sought to further refine and tailor the materials.

Another constraint on longer-term partnerships is making the transition from a partnership nurtured by shared funding into the wider competitive arena of higher education institutions. Here, as Carter (1997, p. 136) puts it, recognising the tensions between the creation of a 'digital democracy or information aristocracy' in web-based programmes and its implications for collaborative work remains an issue.

Conclusion

At the time of writing this chapter, the course has yet to reach a stage where it has been fully piloted and evaluated, so how the final product will actually be used is unknown. Perhaps the biggest hurdle in the development process was, in the end, evaded because the Project finished and a longer-term solution for how the curriculum could be managed and updated as a collective endeavour was not found. As McLaughlin et al., (1999) suggest:

'the factors that determine the effectiveness and success of a technological system do not lie solely in the technology itself but depend on the acquisition and implementation process' (McLaughlin et al., 1999, p. 222).

There were, however, some valuable lessons to be learned from the process of building the curriculum about the way people interface with technology and the strengths and potential limitations of using the world-wide web as a teaching and learning media. Different Project partners had previously had varying experiences of technology. There was a significant learning curve for many of those involved to address. This was particularly important with regards to reconceptualising the teaching and learning process through a world-wide web-based resource.

The development process also helped those involved, but particularly the course writer, to develop a personal understanding of a globalised social work and with it, recognition of the need for global responsibility for the welfare of children, young people and their families. It is not possible to assert that just because a concern about children is situated outside one country's border that it has no part to play in the resolution of that concern more broadly.

Editors' Note

The Child Welfare across Borders Course can be accessed through the website of the Centre for Human Services Technology at: <http://www.sws.soton.ac.uk/cwab/>.

PART III

BROADENING HORIZONS – CREATING LEARNING OPPORTUNITIES ACROSS BORDERS

18 Visioning International Student Exchanges
LENA DOMINELLI

Introduction

Social work is a demanding profession for it requires its practitioners to be able to work with contradictions as a matter of routine. One of these is that of transcending the limitations of the local to become a discipline that engages with the global and is recognised world-wide. This goal is linked to social work's desire to help excluded and marginalised peoples to become full citizens who can participate fully in mainstream society. Learning from and impacting upon the international arena in pursuit of this dream has occupied the ambitions of social work educators and practitioners during the past century.

The endeavours of the many indomitable pioneers who have moved freely across borders to learn about social work curricula and cultures from people in countries other than their own have kept the vision of internationalism alight. The efforts put into this task over the years by women such as Jane Addams (2002), Alice Salomon (1937), Eileen Younghusband (1958) and Katherine Kendall (1998, 2000) typify the enterprise and courage expended in living up to these ideals.

As a result of the activities of these women and others like them, social workers across the world have borrowed from each other in both the theoretical and practice methods domains. These initiatives have given the discipline its recognisable contours while at the same time maintaining the significant features that give social work an approach that is distinctive from that utilised by other caring professions. Being a client-centred and empowering profession is crucial to social work's individuality and provides the discipline with a value base that is shared across continental divides and enables social workers to transcend the limitations of geography.

In this chapter, I examine the strengths and weaknesses of the vision that drove me to bring together a group of colleagues, most of whom had not met each other before, to work on a project that focused on exchanging students across the Atlantic – a venture that challenged all of us in many respects.

Building an International Coalition

As a committed internationalist, I had previously encouraged students to undertake social work placements overseas on an ad hoc basis. But the European Union–Canada Project, *Child Abuse, Protection and Welfare*, provided my first experience of a planned programme of exchanges. The possibility of embarking on such an enterprise was brought to my attention through means of the mailing list for academics with an interest in Canadian Studies maintained by the Canadian High Commission in London.

Seeing the call for applications to the European Union-Canada Programme for Co-operation in Higher Education and Training, I wondered whether I could bring together a group of colleagues that I knew to network with each other and quickly form a consortium that could apply for this funding.

The consortium had to cover at least three European countries, and three Canadian institutions, each of which was accustomed to different frameworks of teaching and learning. Thus, the consortium had to transcend the heterogeneity of its constituent parts to work effectively in supporting a range of international exchange students, including the many of them who would experience the Project vicariously because they would be unable to cross the Atlantic during its period of tenure.

And so, I thought about the values that could bridge a range of social divisions and different ways of working with students. My visioning was guided by anti-oppressive social work principles, theories and forms of practice. I thought that our individual commitment to anti-oppressive practice might provide the necessary links, and this proved to be a sound assumption.

Anti-oppressive practice emphasises the values of: respect for the dignity of the person; equality; power-sharing; celebrating diversities and strengths amongst those involved; interdependence; mutuality; reciprocity and solidarity (Dominelli, 2002, 2002a). Though these values are well-known to contemporary social work students and tutors, their practice can be challenging and difficult to implement at the best of times. Attempting to realise these across six institutional divides was a tall order, but one which we were determined to meet.

These values were to lay the groundwork for non-exploitative relationships in reciprocated exchanges where each could learn from the others, particularly in considering how structural inequalities were addressed in our practices. Trust and goodwill were also necessary if we were to collaborate effectively with one another and not engage in debilitating competition with one another.

The demands of globalisation, particularly those elements that foster homogeneity and competition at the expense of uniqueness, individuality and collaboration also had to be countered. Global contexts challenge anti-oppressive values by undermining heterogeneity. Thus, globalising the local and localising the global has to be done with care and sensitivity.

This goal was further complicated by the desire of Canadian social work educators to transform dominant models of social work by promoting First Nations perspectives which emphasise healing the ravages of a colonialist past. Identifying colleagues who shared these values and commitments became an important part of the decision-making process and guided my views of who could be invited to participate in the proposed project.

I discussed my ideas and the possibilities at length with one of my well-known colleagues in Canada, Marilyn Callahan, at the University of Victoria who gave the intended project her enthusiastic support. Although we had very little time in which to pull our application together, with her and I taking the lead roles on our respective sides of the Atlantic, we submitted our proposal. Sadly, our first attempt was unsuccessful. But we learnt a lot about how not to write up a proposal and did better the second time. The next submission was the successful *Child Abuse, Protection and Welfare Project.*

Visioning and Practising Social Work as an International Activity

The people who joined the consortium shared a vision of expanding the horizons of social work from its national base within a value framework of equality and respect for diversity. All of the staff in the institutions involved were committed to and stood at the forefront of curriculum and practice developments that aimed to enshrine empowerment approaches and children's rights, cultural sensitivity, and anti-racist and anti-sexist perspectives in work undertaken with children and their families.

Our value base and commitment to making the Project work as an international egalitarian and collaborative venture were important ingredients in our work together and ensured that when the going got tough, we were able to work through our differences to find solutions that met the needs of all. We also had to have a sense of humour. As a result of this, we certainly had a lot of fun with each other and laughter amongst us whenever we met.

This egalitarian approach, we later found, differed from many of the other projects that had received funding approval at the same time as ours. Those tended to favour more traditional, hierarchical approaches to working with colleagues. Whilst these had the advantage of certainty, many failed when anticipated progress did not materialise, or things went wrong. Our Project flourished because our willingness to engage fully with each other served to release our creative energies so that a problem encountered was always considered as an opportunity to learn how to overcome the difficulties that came along. This problem-solving approach within a framework of respect and equality reduced the development of personal hierarchies amongst us and we struggled against structural hierarchies together.

This included not getting upset with one another when plans went awry, or individuals failed to respond as and when required. Instead of pathologising each other, we understood that Project work was only a small item in overflowing in-trays, and looked for alternative ways of handling the situation. The development of a web-based course which Julia Waldman describes in the previous chapter is a good example of how we sought to overcome the barriers that our co-operative venture inevitably encountered.

Although Marilyn Callahan and I, and then Wanda Thomas Bernard had all accepted the challenge of developing this web-based course, we were defeated by its demands under the heavy weight of our normal workloads. So, when we next met to evaluate our limited progress, we decided it was time to find the resources with which we could employ a course writer alongside a colleague with the appropriate technical skills.

We were extremely fortunate to get the support of Jackie Rafferty, the Director of the Centre for Human Services Technology (CHST) and Jackie Powell, the Head of the Department of Social Studies in enabling Julia Waldman and David Columbi to complete this work. The CHST subsidised our endeavours so that despite the limited resources that the Project was able to provide for the course, we were able to see it to completion.

However, our first challenge preceded that of developing a web-based course. It involved the continuation of the partnership when one of the original European partners had to pull out of the Project because there was insufficient funding attached to it. Financing is a key factor in determining who can participate in international exchanges and we were subsequently to discover that inadequate funding featured prominently in the decisions of which students participated in the Project as well.

The withdrawal of one of the original partners had the potential to endanger the entire Project unless a solution was found quickly because we would be no longer able to meet the criterion of involving at least three countries in Europe.

Ironically, the reason that this partner had to pull out was that they were overcommitted on the international front and that cutbacks at their institution meant that as a poorly funded project, this was one of those that had to be axed. Fortunately, the commitment to one another and the personal connections within the consortium ensured that the partner that had to leave found a suitable alternative partner in the same country and in a similar type of organisation for us. And so, with the approval of the European Union (EU), our new member was welcomed into the fold.

However, this problem delayed the start of the Project somewhat. Additionally, the feeling that there was a missing part to the history of the Project seemed to intrude into our new partner's consciousness in a way that the Project as a whole had not anticipated and, on reflection, I think that we should have taken greater care in helping them integrate more effectively into the Project. What we had forgotten was that no one in the group that eventually came to form the consortium had had experience of working with our 'new' member, and as a result, we took too much for granted.

We had been lulled into a false sense of security by the success of our first full meeting as a Project in the conference called by the funders in Cagliari, Italy, which was also attended by our new partner. This proved to be a rewarding encounter that enabled us to cohere as a group, even though this was the first time that most people had met one another. We were fortunate to come together so well. In discussions with other grantholders at the European Union-Canada consortia conferences later, we discovered that this was not the norm.

Our grant was considerably less than we had anticipated. So, dealing with the shortage in financing was our next hurdle. The contribution that came from the Project funders was never intended to provide the bulk of the monies needed to sustain the Project during the period of the award. But this constituted a strain that was never effectively dissolved.

Limited funds meant that the partner institutions and practice agencies ended up having to support the Project to a much greater extent than had been anticipated to be the case when the application had first been drawn up. Nonetheless, we felt that we had to meet our obligations to the Project's objectives and the people that had already been drawn into participating in this venture. So we went ahead and were constantly looking for new sources of money. However, for the academics involved in the Project finding alternative sources of funding to support all of the activities that we had planned required even more of our highly pressured time. But we felt we had little alternative than to search for these. Without these additional monies, the Project would not have been as enriching an experience as it became.

We became fairly adept at securing additional resources and were thereby enabled to extend the reach of the Project to practitioners and other academic staff who were less directly involved in its work. This was particularly important when we held our Project Conferences to share research findings, curriculum ideas and experiences. This additional funding enabled the Project to contribute towards the expenditures people not normally involved in the work incurred when participating in venues away from home. The Swedish partner was very successful in obtaining such funds. Our differentiated ability to obtain monies reflected the inadequate infrastructures and importance given to international links in higher education. Some universities are better equipped than others to contribute towards or to handle international projects.

International work, whether it is to exchange students or to disseminate research findings does not hold a high priority in the budget lines of many institutions in higher education. So, we had to work harder to make possible the dream of internationalising the experiences of our social work students. Indeed, all of us directly involved in the Project were surprised to find that the levels of understanding of the demands that such projects place upon the normal run of everyday life in busy departments and on the individuals directly involved in international exchanges were fairly superficial and that these attitudes were rather widespread. Several Project participants reported that whenever they returned home from a busy and usually exhausting Project meeting, they would be asked, 'How was your holiday'?

At the same time, the support provided by immediate colleagues to the work of the Project, particularly in supporting exchange students was freely and warmly given. But this relied upon individual goodwill and the costs of providing it on the relevant institutions' ledgers was insignificant. Nonetheless, this additional work has to be acknowledged as another pressure point in international exchanges because its absence could easily result in the failure of a project to deliver its intended outcomes.

Universities were most reluctant to provide additional secretarial, academic or placement support. Their hesitancy had knock-on effects on overseas students' experiences and impacted greatly upon them if they began their placements when academic staff went away on research leave and other academic-related activities or home students were away on vacation. There were no supplemental financial resources to purchase replacement support, and without these, the normal anxieties of exchange students intensified.

A further fear, evident during parts of the Project, was to crystalise most strongly after it ended. This came to a head when we were thinking about applying for another follow-on project on the same subject. Then, the implications of international exchanges upon the availability of scarce child welfare placements for 'home' students if these were used for overseas ones became a determining issue. Given the difficulties that universities face in securing adequate numbers of high quality placements for their own students, some potential project participants felt that it was unfair to prioritise these for exchange students as had happened during the initial project.

I personally feel this viewpoint conceptualises the matter around a false dichotomy, because the requirement of providing excellent practice placements holds for all students. Moreover, 'home' students in one institution would become the 'overseas' students accessing equivalent high quality placements in the receiving institution. And, I wondered if the other outlook indicated an underlying mistrust around equivalences. However, I accept that it is easier to control the resources that are under one's own jurisdiction than to rely on what might be supplied by another, whether or not there are contractual guarantees affirming quality.

Conclusions

Organising an international exchange project is a daunting but stimulating endeavour. Those who participate in its activities have to be prepared to put in a lot of hard work, be flexible in their approaches to problems, and welcome meeting and working with others who are different from them. This calls for putting anti-oppressive values into social work practice and our relationships with one another. But even with these ingredients at one's disposal, it is impossible to predict the outcome of a project if it lacks every participant's commitment to egalitarian and collaborative ways of working.

At the same time, it is crucial that managers in the universities and agencies fully support and resource international exchanges and deem these an integral part of their employees' workload rather than an 'extra' that individuals can 'choose' or not, to engage in.

19 Dialogue with the Field
JOAN GILROY

Introduction

This chapter is about working with child welfare practitioners who supervised and assessed the field practice of international social work students. It stems from my experience of co-ordinating Dalhousie University's participation in an international project entitled, *'Child Abuse, Protection and Welfare'*. Student exchanges formed a significant portion of this three year project among schools of social work in Canada, Sweden, the Netherlands and the United Kingdom.[1]

Students were selected by each of the participating universities to do field placements abroad. Dalhousie University's Maritime School of Social Work sent seven students to the Project's three European partners, and received eight from these same universities.

Over the three year life of the Project 45 students were exchanged. One of the Project's goals was to design a child welfare curriculum that could be used internationally. The experience of students learning about child welfare by doing field work in another country was an important source of information for papers, publications and a web based course called *Child Welfare across Borders.*

What follows is an example of how Project faculty worked with local social work practitioners to design and implement field placements that met the requirements of the European universities and at the same time were rich with learning about child welfare in Nova Scotia and Canada.

Student Placements

Preliminary planning for the field placements was done by Dalhousie's faculty team[2] in co-operation with the Canada–European Union Project team. The placements occurred in the fall of 1998 and the spring and fall terms of 1999.

Students selected for the Project were registered at, paid fees to and met the programme requirements of their home universities. Their field or practice placements were governed by the criteria of their own universities in terms of length of time, types of experience required, demonstration and documentation of knowledge and skills, and assessment procedures and evaluation.

Of the eight students who came to Dalhousie, three were from the University of Southampton in Britain, three were from Hogeschool West Brabant in the Netherlands and two came from Stockholm University in Sweden. Seven of the eight were women in their 20s; the one male student was in his 30s; none of the students had children.

All but one student were in their final year of first degree programmes and had completed at least one field placement in their home countries. The exception was the male student who was on a Masters programme. But he too was on his final placement.

Six of the eight students were placed in traditional child welfare agencies legally mandated to provide child protection and other basic services such as adoption, residential and foster home care. One student from Britain was assigned to the intake unit in the largest district office of the provincial department of community services and was supervised by an intake supervisor. Two other students, also from Britain, were in family care (child protection) units of a large semi-private[3] children's aid society and supervised by the unit supervisors.

Three students from the Netherlands were assigned to the same provincial government district office mentioned above. These students had completed their formal field requirements and were doing research on aspects of child welfare and related topics of special interest. Instead of doing hands-on work, they became participant observers, shadowing child welfare workers, learning about legislation and services, and attending staff meetings and workshops. A supervisor in child protection organised and oversaw their placements.

The two students from Sweden were assigned to a family agency where they were supervised by the executive director and staff. This agency works with families who are having difficulties raising their children because of poverty, lack of employment and related problems.

Since it is not a statutory child welfare agency and not mandated to remove children from their homes, the staff work with parents on a voluntary basis and have more flexibility to focus on prevention of child neglect or abuse, as well as parent education.

The six supervisors[4] involved were all well-qualified and registered to practice social work in the province of Nova Scotia. They had considerable experience in the field and in supervising students from Dalhousie's social work programme.

The Placement Process

Preliminary planning for field or practice placements was undertaken by the faculty (academic staff) Project team, which identified the needs of the students and placement possibilities.

Following these discussions, team members approached agency personnel to inform them about the Project and explore their willingness to supervise international students. We tended to talk with people we knew. They had had done previous agency field instruction in family and child welfare, and for the most part we met with a positive response to our requests for assistance.

Because of personnel changes in the school's field placement co-ordinator position, we did not follow the normal process of arranging placements through the field co-ordinator from the University. Instead, we made the placements directly, informing and working in co-operation with the coordinators.[5] In arranging the placements for the international students, we recognised that we were competing to some extent with Dalhousie's own students for scarce and valued placements in the child welfare system.

Although we had done a considerable amount of background work with child welfare staff, the supervisors and first line workers had limited information about the international project which is not surprising given the demands of their workloads. It was important, therefore, to approach specific supervisors with information and to brief them as thoroughly as possible about the project, individual students and their requirements in terms of supervision and the evaluation criteria used by the students' home institution.

In Nova Scotia, and elsewhere in Canada, practitioners generally provide the supervision of social work students without either getting paid or securing workload relief for this commitment. Given their heavy workloads, difficult working conditions, the stresses involved in investigating child neglect and abuse and making decisions about whether to take children away from their parents, adding the supervision of students or practice teaching responsibilities represents a very considerable commitment on the part of the supervisor.

Once supervisors agreed to take international students, we met with them and the students to review the Project, provide further information about that particular student's European school's fieldwork objectives and requirements, and supply copies of field work manuals and student handbooks from the partner European universities.

We also discussed placement contracts or agreements and completed the contract or letter of agreement required by the school of the individual student concerned. Additionally, we set up a schedule of meetings and established an understanding that supervisors could contact a member of the Project team (principally the co-ordinator) at any time about their concerns or issues they wanted to raise.

The Placement Experience

Five of the eight students kept field journals or logs which they shared with their placement supervisors (called practice instructors in some universities), home university faculty advisor or tutor and with me as the local Project co-ordinator. I responded to these journals both on e-mail and in-person sessions with the students. Several students were able to participate in a field seminar with Dalhousie students in child welfare for whom I was serving as faculty field instructor and advisor.

At the same time, another Project team member, Wanda Thomas Bernard, was doing on-line instruction with Dalhousie students who were on placement in Europe and Dalhousie students who were doing field placements at a distance from the University.

Wanda welcomed the European students to participate in the on-line programme. I was also corresponding by electronic mail on a regular basis with Dalhousie's students while they were in Europe. Other Project faculty members also had contact on a less intensive basis.

While they were doing field work, the international students simultaneously had the opportunity to enrich their experience by participating in the following complementary activities:

- orientation sessions in child welfare given by a member of the Project team who was past director of a large statutory child welfare agency, a part time lecturer and supervisor in child welfare and a member of the project team
- auditing a course in child welfare offered in Dalhousie's undergraduate social work curriculum which included the history and philosophy of child welfare in Canada, provincial legislation, policy and practice issues
- auditing an elective in counselling in the undergraduate programme at Dalhousie
- attending a two day addictions workshop offered by the professional staff from the provincial government drug dependency services, as part of Dalhousie's field education programme
- visiting resources such as a youth centre for children under sixteen sentenced by the courts, shelters for battered and transient women, a First Nations (Mi'k maq) Family and Children's Services Agency, the Nova Scotia Black Cultural Centre and African Nova Scotian communities
- participating in individual and group supervision sessions with a team member as faculty advisor
- attending lectures related to social welfare policy in Canada, Canada's Royal Commission on Aboriginal Peoples, Africentric theory and sessions on anti-oppressive practice given by faculty members
- meeting with senior personnel in the provincial department of child welfare.

Faculty team members were involved in several ways, such as giving lectures and holding discussions with the international students, taking them to visit out of town agencies and hosting social events which were very important to the success of the Project.

Updates about the international child welfare Project were published in local professional newsletters; and papers about child welfare in Canada and Europe were given at international conferences and distributed to field supervisors and other social workers.[6]

At the end of the exchange, the international students gave seminars about their experience in the Project. In these seminars, students described their learning in field placements, compared aspects of law, policy and practice between Nova Scotia-Canada and their home countries, and reflected on their individual learning as a result of the exchange.

The students felt that they had good experiences in their field placements and learned a great deal about child welfare and how it compared to what was known and practiced in their home countries.

They were very positive about their supervisors and credited them and the staff in the placement agencies with providing meaningful learning opportunities, good supervision and support. The students acknowledged that the amount of time involved in supervision was considerable and that it added to the supervisors' workload. They expressed deep appreciation to their supervisors for their contribution to their learning.

Issues Arising from the Project

While working with practitioners, several issues emerged from Dalhousie's experience with regards to the supervision and assessment of the field work undertaken by international students. These issues concerned funding, workloads, communication, learning requirements and assessment of learning and they arose in the context of the broader international child welfare Project. They have been identified as follows and are discussed below.

Funding

Students from one of the partner schools were less well funded than those from the other two European universities, and the Canadian students doing field placements abroad. Differences in the value of currencies also meant that living in Canada tended to be less expensive for students from the United Kingdom and Sweden, and more expensive for those from the Netherlands.

Students could not anticipate fully the outlays for accommodation and differences in the cost of living. And some students found that they had to take out student loans to meet their financial commitments and expenses during their exchange period. As the faculty Project co-ordinator, I sorted out any money and housing difficulties with the students, but the field supervisors needed to be aware of these problems as they created a certain amount of initial anxiety and stress, which naturally affected the students' involvement in the field.

Academic Workloads

Several international students from both Canada and Europe found their workloads heavy because they were carrying courses and writing papers or dissertations whilst overseas to meet programme requirements at their home university. The amount of work was at times a barrier to taking full advantage of time abroad. Again, as faculty Project co-ordinator, I carried major responsibility for advising on academic matters, but field supervisors also listened to student concerns in relation to courses, papers and dissertations for their home university and were very supportive.

Communication

International students and faculty had to manage a rather large number of relationships and complex communications. Students, for example, had to communicate with their home university faculty including their field placement co-ordinator, faculty advisor or tutor, course instructors and dissertation supervisors where applicable; with Project co-ordinators and team members at both the home and exchange university; and with their field supervisor and staff in their exchange placements.

The distance between them and home university faculty advising them on academic work created a certain degree of anxiety and emphasised the need for clarity among all participants. All of the students were computer literate and used electronic mail extensively for communication. Indeed, computer technology contributed significantly and positively to this entire Project.

Language differences were important and made the direct provision of services somewhat limiting and stressful. In this Project, language considerations posed particular difficulties for international students whose first language was other than English. Language issues rose to the fore in several ways. The students from Sweden and the Netherlands were proficient in English, but were apprehensive about whether their level of understanding of the language was sufficient to talk with clients about personal and family problems and to make formal presentations in English.

Canadian students on exchange in non-English speaking parts of Europe also found that their lack of fluency in the language was a significant barrier in some aspects of their field work. Despite the common language between England and Nova Scotia, the British students also took time to adapt to Canadian accents, idioms and the cultural context in which these were embedded.

Communication is very important, indeed a foundation for social work practice. In spite of differences, the students were able to learn a great deal about the importance of shared language and culture in social work. One student spoke in her final seminar about learning to allow and accept client help with finding the right words to reach a mutual understanding of problems and goals. All the students discussed their heightened awareness of difference, of being an 'outsider', and how this increased their sensitivity to clients of social welfare services.

Supervision, Assessment and Evaluation Requirements

As we knew from the outset, there was considerable variation among the Universities in the Project (within Canada as well as among European partners) in relation to field learning objectives, expectations and procedures for assessment or evaluation. Dealing with these was a major challenge of the exchange.

Students from Britain, in accordance with the requirements of the accrediting body, were required to spend a specific number of days in placement over a period of six months, have a minimum amount of time per week set aside for supervision, undertake a minimum number of interviews that were directly observed by their supervisor, and document their competences in values, knowledge and skills according to set guidelines. They also had to complete academic evidence sheets and do a placement essay.

The students from Sweden were also required to do a certain number of weeks (fifteen) in this, their second and final undergraduate placement. Their practice guidelines emphasised the importance of counselling and the responsibility of supervisors to help students to prepare for counselling, stimulate reflection, schedule sufficient time for discussion and reflections on field work activity and its connection with knowledge and personal experience. Evaluative reports were required from the project co-ordinator and the agency supervisors.

The exchange students from the Netherlands had completed the official field requirements and were doing participant observation and independent study. While there was considerable contact with the field as a basis for learning about child welfare, there was no requirement for formal assessment of performance in the field or an evaluation. As faculty advisor, I met with the students on a regular basis and wrote a report for their school, describing the field or project activities undertaken by the students and my impressions of their learning and professional development.

The experience with the first student who came showed that there was some lack of clarity about the requirements related to the amount of time for supervision, number of observed interviews, and the documentation of specific skills and assessment procedures. In addition, the designated supervisor (or practice teacher) was dealing with an unanticipated personal crisis which kept her from being available for consultation and meetings with the faculty Project member for part of the placement period.

This resulted in the student experiencing a high degree of anxiety about not being able to meet the requirements of the home programme and, therefore, not passing the internal and external assessments. Although this situation turned out well, in the sense that the student was able to meet all the requirements and was ultimately positive about the overall experience, the concerns expressed were not sufficiently addressed at the time of the exchange.

Team members had read and discussed requirements with faculty in partner institutions, but we were new to the implementation of the different European field programmes. It was not until we were actually working with the students and supervisors that the requirements came alive. As Project faculty, we learned a great deal from the first exchange placement and were able to correct mistakes and adapt the advisory roles in subsequent placements.

Seminars

Students gave a seminar at the end of their placements describing their experiences in the field, courses and related educational and social activities, comparing and contrasting selected aspects of child welfare legislation, policy and practice between Nova Scotia-Canada and their home country, and reflecting on their learning. As stipulated in the project agreement, students held these seminars in both host and home universities.

At Dalhousie, the faculty team invited field placement supervisors and agency staff, faculty and students from our School, and members of the professional and university community to these seminars. Attendance ranged from ten to thirty five and included people from all these groups. The seminars proved to be a valuable vehicle for demonstrating what had been learned and accomplished, and for acknowledging in a more formal and public way, the amount of work and support given by field supervisors.

In these seminars, the students had a chance to pull together and highlight their learning. Field supervisors were given a great deal of credit for their work and they learned more about the Project as it developed. Seminars were a concrete example of the positive accomplishment by all the participants and partners in this international venture.

Reflections

Overall, the international child welfare Project was highly successful for the participants at Dalhousie University. This was due in large measure to the quality of the exchange students, the support of local child welfare and family agency personnel, staff from Dalhousie University, and the considerable amount of work students, supervisors and faculty devoted to this Project.

While mistakes were made and there were gaps in information, communication worked well on the whole. This can be attributed to the quality of the participants and their commitment to the significance of cultural and other forms of diversity in child and family welfare and the need to provide international content for practice in an increasingly globalised world.

In an effort to assess the Canada-European Union international child welfare Project from the perspectives of participants, Dalhousie's Project team surveyed participants asking what was best about the experience, what lessons had been learned, what could have been done differently and what suggestions they had for future projects. Responses were strongly positive from all the participants – the students, field placement supervisors and Project faculty. The findings revealed that we had underestimated both the amount of work and learning involved and the high degree of satisfaction achieved by all those who took part in the Project.

The supervisors expressed appreciation for being part of this Project. They felt that they had benefited personally and that the experience had contributed to other staff in their agency. They found the students 'positive, energetic, keen, mature and insightful'. They also enjoyed the student seminars and felt these had given them an opportunity to learn more about the Project as a whole.

One suggestion that was made by respondents was to arrange an exchange project for child welfare supervisors and workers. Although supervision involved a considerable amount of work over and above their regular duties, the field supervisors found it stimulating and refreshing and looked forward to building on the work that they had undertaken already.

One supervisor commented that the experience gave her work a much need lift, and that she would not change anything about the Project except to develop it to include practitioners so that they could acquire experience in other countries. The supervisors all felt they would benefit from exchanging places with their counterparts in Europe.

If such an exchange were possible, they felt that they would be able to learn directly about similarities and differences in family and child welfare legislation, policy and practice which help to rethink underlying values and services in this province and country. Among the family and child welfare supervisors and practitioners involved in this Project, there is a strong interest in an international exchange aimed at meeting their needs.

Conclusions

In summary, it was the view of Dalhousie's group of participants to the *Child Abuse, Protection and Welfare Project* that the objectives of the field exchange and entire international child welfare venture were accomplished and exceeded in every area – increased student mobility and knowledge of child welfare, more school-field interaction, international conferences which involved practitioners and students as well as academics, publications and related scholarly and professional work.

Whatever the problems and issues, people felt that we had tackled them co-operatively. Thus, the Project had enabled all of us to learn more about how to work cross-culturally and in a broader, more diverse context.

While it is difficult to measure the impact of one project on longer term curriculum development and professional practice, clearly increased awareness of global issues and comparative knowledge about child welfare in Canada and Europe were achieved. As a result, participants felt they were better prepared to graduate, practice and teach in child welfare and the social welfare field.

Notes

1. In tandem with the international child welfare Project, Dalhousie's Project team also interviewed first line, supervisory and administrative staff about what they viewed as the most critical issues facing them in their jobs. We presented findings from these interviews and reported periodically on the progress of the Project at meetings with field personnel, exchange students, academic and professional colleagues.

   Findings from the interviews were published in 'Critical Issues in Child Welfare: Perspectives from the Field', by Joan Gilroy, in *Community Approaches to Child Welfare* edited by Lena Dominelli (Ashgate, 1999); and in 'The Changing Face of Child Welfare', by Joan Gilroy in *Valuing the Field: Child Welfare in an International Context*, edited by Marilyn Callahan and Sven Hessle with Susan Strega (Ashgate, 2000).

2. Members of the Project team at Dalhousie's Maritime School of Social Work were Wanda Thomas Bernard, Joan Gilroy (co-ordinator), Marilyn Peers and Gwendolyn MacDonald Slipp. They represented a range of scholarly, educational and professional interests including Africentric and feminist theory, child welfare and field education. Professor Lena Dominelli, University of Southampton, was the overall Project Co-ordinator.

3. Semi-private in this case means an agency operated by a volunteer board of directors providing statutory child welfare services under provincial government legislation, standards and funding.

4. The supervisors were Peggy Anderson, Mary Craig, Marika Lathem, Donelda MacDonald, Jane Sinclair Bond and Barbara Williams. In Canada, registration for social workers is a provincial matter. Under legislation passed in 1993, the Nova Scotia Association of Social Workers has the power to regulate both the title 'registered social worker' and the practice of social work.

4. Wanda Thomas Bernard negotiated with agency staff on behalf of the first international student and I did the same for the other seven students. Marilyn Peers and Gwen MacDonald Slipp discussed potential placements with many colleagues in the field and their knowledge of child welfare and the field placement process were essential to securing suitable placements.

6.   Many of the papers distributed to Dalhousie's participants were published in Dominelli (1999) and Callahan, Hessle and Strega (2000) cited above.

20 'What am I Doing Here, Really?' – Students' and Teachers' Reflections on International Placements

CAROLYN NOBLE

Introduction and Context

The idea that social work is a local, culture and nationally bound profession is fast being challenged as social work programmes spread across the globe. Schools of social work are opening up in many countries once closed to Western influences, as the reality of global interdependence breaks down previous communication and ideological barriers. At the same time, the rapid growth of changing demographics in many Western countries has demanded social work academe to foster a culturally aware programme in the curriculum that prepares students and practitioners for the realities of practice in increasingly multicultural communities.

Many programmes in the more developed counties such as the United States, Canada, the United Kingdom, the Nordic countries and Australia are extending their social work programmes to include international placements as part of the field curriculum. Such an activity has appeal to many students interested in immersing themselves in another culture so as to experience different views of human behaviour and welfare systems. An international practicum is a potentially powerful experience for learning about cultural differences and is a particularly important preparation for international practice (Healy, 2001).

This chapter explores the rationale, educational concepts and experiences arising from international placements in a university in Sydney, Australia. Drawing on the experiences and reflections of a group of social work and community work students and support teachers' experiences of placements in developed and developing countries, the organisational framework and placement structure are described in the context of the 'value' for the students and international agencies as well as the academic learning available. Challenges and obstacles that emerged during the placements are identified. The concluding section identifies lessons learnt from the experiences and suggests guidelines for future international arrangements.

Professional Education – International Perspectives

Professional education that includes an international placement is designed, in part, to make the connection that many social issues facing social workers at 'home' are inextricably linked to global and transnational concerns. Immigration, refugees, asylum seekers, family reunification and resettlement issues are examples of practice that transcend local and cultural boundaries. Academics keen to facilitate students' access to, and knowledge of, international issues and the effect on peoples' lives of the growing interdependence created by the global flow of information, capital and technological advancements (Razack, 2002) will encourage students to undertake international placements. Many academics regard international placements as one way of counteracting local prejudices by including a global perspective on local issues.

'Modern' social work includes an ongoing commitment to social justice beyond national borders such as international peace initiatives, anti-imperialist and anti-racist social work and work on international human rights (Razack, 2002; Ife, 2002). International policies, treaties and programmes have an indirect effect upon national and regional policies and thereby large parts of the world's population. Exploring and understanding specific cultural beliefs, practices and historical intergroup connections inform culturally sensitive practices and facilitate multicultural awareness (Mama, 2001).

Community development curricula make connections with international projects and initiatives as models for practice; international material permeate many core subjects; while many social workers involve themselves in international service organisations and social welfare activities (Razack, 2002). International research is also gaining momentum as social work extends beyond its national and regional concerns (Barlow 2002). Global interdependence is relevant to contemporary social problem analysis, more generally, and social work education more specifically. International exchanges can broaden individual student's life experiences.

The literature talks about international placements as being a 'life altering' experience for many teachers and students who have involved themselves in such activities. Despite this positive feedback many academics are cautious about the experience. In particular, Mama (2001), Healy (2001) and Midgley (1990, 1999) in the USA, and Barlow (2002), Razack (2002) in Canada and Lyons (1999) in UK identify the philosophical, organisational, methodological and pedagogical challenges.

My own experience as a field academic in Australia supports their concerns. The promotion of international goodwill, the personal gains from such an experience and the commitment to international social justice that are the raison d'être of many of these exchanges, bring a heightened awareness of moral and ethical responsibilities. Caution and reflection are needed to avoid these international exchanges, especially if these placements are mostly unidirectional, becoming another form of colonising behaviour from the West (Razack, 2002).

Curriculum 'transportation' poses a particular challenge given the dominance of Eurocentric theories and practice approaches especially as students set their leaning goals within the context of their 'home' programme. Referred to by Spivak (1993 cited in Razack, 2002) as 'pretentious internationalism' any international activity must continuously assess how discrimination and domination is produced and organised. This concern also applies to student exchange programmes which cannot be naively considered as 'innocent' activities that are conducted in the international domain.

International Placements

Practice experiences generally are designed to assist students with the integration of theory with practice, and practice with theory, and are a significant and memorable component of social work education (Noble 1999). For students, the acknowledgment and affirmation of their own development, values and skills through placement experiences is regarded as important (Starbuck and Egan, 2000). Also significant in their development, are the opportunities to promote professional confidence, overcome doubts and a sense of powerlessness, and being provided with possibilities for dealing with 'real' problems, issues and dynamics (Starbuck and Egan, 2000). Field placement in a different country enhances and further develops these experiences by giving students occasions for undertaking and reflecting upon different kinds of agency work, agency dynamics and organisational and philosophical practices.

International placements extend students' professional knowledge and skills by exposing them to different systems of social welfare and the opportunity to engage with issues and problems that may exist in their 'home' countries, but are viewed and remedied in very different ways (Healy 2001).

In the professional courses in my university – the University of Western Sydney (UWS), international placements are offered to those students who want to expand their practice experience by working in a different culture and immerse themselves in a different way of life in order to further their understanding of social welfare systems from a cross-cultural perspective. International placements complement multicultural issues addressed in the curriculum. They are also a significant part of the Bachelor of Community Welfare (International Social Development) award at UWS.

By submerging themselves in other cultures, students have the opportunity to experience first-hand the realities of practice in a different setting within diverse ideological, political and religious contexts. Separated from their own culture, friends and familiar learning environments, students have to confront different perspectives about the nature of their professional education by locating themselves, for a short period at least, as the 'Other' in relation to cultural and socio-political practices. The challenge for social welfare and social work academics is to ensure the appropriateness of such placements and identify the educational frameworks that are suitable for international exchanges.

About the Study and the International Placements

In the discussion that follows, I report upon international placements in the social welfare field that form part of the practicum curriculum at UWS. In it, I quote from comments given by students and teachers in respect of several of these programmes to give a flavour of the quality of their experiences. Student placements have occurred in countries such as Indonesia, East Timor, the United Kingdom, Chile, Nepal, Bosnia, Thailand, Vietnam, Fiji, China and Malaysia. In these placements, students have been involved in programmes as diverse as slum redevelopment; peace and reconciliation projects; working with street children, people with disabilities, street schools, and programmes for HIV/AIDS education.

While the experiences for all the parties involved in these exchanges create opportunities for new and shifting contexts in education, deeper inquiry is needed to fully evaluate these developments. Reflection on their experiences shows varying responses to the challenges, obstacles and value of international placements. I have excluded from this discussion the experiences of students from developed countries who have come to Australia for cross-cultural exchanges.

All students undertaking international placements in the programmes I co-ordinate either volunteer for the additional experience or have to do it as part of their course. A small number are familiar with the language and culture as they are 'going home' to their family's country of origin, but most have not travelled abroad before, let alone ventured to places where the language, culture and social life is different from their own. Some go in pairs; others small groups. Many also travel to the placement under their own initiative. All pay their own costs with minimal financial help from the University.

Some agencies receive a small remuneration, but most volunteer to take students and meet the costs out of their own meagre budgets. As far as possible, placements are selected where it is agreed that students would 'add value' to the agency for the time that they are there. Barlow (2002) refers to this 'value added' consideration as a way of militating against unidirectional relationships where students could be seen as taxing the already strained resources of agencies without obvious advantages to them. Overall, the goal of these international placements is to offer participating students an experience of cross-cultural work while remaining attentive to the 'host' agency's needs, difficulties and the extra demands that having overseas students would create.

International Placements – The Issues

There are many issues involved in arranging international placements, the most obvious being organisation, structure, preparation, partnership with international agencies, curriculum expectations, the learning requirements, the learning opportunities available, support and follow up, and the debriefing and integration of the experience into current and future learning opportunities. I agree with Healy's (2001) comments that unless the university curriculum and the participating students and teachers place a high value on cross-cultural learning, international placements should not be given a high priority, or even be attempted. Preparation for the many issues that arise must be informed by a solid and critical pedagogy and allocated adequate educational space for preparation, supervision, support and debriefing.

My experience in supervising and coordinating international placements suggests that students and supporting teachers going overseas must be prepared to identify and accept differences and be well-versed in cross-cultural practices. The 'host' agency needs to have agreed to participate without being coerced into doing so and regard the placement as having value for them and their service users.

The 'host' agency's familiarity with the visiting student's courses and culture is also an advantage because it helps the student to get immersed into the different cultural experience and obtain the most out of the learning opportunities that are provided. Students, if possible, must be familiar with the local language, culture and type of work that the agency undertakes. They must be prepared to deal with uncertainty and the unpredictability of the experience and have curriculum requirements that integrate the cultural experience throughout their placement. Teachers must ensure the safety of the students while on placement as well as the travel arrangements as far as possible. Pre-placement preparation is, therefore crucial.

Structure and Organisation

All students undertaking international placements are directed through the following process. All of them are interviewed and assessed as to their particular learning goals, motivation and ability to undertake such a venture. Approval from the field teachers is the next step, followed by screening of the proposed agency for its learning opportunities and willingness to take students. Where possible, the local university is contacted and 'on the ground' support is arranged and formalised. In Indonesia, for example, local students as well as teaching staff from the university sometimes volunteer themselves to support these students, so this service is explored. Contact is then made with the 'host' agency supervisor by either email or fax.

Before their departure, all students have to attend a pre-placement workshop for several days. This pre-placement class addresses issues such as orientation, expectations, time and task management, networking, organising support and contact with 'home' university staff, and other administrative details. Particular attention is given to refresher classes in cross-cultural awareness regarding customs, dress, behaviour and issues concerning power relations, privilege and racist behaviour. This structural analysis permeates the curriculum and students explore the way ethnic, cultural and racist issues might arise during their stay.

Additionally, those going to developing countries such as Indonesia or East Timor are encouraged to undertake either an intensive language course for a semester before they depart, or participate in a cultural immersion course if this is available prior to their placement starting in an agency. If language courses are not available at the university, students are encouraged to make their own arrangements for cultural immersion or at least learn the basics of the language and customs before they leave.

Workloads are set within the context of their 'home' course and adjustments are made according to the learning that is available. Students are encouraged to write journals. And, each student is required to write, at least, two critical incident reports from their experiences. Debriefing is done, either during the placement if teaching staff accompany the students, or on return for those students who went abroad without support staff. Because international placements at UWS are usually done in a block during the semester breaks, the classroom component (integrative seminar) is, in some cases, completed in the following semester where the further integration of theory and practice in an international context is explored. Other students in the class are interested to compare learning on the international placements with the learning that has occurred in local agencies.

Collaborative efforts in organisation and support are, therefore, required from many people. Local support and educational staff have to become involved in these exchanges. Teachers are needed to accompany students. And, people supporting the placements from 'home' via phone and email contact are also required. All in all, arranging and supervising international placements is very labour intensive. In addition to establishing an extensive support structure, the university placing these students needs to have a well-resourced and reliable infrastructure. This level of infrastructure support is often ad hoc and in most cases not pervasive enough. 'Host' agencies are also required to provide access to contact back home for the students via email, fax or phone. Additional travel and health insurance is compulsory.

Support

Teachers and students participating in these international placements acknowledge that international placements should be structured with as much support as possible from a variety of people. As mentioned above, teachers accompanying students or designated teachers at the 'home' university most commonly provide support. However for two placements in Indonesia, a teacher from the Education/Language School who was well-versed in the language, culture and customs of the country provided additional support to the students concerned.

Students and accompanying teachers thought this person's role was pivotal to the success of the placements. Her wealth of experience and overview of cultural issues as well as having the language skills helped with both orientation and ongoing support. She successfully motivated and enthused the students before and during their stay. On her return, one student commented on this particular experience as follows:

'having the support of (name of teacher) was invaluable. Our first two weeks in Indonesia would have been chaos without her. Learning Bahasa Indonesian was an intimidating experience...without her help to negotiate and translate for us the first two weeks at the (Indonesian) University would have been wasted' (Louise).

Another student said:

'without her support and knowledge of the customs, beliefs and religion, I don't think I would have thrown myself into the experience as much as I did. (She) encouraged us to spend time with the Indonesian people and to form strong friendships, to discover as much as we could and to share our information with each other' (Imogen).

Valuable support was also gained from the English-speaking Indonesian students assigned to work with each student:

'Linking up with (students from the local university) ... was also a valuable support. They were able to share with us what it was like to be an Indonesian man or woman living in Indonesia' (Annie).

Teachers from the 'home' universities who were on-site for placements in Indonesia were also very much appreciated by the students as they helped them to identify cultural meanings and contexts arising from their experiences at the point of contact. As one of them declared:

'debriefing with them (home supervisors) after a day at the agency was very beneficial in that they added the social work (perspective) and helped us deal with the culture shock ... they helped us bring us into the world of international social work reality which is that we can do as much as we can to help people and make the societies in which people live better but we can't save the (situation) in the two months we were there. Without this reality being talked about I think I would have felt so disheartened and displaced and asked, 'well, what I am I doing here, really?' (Suzie).

Relying solely on support from the host agency in a developing country, without additional support from 'home' supervisors can be difficult as this particular student comments:

'support was different as workers were coming from different beliefs, religious background, values and work ethics and much more' (Kate).

On-site 'home' supervisors are not as crucial in countries where English is the main language, as this student's experience of her placement in Scotland made clear:

'the (local supervisor) helped with orientation, goal setting and supervision ... Introduced us to touristy things as well as helping us make friends ... (we were) encouraged to work independently and learnt a great deal about the welfare system and this (particular) agency' (Carla).

Additionally, students reflecting upon their experiences in Scotland said that going to an agency used to having students and who was ready and prepared for them was crucial in helping to make the experience more pertinent to their particular learning needs and desire to acquire new skills. This agency's preparations also supported the students in negotiating their transition from one culture to another. And, it helped the students to settle in and establish contacts with and gain support from the local community for the duration of the placement.

Conversely, the lack of appropriate support from the 'home' university was a principle reason that one placement was ended prematurely. Two highly motivated and well-prepared students came home after less than a week from a 6-week placement in a developing country because there was a breakdown in support from the 'home' university when they most needed it. Disorientated, anxious and isolated from university support, they relied on friends and family and the 'host' agency to talk through issues that arose for them, especially when they became sick after arriving in mid-summer when the pollution was very heavy as a result of the huge fires in the country's rain forests.

Disappointed with the slowness of their 'home' university's response to their concerns, and angry about the assumptions that they were not trying hard enough when contact was made, they terminated their placement and came back feeling angry about the lack of support, encouragement and follow-up arrangements from the 'home' university. Frustration about organisation and accountability for following up students on placement also emerged as an issue as a result of this incident.

Value

Most students on returning from their international placement acknowledged the usefulness of acquiring new concepts for practice as well as being exposed to different and challenging cultural traditions. Generally, students regarded their experience as a valuable opportunity to rethink cross-cultural issues in both teaching and practices in their own culture. Several commented that is was indeed a 'life altering experience'. However, Midgley (1999) and Razack (2002) challenge this notion of 'feeling good about the experiences' as needing a critical knowledge base, one which sustains a critique about the forces of imperialism and challenges students to think about how seeing new practices through imperialist eyes actually impedes real cultural dialogue and impedes their professional growth.

My experience of most students going to developing countries was that, in the main, they were sufficiently culturally aware and prepared to reflect on their dominant and privileged position as Western students. However, it is difficult to monitor all students' responses and behaviour in a culturally appropriate way. Moreover, giving attention to culturally sensitive practices is an ongoing challenge.

One student returning from East Timor just after the independence struggle commented that she was humbled by the experience and felt a great personal challenge as a result of putting herself outside the 'box of Western security'. Although she was still seen as 'special' because she was from a Western country (a country involved in the liberation struggle as well), her experience of being a minority, that is, on the other side of the language and cultural barrier helped her to develop a real empathy for understanding difference from the position of 'Other'.

If there is any value in the experience of undertaking international placements, it is the challenge to build theories and practices, deconstruct present knowledges and open up the debate to experiences of being vulnerable to criticism of one's dominant position in world politics and learning how one's own complicity in cultural hegemony can be exposed. International placements provide the opportunity for cultural immersion and the possibility of undertaking a personal and professional critique of daily life that are not possible in one's own specific culture. These are of significant value when the culture in question is a hegemonic one that by virtue of its dominance precludes such questioning and reflection.

Students' reflections on their experiences of working in another culture highlight the nature of the privileging and assumed superiority of their own cultural heritage in a way that is not accessible to them when they are at 'home' in their own country where much can be taken for granted. As students can't 'escape' being confronted by difference, their exposure requires them to immerse themselves, educationally, socially and personally in the new culture.

Submerging themselves in it is essential if they are to get any value for themselves out of their experience and respond to the personal challenges that arise from the contrast between the way that others live their lives and how they conduct their own. The following two comments are typical of other students who make similar points:

'Going to Indonesia was the most powerful and life changing experience of my life. I learnt more about myself, about different cultures, different lifestyles and what it was like to live in poverty' (Maria).

Another student claimed that in:

'(undertaking this placement) I learnt so much about my own values and beliefs. I had to reassess everything I had once believed in and alter some other aspects and fine-tune others. The upsetting thing is that I cannot honestly say how beneficial I was to that organisation in terms of the work I did for them. I still feel as though I did not achieve much for them' (Felicity).

International exchanges also enable 'host' agencies to explain their country's issues and welfare practices from their own cultural, historical and political perspectives.

Travelling overseas, living in another country and attending a different practice agency and organisation can, if well-supported with appropriately developed curricula, make a substantial contribution to students' ability to develop their own independent professional practice. Relying on their own problem-solving skills and initiatives, students are forced to attend to the issues as they arise. This is especially relevant for students who are without university support whether from their 'home' university or the local supporting university because these students are on their placement alone.

Educational value is gleaned from the integration of these experiences with curriculum expectations, assignments and online debriefing and discussions. As contact with the home university can be slow and access to internet technology limited most students in developing countries have to improvise in many situations to get the best out of their opportunities, thus reinforcing independence and autonomy in practice. A good placement experience can make the student think laterally and critically.

Although some students felt they were a burden to the agency, there was potential for reciprocity with agencies that welcomed overseas students' involvement in their projects and the resources and ideas that students brought with them. In placements where students were accompanied by university staff, it was possible to relieve the receiving agencies from the difficult and time-consuming task of supervising and debriefing these students. Those students who went on their own reported valuable work was done, often by providing the agency with additional person power in situations where the agency was short-staffed and under-resourced.

For teachers involved in developing and supervising the international placements all commented that there was much for the students to gain from these experiences. In particular, awareness of global issues in a local context and an opportunity to relate their experience to a comparative analysis of social issues were regarded as having immense value to teaching theory and practice in the 'home' curriculum. Exposure to particular types of community development work different from that being undertaken in Australia was extremely beneficial for teaching cross-cultural work.

Conversations between agency staff and support staff were reported as meaningful, each learning and earning a respect for each other's positions and differences. It also provided an occasion for the 'host' agency to share its model of working and articulate its particular philosophies and practices at the same time as engaging with other 'foreign' workers in the exchange of information, ideas and differences. Cultural alliances were developed and in some cases the dialogues between them continue.

Challenges

It will come as no surprise if I note that as a result of international placements and their experiences, everyone identified the emergence of many challenges to their values, privileges and position. Time constraints, the culture shock of living conditions in developing countries as well as seeing the limited and frustrating work of non-governmental organisations (NGOs) and agencies struggling with little or no direct support from government were readily discussed in the debriefing sessions.

Some students who were involved in projects designed to militate against discriminatory practices from 'repressive' governments experienced the very real dangers of oppositional political work being undertaken by some agencies where they did their placements. For example, some were actively working 'under ground' by providing information on birth control and sexual health that was directly counter to government and the prevailing religious beliefs of the country concerned. As a result, there was an ever present sense of danger.

Others were visibly shocked at the conditions and organisational practices of local agencies that seem to treat people with a severity not so evident in their own countries. What were seen as violations of basic human rights created stress and concern for the students. Not feeling that they were in a position to challenge these practices because they were students was difficult for them. This situation was particularly hard for those students who felt that social justice issues were compromised as a result of their inability to confront these issues.

This student's comment sums up what many identified as overall challenges in undertaking a placement in a developing country:

'Challenges for me were the language barrier, but also having the courage to get on the plane and say, 'goodbye', to my family and friends for two months was a challenge as I had never been away from home before. Witnessing poverty I saw everyday was a challenge. It was a challenge not to cry ... having to come to the realisation that I could not change anything in two months was a challenge. While studying, I guess I still had the ideal to save the world and that was totally gone by the time I got back. Not that I don't still want to save the world, as everyone would if they could, but knowing that I may now only be able reach a handful of people in my lifetime ... but I am now OK with that' (Laura).

Conversely, students who went to developed countries talked positively about being exposed to new and different approaches to welfare work and social work and the similarities and differences in practice models and outcomes. More advanced and emancipatory practices were identified. And, as each student could speak the language, they felt able to do some productive work for the agency, while at the same time acquire more professionally appropriate knowledge and skills relevant to their course back home. As one of these students said:

'Work was more rewarding in that I could actually do work that I knew was of benefit to the agency ... seeing the reactions (of the clients) when they saw what they had created and the launch of the project was truly inspirational and fun' (Carla).

As well as learning new skills and making a contribution to agency work, there were generic challenges identified by all students and teachers from all placements. These included: time constraints; having to establish rapport with many different staff and clients; learning about new welfare systems or ideologies of care; learning about the history and culture of the agency; and understanding the agency's relationship to the overall social welfare system in a short period of time. Even when there was a language in common, cultural differences in an agency's history, practices and philosophies were still evident.

Challenges identified by teachers who accompanied students on placement were many. Specifically, these teachers had to deal with: differences in an individual student's ability to address, confront and deal with cultural issues; the frustration of students who were not being exposed to new experiences but acting as 'baby sitters' or being marginalised because of lack of language; and the complaints from students who found the culture shock of living conditions difficult to adjust to.

Other challenges identified were: working positively with students who lacked initiative and wanted to have the agency define their role and learning opportunities with minimum involvement from themselves; awareness of not wanting students to be a burden on an over-stretched agency's resources; students who were very outspoken in their criticism of the agency being seen as abusing basic human rights; and balancing an appreciation and understanding of cultural sensitivities and practices against real problems with living conditions and agency practices.

One teacher, in particular, said that the pressure from the 'home' university to take international students added another problem as the 'host' agency was offered limited support. This action creates an unnecessary burden on an already overloaded and under-resourced organisation.

Briefing, supporting and debriefing students individually and together was a particular challenge when support teachers and students shared the same living space as it was, at times, difficult to separate out personal and work issues. Support teachers sharing the same accommodation with students on placement had to be culturally aware at all times and act as a role model for the students even when they got sick, hot and lonely themselves. Several commented that dealing with students' cultural trauma during placement generated by, for example, incidents of violence against clients, was often very demanding. Further, as these teachers were not involved with the agency or students during the day they felt they had to fill their day with 'productive' work such as reading or visiting agencies so as not to be seen as having a holiday while the students worked hard.

Language difficulties emerged for the teachers as well. Even when English was spoken and interpreters were present, the language barrier created obstacles preventing any deep engagement with the agency about the nuances of the work, or an opportunity to grasp an understanding of the cultural and socio-political situation in which the agency was located. The dilemma about their role as teachers or 'in loco parentis' also emerged and was not resolved satisfactorily. Students needed their support during the day, but often wanted no control or cultural reflection at night in what they considered their leisure time.

Another important underlying challenge involved the levels of financial commitment necessary for the exchange. Students had to meet all their expenses while support staff were financed by the university. When university funds were no longer available, 'on the ground' support from the 'home' university was stopped.

Lessons Learnt

International placements and student exchanges are now part of many social work programmes. Rather than avoiding the issue and challenges they present, a way forward is to identify lessons learnt and to suggest strategies to make sure that students, staff and participating agencies and universities achieve optimal experiences. To this end, students and staff from this Sydney-based programme have identified several such strategies resulting from their experiences. These are listed below.

Core Considerations

University teachers responsible for international placements 'must' undertake the following:

- Interrogate the almost universally unidirectional nature of these placements taking into account the legacies of colonialism and the positioning of notions of privilege and marginal status of agencies involved in the exchange (Razack, 2002);
- Develop and have in place a cross-culturally sensitive curriculum to inform the learning so as to engage in culturally appropriate theorising about international placements;
- Incorporate adequate educational space in the curriculum to interrogate and incorporate these experiences into 'home' courses;
- Engage in research, cross-cultural dialogue and critical reflection so as to avoid the possible dangers of domination and exploitation in the exchange;
- Ensure this dialogue is ethical and appropriate to the international setting available; and

- Investigate whether there are *real* and/or *potential* opportunities for reciprocity in these placements and avoid placements where the experience might be unidirectional.

Educational and Curriculum Considerations

Pre-placement organisation requires consideration of such things as:

- Development of international placement packages for staff, students and overseas agencies;
- Establishment of formal arrangements or Memorandum of Understandings (MUI) with local universities and agencies to ensure mutuality in learning;
- The identification of local support people and supervisors well in advance of student placement;
- Sending draft learning contracts to the 'host' agency before the student arrives;
- Ensuring that students have knowledge of or basic instruction in the language of the 'host' agency and undertake cross-cultural awareness workshops and orientation at least three months before starting placements. This allows for screening of both agency staff and students, thus minimising anxiety and uncertainty;
- Making clear and explicit what the expectations are from the 'home' university and check it against the expectations of 'host' agency;
- Brainstorm issues with 'host' agency and students about the issues likely to emerge and strategies for addressing them before placement commences;
- Establish as many forms of communication as possible including fax, phone and email if available;
- Thorough screening of the agency for the appropriateness of the placement on offer and the opportunities for mutuality and reciprocity in the exchange;
- Use only agencies that are in agreement with the exchange;
- If possible the 'home' university should offer some form of financial support to the 'host' agency for time and effort involved;

- Interpreters should always be available for both agency and students to minimise communication difficulties; and
- Students and 'host' agency should be prepared with curriculum expectations that address cross-cultural issues.

Orientation

- Where possible support staff should accompany students for at least the first week of placement to ensure that the agency is appropriate, establish ongoing contact and identify and address possible difficulties before the students continue. This minimises stress on the agency if students are experiencing any cultural dissonance or difficulties;
- Students and staff should have a least two or three days before placement starts to get orientated to the climate, culture, agency location and expectations of the agency for themselves as students; and
- Identification of common interests in the placement and mutual awareness of cultural differences need to be explored before and during placement.

Evaluation and Debriefing

- The 'home' university should have clear outcomes established for international learning appropriate to level of placement in order to evaluate students' skill and knowledge;
- Ongoing monitoring of students progress should be done by 'home' university staff in consultation with 'host' agency; and
- Ensure appropriate educational space is available for debriefing students and teachers on return and for interrogation of experiences in relation to 'home' course content and cross-cultural awareness gained as a result of this experience.

Conclusion

International placements are here to stay, especially as the globalising nature of social work education expands to include cross-cultural exchanges. However, even the lists above which were generated from of a university committed to cross-culturally sensitive practice pose problems for a successful and culturally appropriate experience. Setting the learning within the 'home' university's professional context immediately raises concern about reciprocity and mutuality in the exchange and the inherent hegemonic practices underlying the strategies. Lists such as these have to become part of a continuing dialogue among participating agencies, rather than a unidirectional undertaking such as this.

We as teachers involved in initiating, supporting and evaluating students' experiences of international placements still have much to learn. Clearly, any experience must include an open, equal and mutually beneficial dialogue with all involved. While most placements occur from developed to developing countries, the dangers of replicating imperialistic and hegemonic behaviours and expectations are ever present. However, in questioning our agenda in undertaking international placements we are at least confronting the issues and this is, in effect, a real beginning to initiating and committing ourselves to meaningful and reciprocal dialogue.

21 Exploring Partnership: Student Evaluations of International Exchanges in London and Durban

SUE LAWRENCE, DONNA DUSTIN,
MADHUBALA KASIRAM and RUBEENA PARTAB

International exchanges raise opportunities and challenges for those who participate in them. In this chapter, we explore possibilities for an international exchange and a collaborative partnership between two social work qualifying programmes in two countries with contrasting national and socio-economic contexts: England and South Africa. Our aim was to consider the compatibility of two specific programmes for possible collaborative teaching and research. The two programmes involved were the University of North London (UNL) in London in the United Kingdom and the University of Durban-Westville (UDW) in Durban in South Africa.

The opportunity to explore collaboration between these two specific programmes arose when Madhubala Kasiram and Rubeena Partab from UDW visited London in July 2000 to attend a conference. They took the opportunity to visit UNL with whom their University already had developed links in other Faculties. At that initial meeting, the staff representatives from the two Universities decided to undertake a comparative evaluation of their two programmes to further explore possibilities for collaboration.

None of us made claims about the representativeness of our two programmes vis a vis their respective national settings. In this, we were sensitive to the difficulties encountered in comparative work.

Comparisons of social work in different European countries have concluded:

> 'that the potential for arriving at a comprehensive approach to comparative social work science is as yet underdeveloped...(but that) such an approach provides an opportunity for analysis, debate and evaluation of both traditional assumptions and emergent (re-)constructions of social work' (Erath et al., 2001, p. 1).

Therefore, the opportunity to engage in such a comparison was fortuitous, but we grasped it enthusiastically.

Sue Lawrence at UNL had already devised a post hoc student survey soliciting student view of their course as part of the General Social Care Council feedback for quality assurance. As a result of the exploratory visit by Madhubala Kasiram and Rubeena Partab to UNL and our desire to investigate partnering possibilities between the two Universities, we adapted the survey for use by UDW.

The two cohorts of students involved in these evaluations were relatively small and methodological issues prevented straightforward comparisons between us. But, the comparison of results generated important issues in relation to the compatibility of the programmes and possibility for a partnership between the two programmes for teaching and learning purposes.

The study raised important issues regarding social work practice in the context of different cultural settings and had considerable implications for social work education. One particularly interesting issue raised was whether social work has a core theory and knowledge base that can be considered relevant across borders. If this were to be the case, this could be taught to social workers in any social context, and would facilitate collaboration between schools of social work in any two national/cultural settings. Or, if social work knowledge is relative to its practice context, it would require schools of social work in different countries to choose what theories and knowledge to teach to ensure their relevance to social work practice in that particular social context. This would limit possibilities for international exchanges.

Aims of the Study

The main aim of this study was to establish whether there were possibilities for collaboration between the two qualifying social work programmes in terms of the teaching of social work students and the learning that they experienced. A further aim of the study, consistent with comparing the two programmes, was the exploration of their compatibility. This required us to explore similarities in the education of social workers in these two specific programmes taking account of the students' learning experiences and the practice context for which they were being prepared. We conducted our exploratory study was conducted over a two-year period between 2000 and 2001.

Demographic Context

We examined the student demographics at both Universities to assess the extent to which comparisons between the UNL and UDW samples were possible. Because social work is located within an ever-changing context (Parton 1996; McKendrick, 1998, p. 99), differences along with similarities need to be acknowledged and understood in view of the purpose of the study. And so, we undertook an analysis of demographic information.

Demographic comparisons were made in terms of the number of students from 'disadvantaged' social groups on each course, the age of the students, the course entrance criteria, length of course and academic level of course. Both groups of students came predominantly from relatively socially disadvantaged backgrounds within their respective country.

This pattern can be attributed to the mission statement objectives of both Universities. UDW has made its mission one of serving persons who had previously been excluded from educational systems during the apartheid era (McKendrick, 1998, p. 101). UDW prides itself in providing disadvantaged persons with the opportunity to obtain a higher education.

The mission statement of UNL proclaims a similar objective. UNL's version states that it:

'recognises and celebrates London as a dynamic and diverse city, but also one that contains poverty and discrimination, which the University must confront and combat' (London Metropolitan University, 2002, p. 1).

While their mission objectives represent a similarity between the two programmes, this does not necessarily mean that the two cohorts of students involved in the study would see themselves as equally disadvantaged in relation to each other.

One distinct difference in the two groups was that students from UDW were predominantly younger, having entered the social work programme upon completion of their schooling. In comparison, students from UNL were adult learners, being required to enter social work training after having acquired work experience.

The students who participated in the study had received two different qualifications, namely, a two-year diploma or three-year degree in the case of the UNL sample, and a four-year degree in the case of the UDW students. Consistent with the purpose of this study, the exploration of similarities and differences between our two programmes for the purpose of exploring possible collaboration, we found another immediate difference. This related to the level of social work experience that the students had on starting their respective programmes and the lengths of their programmes of study. Both of these differences would have implications for any future collaborative arrangements and would need to be addressed.

A further difference between the two student cohorts was that at the time of their inclusion in the study, UDW students had just finished their studies and were about to start their professional practice. UNL students had been in practice for a short period at the time of their inclusion in the study. This meant that their knowledge of what happened in the field of practice varied. The differences in the level of development of the professional expertise of the respective cohorts could have made a considerable difference in respondent's perspective on the content of their studies (Fook et al., 2000), and must be taken into account in considering students' evaluations of their respective programmes.

Methodology

The researchers from the two programmes met on two occasions. The first meeting occurred in July 2000 to discuss the aims of the study and the research methods to be used. The second meeting took place in September 2001. At this time, we compared the data that had been collected between us. Communication between meetings was maintained via e-mail and fax.

The research design was exploratory to enable us to obtain comparable data on the two programmes. We carried out post hoc student surveys and compared social workers' experience of their professional education in these two specific programmes.

The comparative components of the post hoc study were in respect of examining demographic profiles and student responses to evaluations of the respective programmes. Hence, the study was essentially qualitative, although some quantitative data was obtained and will be presented where applicable below. Additionally, we contextualised differences where these apply by taking into consideration the characteristics of the research sample.

As we explained earlier, the social workers in the UNL cohort had left education and were practising at the time of their survey. The social workers in the UDW cohort had just finished their education. Thus, they were about to start their practice at the point of their inclusion in the survey.

The research instrument was a questionnaire, which was similar for both institutions except for a few specific questions related to the special characteristics of each University's sample and programme. Both closed and open-ended questions were used.

The students' responses in evaluating their learning experience in these two programmes were compared for the purpose of exploring the compatibility of the two programmes in relation to possible collaborative teaching and learning. Differences were observed in the appreciation of the theory taught in the two schools. There were limitations to the study, which prevents us from generalising from the results beyond the aims that we set for the study. We comment on these further below.

Sample Details

In terms of the histories of the two universities, UDW had a history of accepting black students before the end of apartheid. This past would seem to make it a progressive institution. However, the social work department is in transition from being a white dominated, casework-oriented programme to one that is more suited to its socio-political and cultural environment.

UNL has a history of radicalism both in the university and in the social work programme. The School of Social Work is associated with and emphasises anti-oppressive practice both in its recruitment policies and in its programme content. One example of its commitment in this is that when the then qualifying body, CCETSW, scaled down its anti-racism policies and removed anti-discriminatory practice as a competency in 1996, the School of Social Work at the UNL retained anti-oppressive practice as a specific competency.

Two sample groups from the undergraduate programmes from each of the two Universities were targeted for inclusion in the study. The two cohorts of students were relatively small. Altogether, 155 questionnaires were sent to students. Of these, 117 were returned, giving an overall return-rate of 75 per cent. At UDW, 93 students in their fourth and final year of training responded to the questionnaires, whilst these were returned by 19 undergraduates and 5 non-graduate (Diploma) students at UNL.

The UDW sample was larger than the UNL sample because of the different way in which the questionnaires were presented to the students. The questionnaire was mailed to students in the case of the UNL respondents, and handed to students in the classroom for the UDW sample. As might be expected, the different methods of questionnaire administration yielded different response-rates, with that of UDW being substantially higher than UNL's.

Thus, the different response-rates from the two Universities are related to the sample from UDW being derived from a 'captive audience' whilst in that from UNL, the students had a choice of responding, as they had already graduated from the programme and were in employment by the time we conducted the survey. Furthermore, uneven sample sizes made straightforward comparisons between the two institutions difficult.

Nonetheless, while differences between cohorts prevented definitive conclusions, sufficient data was gathered to allow consideration of comparison of the two programmes on some levels.

Another key limitation of the study was rooted in the uneven size of the samples and the differences in the levels of experience held amongst the students. Therefore, while no claims are made for the empirical generalisability of our findings, the information which we obtained from the study generated important issues in terms of the aim we set, which was to explore possibilities for collaboration.

Analysis and Discussion

At UNL, the sample comprised students who had graduated from the programme and who were practising as professionals. Fourteen students from UNL had less than one year in practice, 9 students had between one and three years, and one student had between three and four years of post qualifying social work experience. At UDW in comparison, undergraduate students in their final year of study responded to the survey. Thus, at the time that they completed the questionnaire, they did not have experience of working as professional social workers. Again, this is a significant factor which must be taken into account when drawing inferences from the data.

Both sets of students considered their investment in the study of social work worthwhile. All of the students from UNL reported this to be the case, while in UDW 68 per cent replied in the affirmative. There 17 UDW students who responded negatively and did not consider their investment in social work study worthwhile. These may have responded in this way because jobs for social workers are scarce in South Africa. The shortage of social work jobs can be linked to the country's economy and the transition in becoming a democratic state. Financial remuneration for social workers is not considered to be commensurate with the efforts and risks of the job. Moreover, staff turnover produces high tensions that limit job satisfaction (Naidoo, 2001).

By contrast, in England, social work jobs are plentiful and there is currently a drive to train and recruit social workers due to recruitment and retention problems in social services departments (Platt, 2000, p. 25).

Students who graduate from social work programmes in England would therefore expect to find employment as social workers more readily than their counterparts in South Africa.

Positive responses from both UNL and UDW students highlighted that social work training made them more confident, self aware and reflective. They had an appreciation of the theories and methods in social work and felt that they had enhanced their practice skills through their studies.

UNL responses claimed that the training had equipped them to work in a specialist area. They had acquired a better understanding of how systems work and could be better advocates for service users; and had an increased perception of client needs.

Specific UDW responses were that it was important to learn about the work environment prior to graduating. They had been able to initiate community projects and had had exposure to social development initiatives. Also, they had gained experience in teamwork; achieved personal satisfaction and fulfilment; and been exposed to multi-faceted societal problems.

Learning about the work environment prior to graduating is considered necessary for the sake of the profession and professional survival. In South Africa, students should be prepared for all eventualities. Amongst other practices, this includes: corruption in the field; bribes; emotional ransom; and keeping social security payments under false guises (Brown, 1999, p. 283). UDW students' exposure to practice education was considered sufficiently extensive and intensive to prepare graduates for the field.

Appreciation for learning about social and community development along with the multi-faceted nature of societal problems merit discussion. In South Africa, it is evident that transforming social work education has to engage in a 'melding' of people-changing and society-changing goals (McKendrick, 1998, p. 107).

Both sample groups were appreciative of being equipped for practice. However, UDW students complained of there being too much theory, some of which was considered irrelevant to the world of practice. Others amongst them wished for computer facilitated learning and more practical work.

The two sample groups indicated that their qualification had generally increased their job prospects. This covered 100 per cent of the UNL and

67 per cent of the UDW sample. As compared to the 100 per cent response rate amongst UNL respondents, UDW students were possibly apprehensive about finding paid employment in social work, as there were fewer social work positions in South Africa than in the UK. In South Africa as in the case of India (Menachery and Mohite, 2001, p. 117), social work graduates may well migrate to fields such as marketing, sales and clerical work in the absence of job opportunities in social work. The shortage of social workers in the United Kingdom has meant that its political representatives are currently aggressively recruiting social workers world-wide (Naidoo, 2001). Consequently, some graduates from these two countries are employed in the United Kingdom to practice social work as a result of aggressive recruitment campaigns mounted by UK agencies (Brindle 2000). This policy can create problems for social work agencies on the ground in India and South Africa.

Programme Evaluation

Three questions were asked to elicit students' evaluation of their teaching programmes. One was a closed question and two were open-ended ones. The issue of the teaching of theory, the value of theory to students and the application of theory to practice emerged as an important issue in these three questions.

The closed question asked students to rank various aspects of their teaching as good, adequate, poor or unsatisfactory. The first open-ended question asked students to give examples of what they found most helpful in their training. The second open-ended question asked what students would like to see changed. Their replies produced comments which seemed to contradict responses to both the closed question and the first open-ended question. These responses raised wider issues of the relevance of theory being taught in the context of students' work in the field.

The responses to the closed question will be discussed first. Because of the size of the sample, good/adequate and poor/unsatisfactory responses were collapsed. When analysed in this way, the majority of both cohorts of students gave positive responses. Two-thirds (66 per cent) of UNL students rated the programme's integration of theory to practice as good/adequate, while one third (33 per cent) rated it as poor/unsatisfactory. In comparison, 86 per cent of UDW students rated the application of theory to practice as good/adequate and 7 per cent expressed dissatisfaction, while 7 per cent did not respond to this query. On the evidence of this question, UDW students would seem to be more satisfied with the application of theory to practice than UNL students.

The responses to the open-ended questions regarding the teaching of theory and the application of theory to practice, however, presented a picture that contradicted the one given in the paragraph above.

In response to the question, 'What aspect of your training has helped you most in your work', both cohorts appreciated learning related to anti-oppressive practice and social justice. These should permeate all practice (Dominelli, 1997; Lynn, 1999). Both cohorts also said that relevant theory was helpful. UNL students specifically mentioned the relevance of theory gained in training to their work in the field. This seems to contradict the view of 33 per cent of UNL students who, in the closed question, ranked the application of theory to practice as poor/inadequate.

In response to the question, 'Was there anything missing or anything you would change about the training you received?' both cohorts of students asked for more integration of theory and practice. In specific responses, UDW students asked for a re-organisation of the programme/curriculum to include more social work modules. They also commented that there was too much theory in the curriculum and wanted a curriculum to suit the South African context of practice. The UDW students perceived a gap between the theory that they learned in the classroom and the realities of practice in South Africa. This would seem to contradict the seemingly overwhelming satisfaction (88 per cent) expressed in the closed question regarding the application of theory to practice.

It would seem then, that there were opposing responses to the same issues. On the one hand, students appreciated theoretical content. On the other hand, both cohorts wanted changes in the teaching of theory. In considering the reasons for these contradictions, the way the questions were constructed may have been a factor. When questions were presented in a global or non-specific ranking form, responses were generally positive. However, when the students were asked specifically to think about aspects of the programme, responses were more detailed and critical. This suggests that in future evaluations of social work training programmes, specific responses should be elicited, rather than broad ranking responses to issues.

Another reason for the differences in the responses of the two cohorts regarding theory could be attributed to the differences in the levels of practice experience represented in the two cohorts. The UNL students were adult learners who must have had at least the equivalent of two years full-time experience in order to be considered for admission to the social work course. In addition, they were surveyed after they had graduated and had had between two and three years of post qualifying work experience to draw upon.

The UDW students were admitted to social work training immediately following secondary education and were just graduating from their programme, so they had almost no practice experience to draw upon. This would seem to give these two cohorts very different perspectives on the relevance of theory to practice and in the development of their professional expertise (see Fook et al., 2000). These factors must be taken into consideration in the analysis of their evaluation of the relevance of the theory taught in their respective training programmes and could have implications for which institutions become partners in international exchanges.

In addition to the construct of the questions, and the relative experience of the cohorts, a third difference between them is the context of their practice. Much of the theory taught in the UK is oriented to work with the individual in a society where individualism is valued. This was true even at UNL which had attempted to maintain a focus on anti-oppressive practice in opposition to the wider social work context where the emphasis on anti-oppressive practice was declining. Students at UNL did not object to the theory taught, but wanted more application of theory to practice.

However, it would seem that UDW students were at that time being taught individualistic theories in a society where the collective was culturally valued and where social justice was important in the progress from apartheid to democracy. Students seemed to be expressing a desire for a change of emphasis in the theory taught to include more theory related to group and community work.

Students identified the need for curriculum change to address the needs of the South African context. They suggested that curriculum development at UDW had not kept pace with the broader social changes in the country. The South African White Paper for Welfare also recognised that training does not equip graduates to respond to the social developmental needs of the country (Drower, 1999, p. 23; Lombard, 1999, p. 97).

From these responses, it would seem that although curriculum development has occurred, the UDW students still perceived a gap between theory and the reality of practice in South Africa. There is a need to balance professional, vocational and academic components in social work programmes (Weinstein, 1996, p. 37). From the evaluation of the UDW programmes, it was apparent that the academic component of the course was generally considered adequate with specific suggestions being for syllabi to keep abreast of the changing context of South African society.

Discussion of Social work in the United Kingdom and South Africa: Differences and Similarities

A significant difference between these two cohorts, aside from their difference in levels of experience, was that they were working in different socio-economic, political and cultural contexts. Internationally, social work is practised around the world in many different contexts. What links social work in different social contexts is its role as mediator between the individual and the state or the wider society (Washington and Paylor, 1998, p. 336).

There are essential similarities and differences in the role and knowledge base of social work wherever it is practised. Social workers adapt their role and knowledge base to the social context in which they practice. The core activities of social workers could be characterised as integration, representation, mediation and surveillance (Philp, 1979). The difference in emphasis on different aspects of these core roles will reflect the different needs of society at different points in history. As Majewska-Galeziak (1998) has pointed out, social work can take an exclusionary role in society or a developmental one.

Social workers draw on a range of theories to enable them to carry out activities relevant to their social context. The focus of social work interventions will thus vary from one context to another, but it is argued that there are core elements of social work knowledge, values and skills that can be identified across different social contexts. If these core elements can be identified and worked with, collaboration may be possible in spite of the different contexts in which social work is practised.

England: Focus on Work with Individuals

England can be described as a post-industrial country. In England, social work, particularly that taking place in the statutory sector, tends to focus on the individual in society. In the late 1960s and early 1970s, social workers were more concerned with social and community development.

For example, the community development projects of the 1970s attempted to address structural issues related to poverty (Payne, 1995:8). The Barclay 'patch' organisation of local authority social work services also encouraged social workers to work with local residents and other professionals within specific geographic areas to improve local social conditions and prevent social problems (Adams and Shardlow, 2000).

However, in the 1980s England experienced the rise of New Right policies. The focus of these policies was to: reduce the role of government in the provision of welfare; close the institutions which formerly provided care to vulnerable people (e.g., older people, people with learning disabilities and people with mental health problems); and subject welfare services to a 'mixed market' of care in the community (Griffiths, 1988).

The purpose of these policies was to promote efficiency, the commodification of services through privatisation, managerialism and an emphasis on value for money. These policies also reflected considerable hostility towards professionals (Cutler and Waine, 1994, p. 14-16) who were regarded as having too much freedom to interpret policy (Lipsky, 1990).

Statutory social work in England is now largely focussed on individual need and cost restriction. With the introduction of care management, there has been a fragmentation of prevention and provision to an extent that now community work and prevention are areas of practice with which social workers in statutory agencies are seldom able to engage (Dustin, 2000) as these areas are now increasingly the responsibility of youth and community work departments or voluntary agencies.

A distinction needs to be made between the effects of these policies on public sector social workers, i.e., those working in local authority social services departments, and practitioners employed in the private and voluntary sector. The effects of this have been felt more directly by social workers in the public sector. However, it could be argued that practitioners in the private and voluntary sector have been affected to some degree by the practice realities.

Private and voluntary agencies have been drawn into the ambit of the state because they now receive funding from local authorities in order to provide services formerly provided by the local authority social services departments. This funding is provided through service level agreements which tie the voluntary sector into providing needs identified by local authorities. The voluntary sector has thus not been untouched by New Right policies.

As Lorenz commented about the role of social workers in the public sector in the UK:

'their mandate rarely extended to proactive, inclusive and universal activities. These remained the domain of the voluntary sector and of other professional groups such as youth workers' (Lorenz, 1994, p. 24).

Indeed, the UK is becoming increasingly identified as an extreme example of a liberal welfare regime, as proposed by Esping Andersen (1999). As a result, social workers have become increasingly unpopular in the public's perception. Again Lorenz comments:

'British social work has born the brunt of public criticism ... . because it is associated so directly with a state that plays very ambiguously with the boundaries of social rights, relying more on coercion than on endorsing civil and social rights for social cohesion' (Lorenz, 1994, p. 24).

The theoretical paradigms which are most commonly used in neo-liberal state social work are empirical-analytic, ecological-systems and construction theories. These perspectives seek to objectify client situations, focus on the individual and emphasise the technical and instrumental purposes of social work. They tend towards short-term interventions aimed at achieving measurable outcomes. They are particularly attractive to societies where efficiency and effectiveness are valued (Erath and Hamalainen, 2001).

In the UK, public sector social work is shifting from concerns for universal welfare and social justice to individual need and value for money. Public sector social workers are being relegated to a circumscribed regulatory role, concentrating on rationing and risk-assessment. Even within this current practice context, social work still retains its radical emancipatory and anti-oppressive stance in relation to the wider context of civil society. It would seem that anti-oppressive practice and a striving for social justice is an element of social work values wherever it is practised. The degree to which the knowledge base that would support these values is taught and the degree to which they can be implemented may vary, but these values are core to the profession (Jordan, 2000, p. 208).

South Africa: Focus on Work with Groups and Communities

Clearly, South Africa is at a different stage of national development from England. South Africa could currently be considered a new post-colonial country. Following the collapse of apartheid in South Africa, nation-building was an important goal of government. Language plays an important role in the social construction of reality (Burr, 1995). For example, the Zulu word 'Simunye' is used among South Africans, which means, 'We are one'. The word 'ubuntu' which translates as 'we are what we are to others' is also used to construct a social connectedness among South Africans who have been historically divided by race.

These words and the sense of community they convey are used by social workers in South Africa to convey the need to build consensus among the diverse peoples of the country. Community development work, and group and community work theory, would, therefore, be important in social work in South Africa (Mazibuko, 1996).

The words used in South Africa to convey social connectedness do not seem to exist in the English social context. This may be related to the

New Right emphasis on individualism as reflected in Margaret Thatcher's much quoted statement that there is 'no such thing as society'. The closest concept in English social work would derive from the literature related to anti-oppressive practice, but the language used generally refers to the individual and anti-oppressive practice with individuals. Anti-oppressive practice is not often geared to building positive links between disparate groups in the wider community. Local authority social workers in England are now working in a restricted individualised way that tends to pathologise and exclude the individual from the mainstream of society. It also considers their needs in the light of a market of care. In England, 'Care in the Community' policies involve the care of individuals in the community (where 'community' means outside institutions) using quasi-market mechanisms to fund care.

Social workers in Durban-Westville are working in a society that is very different from English society. They seem to be working towards forms of practice that promote inclusion, community building and nation building. Since 1994, the new democratic government in South Africa has had an overall developmental strategy. The South African Parliament adopted the White Paper for Social Welfare in 1997. This favoured the developmental approach described as:

> 'a type of social work which diverges from the residual, service-oriented approach directed at special categories of people in need, and tends toward holistically planned development strategies which place people and human rights at the centre of social planning' (Chetty, 1999, p. 73).

The theoretical paradigms that best support developmental activity and 'nation building' take a hermeneutic and critical theory perspective. These perspectives favour the subjective nature of the client situation with individual and societal development as the targets for intervention (Erath and Hamalainen, 2001, pp. 17-23).

In contrast to social work in the London context, social work in Durban-Westville is moving from an era when it was strongly associated with the authority of white supremacy and individualised methods of work with a psychodynamic theoretical base which may have served the purposes of the apartheid regime. Social work in Durban-Westville seems to be moving from this position to one in which social work serves the new anti-oppressive practice, integration, cohesion and developmental goals of its society. It may be that both traditions are still part of the experience of UDW social work education. This could explain the seemingly contradictory responses of UDW students.

Possible Similarity between England and South Africa

Informal care, or care within families, may be at similar levels in London and Durban-Westville but for different reasons. In London, family members may care for each other because the current neo-liberal ethos in England limits the investment of government money into care. In South Africa, informal care would be the norm because there would seem to be a level of traditional family life wherein there is an expectation, and indeed a necessity, that families will look after their own members. Another reason that levels of informal care are high in South Africa would be that because the welfare state is not well-developed and state resources are being used for more pressing needs.

Durban-Westville students in this survey said that they would have liked theory to be more relevant to the South African context. This perception on their part may stem from the fact that they are studying theories, which are essential knowledge in Western social work oriented to working with the individual, but may not be considered by some to be relevant in South Africa. There may be a perception that such theories are not relevant to the social and community development work that will contribute to nation building in South Africa.

However, social work is always about balancing the needs of the individual and the community. Both need to be kept in the equation of social work practice. English social workers would perhaps like to return to more preventive community-based work, but are restricted from doing so in the current socio-economic and political climate. Social workers in South Africa seem to be engaged in the excitement of nation building and developmental social work, but need to maintain the attention to individual need that is central to the practice of social work.

It would seem, therefore, that social workers in England concentrate on Philp's (1979) representation role, representing individual need to the bureaucracy of welfare and surveillance. This results in means testing and encouraging independence from the state provision of services, in a way that could be considered exclusionary. South African social workers, on the other hand, are focussing on Philp's integration, working in community development projects to integrate formerly oppressed peoples into full membership of their new nation. This could be considered developmental social work.

While these differences could be considered obstacles to collaboration, it is possible that they could be used as building blocks in such endeavours in that each cohort of students could gain a new perspective on their own work by comparing their professional experiences.

Conclusions

In evaluating social work programmes at both Universities, it was evident that students were generally satisfied, believing that the University that had provided them with the opportunity to study was equipping them for practice. Some students made specific suggestions regarding the theoretical content needing to keep abreast of changes and adjustments to practice education. These suggestions are significant and warrant investigation in a further study.

Students' comments on their use of theory raise the issue of the relevance of social work theory in different cultural and policy contexts. Whether the same theories can be of use in social contexts that are exclusionary and those that are developmental remains a question for further exploration.

Regarding partnering possibilities, both programmes offer students a generic training albeit within different time frames. However, in England, plans are underway nationally to increase the length of qualifying professional social work training to three years, from 2003. This will bring the UK in line with the agreed length of undergraduate training in Higher Education in the European Union, under the Bologna Declaration (Lawrence and Reverda, 2000). Therefore, partnering prospects may be limited but not impossible, given other shared characteristics such as student diversity and the aim of both Universities to widen access.

While collaboration could be undertaken in view of core similarities in theory and values that exist in the two programmes, the physical difficulties of communicating would limit the degree of collaboration that might be possible. Ideally, student exchanges would be useful for students, but this would involve a requirement for funding which is currently out of reach of either programme. Communication between staff and students could be undertaken using electronic mediums such as electronic mail and interactive learning platforms.

The use of electronic information technology (IT) would facilitate the exchange of teaching materials between staff. IT could also be employed by students to exchange anonymised case studies. These could illustrate the situations they are working with, the role they play in these situations, the skills they use and the strategies they have employed to address the problems encountered. However, one of the difficulties identified by students at Durban-Westville was insufficient IT support, so this approach might not be feasible at the current time. Of course, written material could be mailed back and forth, but this would involve cost and time delays.

A further difficulty might be that students would not want to engage in work that was not part of a recognised programme. Students are often quite instrumental in their learning strategies and might not be willing to engage in activities that do not relate directly to their own programmes. The viability of voluntary exchanges under these circumstance is, therefore, somewhat questionable.

Whether or not collaboration between these two programmes is possible, the exercise to consider comparability between social work education in two different national and cultural contexts has raised interesting issues about the nature of social work. This exploration regarding the possibilities for collaboration between UNL and UDW has confirmed that the potential for arriving at a comprehensive approach to comparative social work science is, indeed, underdeveloped (Erath et al., 2001). However, efforts to explore collaboration can contribute to the debate about the construction of social work in different national and cultural contexts. This makes it an endeavour that we think is worth considering further.

Postscript

Since this study was undertaken, both UNL and UDW have been the subjects of merger within their own countries, a trend in higher education which would appear to be happening in a number of countries. The University of North London merged with London Guildhall University on 1 August 2002 to become London Metropolitan University. Meanwhile, plans are afoot for the University of Durban-Westville to merge with the University of Natal. Both events have contributed to delays in the proposed collaboration, but we, the authors of this chapter, continue to be committed to furthering our partnership in the future.

22 Reframing Epistemologies and Practice through International Exchanges: Global and Local Discourses in the Development of Critical Consciousness

VISHANTHIE SEWPAUL

The process of education and the process of liberation are the same
(Connell, cited in Giroux, 1983, p. 114)

Introduction

South Africa is fast becoming one of the most popular destinations with regard to international students. As international social work expands, so do the debates around global and local issues in social work education and practice. Professional social work has a history and tradition of being rooted in colonialism and western hegemony, with the professionalisation process as defined within the logical-positivist paradigm, which constitutes one of social work's major dilemmas and challenges, being firmly entrenched in Europe and North America (Pozzuto, 2001; Sewpaul, 2001; Dominelli, 2002).

In this chapter, I argue that with the uncertain and fluid status of social work in South Africa, emerging from recent major socio-political transformation, the social work discipline has much to offer in terms of alternative conceptions of welfare and development locally and in the international arena. Pozzuto, an American writer contended that:

'there is an opportunity in South Africa to create a socially just society. The diversity both in terms of cultural groups and forms of economic development provide for this opportunity. The diversity also makes the task complicated. South Africans know that societies can be transformed. This is a lesson they have provided for the rest of the world' (Pozzuto, 2001, p. 163).

The contradictions and tensions in South African society broadly, and in the welfare sector more specifically, do make the task complicated, and pose major challenges for the social work discipline. Yet, these very contradictions and tensions present us with possibilities for change and development and for a deepening of democracy.

The educational and cultural penetration of the West has long been acknowledged (Nettleford, 1995; Tsang, Yan and Shera, 2000), with the general notion that anything that is European or American is better than that which exists in other parts of the world. Even as I use them for convenience of universal understanding, I have elsewhere (Sewpaul, 2001) acknowledged that dichotomies of the North-South, East-West, developed-underdeveloped, left-right and First World-Third World, are associated with linear modernist views of development.

They also reinforce an archetype of economically deprived regions of the world as primitive and 'less than' the so-called developed world. By some illogical extension, economic and political power and military capacity have come to be seen as synonymous with intellectual and academic integrity, contributing to the Western exploitation and hegemony that exists in almost all of the Two-Thirds World.[1] Nettleford has cogently argued that:

'legitimacy has ... been too long and blatantly reserved for those who will have proven their worth in terms of their ability to subjugate 'lesser peoples' whether by military means, or by the mystification of technological and scientific knowledge as a weapon of intellectual and psychological control, or by systematic mythmaking about the superiority of artistic culture produced in those parts of the world generally known as 'the North' in the jargon of development economics' (Nettleford, 1995, p. 31).

The following factors contributed to my re-examination of South Africa's potential contribution to broadening the horizons of social work education and training: my personal biography as an Indian woman growing up in apartheid South Africa and the lessons learnt from that; my brief experience of teaching at an American institution;[2] students' commentaries on their field practice; American students' general lack of awareness of America's place in global economics and politics; and the effect of dominant discourses on, and the impact of North-South relationships in the South African sphere.

This chapter discusses international social work by detailing, primarily though not exclusively, the partnership between Grand Valley State University (GVSU), Grand Rapids, Michigan and the Centre for Social Work, University of Natal, Durban, South Africa. The importance of developing resistance to educational and cultural imperialism, and the use of the experiential and emancipatory theories of Gramsci (1988, 1971, 1977), Freire (1970, 1972, 1973) and Giroux (1983, 1994, 1997) are discussed.

The 'intellectual and psychological control' mentioned by Nettleford (1995) has impacted upon the psyches and identities of the Two-Thirds World in profound ways and contributed to our inability to de-colonise our minds. In internationalising social work education and practice we need to ensure that we do not reinforce Western hegemony and control, and that we do not promote the skewed development that exists between the North and the South (Sewpaul, 2001). Part of the answer lies in following sound principles of partnerships. Tsang et al., (2000) contended that with the growing awareness of professional imperialism, international partnerships are increasingly being characterised by reciprocity. The success of the GVSU-South African partnership is, in large measure, due to adherence to the principles discussed in the next section.

Principles of International Partnership

Constructive academic social work partnerships are (or should be) characterised by mutually beneficial and co-operative relationships, among relevant persons, which enhance education and the learning environment. International partnerships should contribute to a dialogical process in the construction of knowledge, with the ultimate objectives of stimulating quality education and developing critically reflective (Schon, 1993) and morally active practitioners (Husband, 1995).

Some of the key principles of successful partnerships include shared vision and commitment, equity, transparency, relevance, mutual benefits and evaluation. I consider each of these below.

Shared vision and commitment

Partnerships may be spearheaded by pragmatic educational and financial imperatives. However, if these are not combined with the commitment and passion of individuals, even sound plans can come to naught. Partnerships, as in community and social development initiatives, involve process and the building of sound relationships that require sustained effort. As Guevara and Ylvisaker (2002), authors from our partner institution, GVSU have noted:

> 'Once the vision for what has to be accomplished is in place, the disciplined work of long distance development begins. This was and is truly a case of 10 per cent creative vision, and 90 per cent dedicated year round collaborative discussions reinforced by mutual enthusiasm and respect.'

Successful programmes have been developed and sustained through the vision and passion of single individuals who believed that they could make a difference, but that they could not do it alone. It is vital that all relevant persons in the partnership have a shared vision so that the partnership works towards the attainment of common goals. Sharing similar conceptual frameworks might be an asset to the partnership, but this does not have to be an imperative. There may be value in partners bringing in diverse world-views that allow for critical dialogue that open each person to new ways of thinking, knowing and doing which may contribute to a respect for difference and a reaching of some synthesis to get the job done.

Equity

In view of the skewed development and the unequal power relations between the North and the South discussed earlier, the issue of equity is quintessential. Each person brings to the partnership different resources: financial, intellectual, expertise and specialisation, organisational, administrative, ethical or spiritual. The assets of each person need to be valued. It is an unfortunate reality that those with the financial resources generally control the nature and shape of the partnership. More disappointing though, is the notion that financial capacity is often seen as synonymous with intellectual and academic integrity. Thus, it is often a convenient co-option of people from developing countries for the purpose of political expediency; they may not be involved in the formulation of the proposal or the planning of the partnership. While I have had this experience in other instances, inclusion and reciprocity have characterised the working relationship with GVSU. All partners need to believe that they are doing things with each other, rather than having something done for them.

Transparency

Mutual respect, openness and honesty are characteristics of successful partnerships. Agreements must include clearly stated plans of actions, objectives and criteria for evaluation. Total egalitarian relationships represent the ideal; the reality is that relationships are frequently asymmetrical. Where such asymmetry exists it is important to confront the differential power locations within the partnership and deal with them realistically. The micro-politics of partnership formation and maintenance must be understood and handled with sensitivity. Poorly constructed relationships can create new and unintended consequences in the forms of exclusion, passivity and dependence thus reproducing the forms of political and social hegemony that we wish to work against. Tsang et al., (2000, p. 149-150) warned that the creation of dependency during partnerships could produce 'a new form of imperialism that might reproduce the problems of colonialism'.

Relevance

Partners need to have a strong conviction about the value of what they are doing. Partnerships work best when people believe that they are dealing with real issues and are contributing to making a difference. The shared vision and the difference that partners hope to make can be achieved in various ways. It is important that different partnership models are explored, and that the most viable and relevant routes are chosen for any given partnership.

Mutual benefit

If the partnership is based on a shared vision and upon mutually agreed goals and objectives, then we may ensure that it is the total partnership that benefits. The partnership should not merely serve the narrow interests of individuals. The plurality of and possible competing individual, programme or institutional interests in a partnership have to be identified and balanced.

Evaluation

Evaluation makes it possible for partners to assess successes and limitations, and to build in mechanisms for accountability. The types of paradigms that we hold need to be clearly articulated as they have implications for the ways in which power is appropriated and for the kinds of authority that might be imposed in evaluation. The purpose of evaluation should be to promote growth and development rather than to exercise control. Both integrative and summative evaluation procedures, based on constructivist views are relevant. Mere results or product-oriented evaluation, based upon traditional logical-positivist paradigms, are often inadequate.

The University of Natal: Scope for Broadening Horizons

Post-apartheid South Africa saw a burgeoning interest from the international community. As a country in transition, with an extremely successful move from a minority controlled white oligarchy to a broad-based democracy, South Africa does, indeed, offer one of the world's best social laboratories. For the young, curious of mind, it is literally a mine of mineral and material wealth that boasts some of the world's best social, political, infrastructural and scientific developments. Yet, its appeal also lies in the tragic representation of sub-Saharan Africa, with its massive poverty, unemployment, inequality, high rates of crime, and the unenviable position of having the highest rate of HIV/AIDS in the world.

The University of Natal was one of the first tertiary institutions to recognise the potential of the international market in education and in 1994 established an International Office, thus strengthening the institutional support for international exchanges. Over the past four years, the Centre for Social Work has offered an International Winter School programme for undergraduate and post-graduate students from Grand Valley State University. In 2001 the programme included students from North Carolina and in 2002, students from New York.

A critical reflection of one's social and political realities and the capacity to develop action strategies consequent upon these reflections is central to social work education and practice. Both local and international student populations need to be viewed as 'consumer' or 'client' groups[3] insofar as we recognise that they enter the classroom and the field-training context with varying degrees of disadvantage. One of these is the control of consciousness by means of the state apparatus and ideology (Gramsci, 1977) in the attempt to maintain capitalist and ruling class hegemony, which is a feature of both western and non-western societies.

American students are generally socialised into unquestioningly accepting the universal applicability of American capitalist democracy, with prominent leaders such as the American journalist, Tom Gjelten, claiming that their country is the moral leader of the world (Gjelten, 2001). Oreskes made reference to the American 'politics of irrelevance' (Oreskes cited in Giroux, 1997, p.217). Referring to poll data, Giroux argued that while youth in some European countries were extending the boundaries of democracy:

'American youth are both poorly motivated and largely ill-prepared to struggle for and keep democracy alive in the twenty-first century. Rather than being a model of democracy, the United States has become indifferent to the need to struggle for the conditions that make democracy a substantive rather than lifeless activity' (Giroux, 1997, p. 217).

Giroux (1983, 1997) also made sharp attacks on American universities, which he believed did not take academic freedom seriously. These insights form an important part of the assumptions that American students carry with them when they engage in international exchanges and can have a profound impact upon their work and experience of an overseas placement.

On a universal level, the impact of oppression is such that oppressed people eventually turn societal and political oppression into self-oppression. Students need opportunities to engage in processes wherein identities and dominant social and political ideologies can be deconstructed. Of equal importance is the aim of providing students with a framework of options for the reconstruction of their identities by identifying external sources of exclusion and oppression, engaging in re-scripting or re-authoring of the self, and the building of action upon their strengthened identities.

Action, reflection, deconstruction and reconstruction, which are central to empowerment-based practice (Sewpaul, 2001), constitute the basis of the micro-foundation for development thinking and practice (Coetzee, 2001). Students need to be engaged in such processes, if they are to successfully engage with 'client' populations in similar ways. Moreover, if educators accept that education 'is a constitutive process of constructing meaning and critically interrogating the forces that shape lived experiences' (Giroux, 1983, p.155) they will accept that educators need to identify how their own ideology informs their own teaching content and methodologies. These assertions are also born out of my personal biography as I describe below.

The Power of Biography: Towards an Emancipatory Pedagogy

Gramsci (1977) saw the starting point of critical elaboration to be in positioning oneself as a product of the historical process. In a similar vein, Giroux has argued that an examination of the historical and social constructs of our lives 'helps to reterritorialise and rewrite the complex narratives that make up (our) lives' (Giroux, 1997, p. 159, brackets, mine). Critical and emancipatory pedagogy raises important issues regarding how we construct our identities within particular historical, cultural and social relations, with the intention of contributing to a more democratic life.

My personal biography confirms that emancipatory pedagogy begins with everyday life experiences and with the particular as the basis of learning, deconstruction and action. For hooks (1989) a feminist writer, one's voice should be the object of theoretical and critical analysis so that it can be connected to broader notions of solidarity, struggle and politics.

Apart from the personal-political identity links, the power of biography lies in its potential to reflect how power and/or powerlessness are reproduced in everyday life experiences. I experienced my most formative years as a child, adolescent and young adult in apartheid South Africa. Such was the power of the internalised oppression of my mother that I grew up in a family setting where the status quo was completely accepted. Here, we were made to believe that whites were demi-gods, to be respected and revered as such. My mother knew no better.

'Subjectivities are produced within those social forms in which people move but of which they are often only *partially* conscious' (Giroux, 1997, p.158, my emphasis). As an aside, later in her life, my mother as part of an organised group, would raise banners and take up certain struggles, although she opposed my engagement earlier on. Widowed at a very young age, with me, the youngest of seven children being five months old at the time of my father's death, my mother worked as a domestic servant for whites for almost 40 years. Thus, her sense of gratitude for whites having provided her with a livelihood; or perhaps it instances Fanon's (1970) thesis of loving the oppressor.

Our subservience to whites was understandable, as the only relationship that we shared with them was one of 'master' and 'servant'. Group areas and separate amenities legislation ensured that we did not get to know whites in any other capacity, let alone as equals. Such was my mother's indoctrination that while walking on the streets where whites lived we were, as children, shooed into silence as 'whites don't like noise'. Under such circumstances my capacity to externalise, and to understand the sources of oppression and of my diminished sense of self (which was quite acute!) were clearly limited.

At the height of apartheid there were innumerable laws such as the Separate Amenities Act, the Group Areas Act, and the Immorality Act that were designed to inform people of colour that we were inferior. On reading signs that said: 'Whites Only' or 'Rights of Admission Reserved', I did not see the problem belonging to an oppressive state, rather I owned the problem and believed that something must have been wrong with me. Yet, I believe that I was more fortunate than most people of colour in South Africa. My experience would serve to confirm Giroux's claim that the 'mechanisms of domination and the possible seeds of liberation reach into the very structure of the human psyche' (Giroux, 1983, p. 39).

In South Africa, the discovery of Freire's (1970, 1972, 1973) method of conscientisation through liberating dialogue and praxis came at just the right moment – during the 1970s when I was in secondary school. At this time Freire's works, which were banned by the government, found their way into South African black universities and into the South African Student Organisation (SASO). His work, particularly the *Pedagogy of the Oppressed*, had a profound impact on young activists of the Black Consciousness Movement (BCM) and contributed to the radicalisation and politicisation of education (Alexander, 1989).

As a secondary school learner, I was fortunate to have had the guidance of black consciousness activists such as the late Steve Biko, Strini Moodley and his wife Sam Moodley who entered our school as a young enthusiastic teacher bent on politicising us. Sam would get us engaged in fantasy trips, free writing and drama, replicating in the classroom the forces of apartheid and oppression. On picking up self-blame and messages of internalised oppression that were characteristic of so many of us, she would confront us with the realities, and made us see that the real enemy was the apartheid State.

Consciousness-raising strategies were coupled with further action, where as school learners we formed, with the help of the BCM leaders, a theatre group called the Chatsworth Arts and Theatre Organisation (CATO). Through CATO, of which I was the secretary, we undertook community political education, wrote Animal Farm into a drama script and produced this as a play. These activities did not come without their own difficulties. Within weeks of CATO's formation we had the Security Branch on us, with threats of suspension from school if we continued our political activities.

Apart from its intrinsic value in helping us recognise our own worth, the activities allowed us to gain a certain measure of control over our lives, and over an unrelenting, oppressive system. This control in turn provided us with a sense of hope for change, an element emphasised by Giroux (1997) in *Pedagogy and the Politics of Hope: Theory, Culture and Schooling*. This hope was born out of some community initiatives, for example, successfully but non-violently resisting the authorities when they planned to terminate a vital bus transportation facility that would have severely jeopardised the working class people of the area that we lived in.

It is perhaps this kind of hope, and the vision of possible change among the generation of school and university learners, that culminated in the well-known 1976 Soweto Riots, where the slogan: *Liberation before education* became popularised. In 1976, as a first year university student in an ethnic institution that fully supported the apartheid status quo, as we chanted, we truly believed, *'we shall overcome someday ... black man (sic) shall be free someday'*. The BCM which was banned in 1977 provided an invaluable source of support, encouragement and guidance as we organised student boycotts and rallies not only against the apartheid regime; the struggle took place within an educational institution geared towards the preservation of political dominance. South Africa still suffers the effect of a lost generation of youth.

But I am sure that many South Africans will agree that we will never trade the liberation and pulsating life of freedom that we have now that our citizenship has become affirmed. We tend to take for granted the 'right to belong' and the 'right to citizenship'. Under apartheid in South Africa, over 80 per cent of the population had been denied these rights, as we had no right to vote until 27 April 1994. It was on the day of the first democratic elections that I felt truly human in South Africa. It is against this background that my educational philosophy is informed. I appreciate the entry of Steve Biko and Strini and Sam Moodley into my life, for they enabled me to develop the confidence to become what I am today.

Through these people and experiences, I realised that I was not a 'passive (victim) of society's control elements' (Coetzee, 2001, p.137), and that I had the capacity to reflect and act upon these elements, a realisation that now also informs my interactions and desired objectives with local and international students. Through this way of living and teaching, I have put into practice the insights of bell hooks (1989) when she argues that the value of the narrative lies in theorising experiences as part of a broader politics of engagement. I explore this in greater detail below.

On Freire, Gramsci and Giroux: Critical and Emancipatory Pedagogy

Having *trained* in an ethnically based, 'Indian' apartheid institution that was preoccupied with the reproduction of dominant cultural and political ideology, with the majority of staff being white, I was certainly not introduced to any form of critical *education* during this period. As a secondary school learner, the benefits derived from critical consciousness and action, that allowed us to 'mobilise rather than destroy (our) hopes for the future' (Giroux, 1997, p. 161, brackets, mine), initially led me to the work of Freire (1970, 1972, 1973) and later to the emancipatory pedagogies of Gramsci (1988, 1971, 1977) and Giroux (1983, 1994, 1997).

Capturing his and the central theses of Gramsci (1988, 1971, 1977) and Freire (1970, 1972, 1973) Giroux (1983) contends that the spirit of critical or radical pedagogy is:

'rooted in aversion to all forms of domination, and its challenge centres around the need to develop modes of critique fashioned in a theoretical discourse that mediates the possibility for social action and emancipatory transformation' (Giroux, 1983, p. 2).

Critical theorists believe in the dialectic of agency and structure, and developed theoretical perspectives that support the notion that history can be changed and provide potential for radical transformation. Giroux (1983, 1994, 1997), Gramsci (1971, 1977) and Freire (1970, 1972, 1973) addressed educational issues as political and cultural issues.

Paulo Freire

Alexander and Helbig (cited in Alexander, 1989) mentioned the following factors as those that allowed for the easy entry of Freire's pedagogy into South Africa.

- Freire's anti-capitalist social theory accorded with the experience and insights of South African liberation movements and of educationalists who were active within these movements;
- The pedagogical situation in Latin America out of which Freire's liberation theology was formed resembled conditions that existed in South Africa;
- Freire's pedagogical method of combining education and culture with conscientisation and politicisation was consistent with the views of the BCM, and was thus readily adopted by the movement; and
- The emphasis of the liberation movement in the late 1970s and the 1980s on grassroots organisation, rooted in small groups and community projects, heightened sensitivity regarding democratic principles. This sensitivity, reinforced by Freire's educational philosophy, became integral to the practice of alternative education.

Writing in relation to the Brazilian people, Freire contended: 'They could be helped to learn democracy through the exercise of democracy; for that knowledge, above all others, can only be assimilated experientially' (Freire, 1973, p. 36). Given the transition of Brazil from a closed to an open society at the time, in *Education for Critical Consciousness*, Freire said:

'I was concerned to take advantage of that climate to attempt to rid our education of its wordiness, its lack of faith in the student and his (sic) power to discuss, to work, to create. Democracy and democratic education are founded on faith in men (sic), on the belief that they not only can but should discuss the problems of their country, of their continent, their world, their work, the problems of democracy itself. Education is an act of love, and thus an act of courage. It cannot fear the analysis of reality or, under pain of revealing itself as a farce, avoid creative discussion' (Freire, 1973, p. 36).

The value of Freire's work lies in his linking *micro-educational* methodologies to theories of *social change*. This understanding combined with his emphasis on the integrative processes of action, critical reflection, theoretical knowledge and participatory democracy, support the contention that the micro-macro dichotomy is a fallacious one. While the underlying assumption of Freire's work is that critical understanding would lead to critical action, there is the possibility that his emphases on egalitarian educator-learner relationships, and action and reflection could become ends in themselves. Although Freire wrote about revolutionary movements he did not clearly identify the role of education within them, or how the increased consciousness of students could be mobilised to promote democracy in the public sphere. However, as elucidated in my biography, Freire's work had a profound impact on the educational and political epistemologies in South Africa during the 1970s and 1980s. His writings have provided the philosophical and methodological foundations for the positive engagement of students, and of wider citizenship groups in processes toward the struggle for democracy. These insights are invaluable when working with international exchange students, as they are with local ones.

Antonio Gramsci

Similar to the thesis of Freire (1972, 1973), Gramsci (1977) argued that education should be used for the creation of a vision of the future through its daily practice, and that knowledge consists of theory and existential experience which is located historically within its context, and is based on action and reflection. Gramsci's theory of education and practical formulations with regard to adult education were developed against the backdrop of his political life. Gramsci's work as a journalist, his ten year involvement in the Italian workers' movement, the ten years he spent in prison from 1927 until his death in 1937, the First World War, the Russian Revolution, and the rise of fascism in Italy (Davidson, 1977) were important factors that influenced his radical educational theory.

According to Bobbio (cited in Davidson, 1977, p. viii), 'There is no personality in the history of the workers' movement ... whose person and work have aroused greater interest than Gramsci's'. Gramsci (1971, 1977) used the concept of *hegemony* as a central explanation of the functioning of the capitalistic system, and elucidated the role of ideology and the state in the reproduction of class relations (the relations of production) and in preventing the development of working class consciousness. Gramsci went beyond Marxist economic determinism by expounding the ways in which common sense and identities are formed within their historical and social locations.

Central to the work of Gramsci is what he called *common sense* (also *contradictory consciousness*) and *good sense*. Gramsci claimed that, 'all men (sic) are 'philosophers'' (Gramsci, 1971, p. 323), with their philosophy contained in a) language, b) 'common sense' and 'good sense', and c) the entire system of beliefs, superstitions, opinions and ways of seeing things and acting which are collectively referred to as 'folklore'. However, he contended that the common sense functioned without benefit of critical interrogation. Common sense consists of the incoherent set of generally held assumptions and beliefs common to any given society, while good sense means practical, empirical common sense, thus the need to transform common sense into good sense.

Contradictory consciousness or common sense is characterised by a dual conception of the world: 'one affirmed in words and the other displayed in effective action' (Gramsci, 1971, p. 326). Thus, ideology is located not only at the level of language but also as lived experience. Gramsci saw the contrast between thought and action to be an expression of profounder contrasts of a socio-historical order. While social groups have their own conceptions of the world, such groups 'for reasons of submission and intellectual subordination' (Gramsci, 1971, p. 237), have also adopted a conception which is not its own. In ordinary times, when such groups are not acting autonomously it is the conception of the dominant group that prevails.

The contradictory state of consciousness, characterised by innocuous ideologies for Gramcsi (1971) did not provide for choice and action, but for 'moral and political passivity' (Gramsci, 1971, p. 333). Thus, in his *Prison Letters*, Gramsci wrote:

'The outbreak of the World War has shown how ably the ruling classes and groups know how to exploit these apparently innocuous ideologies in order to set in motion the waves of public opinion' (Gramsci, 1988, p. 171).

However, as Giroux pointed out contradictory consciousness does not only point to domination and confusion, but also to 'a sphere of contradictions and tensions that is pregnant with possibilities for radical change' (Giroux, 1983, p. 152).

Gramsci (1971) argued that innovation could not come from the masses, at least not at the beginning, except through mediation of the elite or the intellectual. The role of ideology becomes critical to the extent that it has the potential to reveal truths by deconstructing historically conditioned social forces or it could reinforce the concealing function of common sense. It is thus vital that common sense be subject to critical interrogation. In the words of Gramsci:

> 'Critical understanding of self takes place ... through a struggle of political 'hegemonies' and of opposing directions ... . Consciousness of being part of a particular hegemonic force (that is political consciousness) is the first stage towards a further progressive self-consciousness' (Gramsci, 1971, p. 333).

Thus, the theory-practice nexus that arises with ideological critique and critical understanding is not merely a mechanical fact; it reflects the need for a historical consciousness. Historical consciousness, as a moment of ideological critique functions 'to perceive the past in a way that (makes) the present visible as a revolutionary moment' (Buck-Morss cited in Giroux, 1997, p.84). Political revolutionary action for Gramsci (1971) could take the forms of war – a war of movement, a war of position and underground warfare. The war of position would constitute the passive revolution that takes place in societies characterised by relative stability.

Henry Giroux

Giroux, a contemporary American writer, embraces the central theses of Freire (1970, 1972, 1973) and Gramsci (1988, 1971, 1977) regarding politics, culture, class, education, critical consciousness and critical action but he adds to his radical pedagogy significant issues of 'race', gender, sexual orientation, ethnicity, multiculturalism, citizenship education and identity politics. Of particular salience to social work theory and practice, are Giroux's (1983, 1997) critiques of modernity and of feminist and postmodernist theoretical formulations, which are not within the scope of this chapter to include.

Given social work's current preoccupation with multiculturalism, Giroux's views are worth mentioning. In what he called an insurgent multiculturalism, Giroux (1994, 1997) called for discourses on multiculturalism which have been used to victimise minority groups, with an emphasis on their deficits and one which presents them as the 'other', to be combined with discourses on power, racialised identities and class.

In doing so, we need to move away from using white, which is a mark of racial and gender privilege, as a point of departure in identifying difference. Whiteness, as 'race' and colour, represents itself as an archetype for being *civilised* and *good,* and in so doing represents the *Other* as *primitive* and *bad.* This is characterised by the textured use of *colour* in the English language as a signifier for such archetypes. Thus all that is bad has become associated with black, such as black-book, black-sheep, black-listed, and black-mail. Would a deconstruction of 'race' from the constraints of such representations mean a deconstruction of the very language that reproduces it; a language that has become embedded in the psyches of people to become, in Gramsci's language, the common sense?

Citing James Baldwin, Giroux claims that 'differences in power and privilege authorise who speaks, how fully, under what conditions, against what issues, for whom, and with what degree of consistent, institutionalised support' (Giroux, 1997, p. 236). Critical multiculturalism must examine how racism in its various forms gets reproduced historically and institutionally, and essentialist views regarding black, female or African must be rejected.

While multiculturalism generally focuses on the *other*, Giroux (1997) calls for a multiculturalism that provides *'dominant groups* with the knowledge and histories to examine, acknowledge, and unlearn their own privilege' and to '(deconstruct) the centres of colonial power and (undo) the master narratives of racism' (Giroux, 1997, p. 236, emphasis and brackets, mine). An insurgent multiculturalism brings into question not only the effects of racism in terms of the nihilism that permeates black communities and of poverty, unemployment, racist policing an so on, but the origins of racism in the historical, political, social and cultural dynamics of white supremacy.

Giroux (1997) contends that Gramsci's thesis regarding *ideological hegemony* as a form of control that manipulated consciousness and shaped daily experiences and behaviour, is crucial to our understanding of how *cultural hegemony* is used to reproduce economic and political power. Advanced industrialised counties like the United States, not only unequally distribute goods and services, but varying forms of cultural capital – 'that system of meanings, abilities, language forms, and tastes that are directly and indirectly defined by dominant groups as socially legitimate' (Apple cited in Giroux, 1997, p. 6).

Within the dominant culture, meaning becomes universalised and historically conditioned processes and notions of social reality appear as self-evident, given and fixed. Thus, as with Freire (1970, 1972, 1973) and Gramsci (1971, 1977), the importance of 'critical reflection lays bare the historically and socially sedimented values at work in the construction of knowledge, social relations and material practices' (Giroux, 1983, p. 154).

Giroux contends that the modes of analysis in radical pedagogy must be underscored by two major questions: a) how do we make education meaningful by making it critical, and b) how do we make it critical so as to make it emancipatory (Giroux, 1983, p. 3). Giroux (1983, 1997) attacks modernist, technical-positivist rationality, which elevates reason to an ontological status, arguing that it does not allow for subjectivity and critical thinking and that it is antithetical to the development of citizenship education.

He posits arguments for citizenship education to be informed by an *emancipatory rationality*, which is based on the principles of critique and action, and which reproduces and stresses the 'importance of social relationships in which men and women are treated as ends and not means' (Giroux, 1983, p. 191). (Note Giroux's gender sensitive language compared with that of Freire and Gramsci).

Emancipatory citizenship education must be used to stimulate students' passions and imaginations so that they may be encouraged to challenge the social, political and economic forces that impact upon the lives of people; to display what Giroux (1983, p. 201) called *civic courage*. Issues regarding citizenship and democracy cannot be addressed within the restrictive language of markets, profit, individualism, competition and choice, which create indifference to inequality, hunger, deprivation, exploitation and suffering.

Educators must have moral courage and power of criticism, and must not, in the name of objectivity, distance themselves from power relations that exclude, oppress, subjugate, exploit and diminish other human beings. We need to create opportunities for the development of critical consciousness and, where possible for transformative action. International exchanges provide one such route to broadening horizons and developing critical consciousness in the manner envisaged by Freire, Gramsci and Giroux. In striving to achieve these objectives we need to begin where students are, within their historical and socio-cultural spaces.

Student Expectations and Identity Confrontation: Challenges to the Host Institution

While South Africa's First World features constitute a pull factor, it is South Africa's characteristics of the Two-Thirds World that tend to really attract social work students. International students arrive with their own agendas and prior lived experiences. But as Guevara and Ylvisaker have pointed out:

'There is no way to fully prepare United States university students for a gut-wrenching confrontation with the levels of poverty in which many of the world's people live their daily lives – or the health and social consequences of this poverty' (Guevara and Ylvisaker, 2002).

It is up to the host institution to remain acutely sensitive to students' needs and experiences and have skilled and sensitive staff to deal with them. This is especially so where students are not accompanied by a Faculty member from their home institution.

African-American students arrive in South Africa with romanticised notions of returning to the motherland to find their roots, often characterised by a euphoric: *'I got up this morning and I still can't believe that I am in Africa'*, or *'It's hard to believe I am home'*. However, this sense of elation is often accompanied by intense mixed emotions, including sadness and anger linked to the African Diaspora and South Africa's recent apartheid past.

Almost immediately students are confronted with the reality that they are more American than African, a realisation which I found often having its genesis in the offence of being mistaken for a local South African and being greeted in the traditional *isiZulu*. The dialect of culture, historical and self-identities, and national identities are indeed complicated. When confronted with the realities, it would appear that national identities gain primacy.

This reaction does bring into question, contested notions of global citizenship (a concept that I believe to be rooted in conquest, colonialism and slavery), and Midgley's (2000, p. 15) assertion that, 'In the future, many people will regard nationality as of secondary importance to global citizenship'. While arriving with a strong identification with Africa, and with slavery and the slave trade in the African Diaspora, African-American students, more often than not, felt insulted about being seen as local Africans. This may be linked to the fact that race and identity are embedded in the politics of social, economic and class divisions (Giroux, 1994).

It is perhaps the signifier of socio-economic class (African-American students do not share the same socio-economic class as local Africans, the majority of whom are poor) apart from national identification that influenced the students' reactions. An empathic and sensitive understanding of students' emotional trauma as they deal with such cultural and identity confrontation is vital to their appreciation of the South African socio-cultural context. If such a confrontation serves to affirm students' American identity (however they might constitute this identity, as the notion of a single national identity is itself contested), this might, in itself, be a growth producing experience, and one that students should proudly embrace.

In this section I explore these issues through some examples. In 2001, a group of students from North Carolina described their reactions to a University of Natal residence, with its high fences, security padlocks and very small rooms resembling prison cells. For them, these produced images of solitary confinement and detention without trial that occurred for South Africans during apartheid, and these were not consistent with their expectations of a 'transformed', democratic South Africa. On visiting the residence, I found their complaints to be justified, for the rooms and the narrow and sterile passages did, indeed, resemble prison cells. Much time had to be spent in debriefing the students and the University authorities were alerted to the trauma that this experience had engendered in students.

We were promised that the particular residence would not, in future, be used as accommodation for international students. Such issues point to serious areas of consideration on the part of host institutions as they extend invitations to students of the international community. Unfortunately, even in its construction such a building was considered fit for the accommodation of local students who spend much more time there than international students!

Many international students arrive with a naïve notion of wanting to 'really make a difference'. Such altruistic ideals are often immediately challenged by students' exposure to the extent of South Africa's deprivation, poverty and homelessness, and highly visible children of the streets. The battle with their own emotional reactions and their compassion are often accompanied by a sense of disbelief that such circumstances could have been allowed to have developed, coupled at times with a more direct question: *'What are you doing about it?'*

Mentoring and debriefing students play a vital role in allowing them to gain a realistic appraisal of their potential contribution, and helping them gain perspective and a cognitive grasp of the situation – strategies that have their roots in crisis intervention. This is by design, as students who confront the realities of South Africa often experience crisis reactions. This is reflected in the example I consider below.

In 1999, on beginning her field placement, and on entry into an informal settlement one student experienced very acute anxiety reactions with constant bouts of crying. Amid the poverty, unemployment and overcrowding, residents of the informal settlement strove for organisation and survival, through the development of community forums and food gardens. For her, it was the sheer extent of the poverty, combined with the infinite hope and faith of people that was overwhelming. She chose to immediately return to the United States. Something about the experience resonated very deeply with this student's own life experiences, and two years later when I visited GVSU, she informed me that she had still not really come to terms with the experience. However, she did say that she would like to return to South Africa in an effort to better understand her own reactions.

In 2001, her boyfriend joined the Winter School programme to try to understand her life-altering experience. What was interesting was that this group of students, prior to the commencement of their field placements, on passing by the same informal settlement wanted to stop and take photographs. We did so from a relative distance. The students found that viewing the informal settlement as a 'tourist' and as an outsider was very different from moving into and beginning to understand the lived world of the residents, as they visited the homes of families, talked with the residents and observed community projects. Most students experience very intense emotional reactions to this environment, but they tend to stay with the feelings and work through their experiences during debriefing sessions, often amid a host of tears and expressions of confusion. The debriefing sessions focus on validating students' feelings, reflecting on their practice, dealing with South Africa's recent emergence from apartheid, examining the role of the international community in South Africa's history and present status, and critically appraising South Africa's attempts to deal with its current realities. The latter is dealt with from both from a national and global perspective.

Student Field Placements: Action and Reflection

Prior to the arrival of the students, the co-ordinator of the host institution is informed about the students' areas of interest, and as far as possible field placements are organised accordingly. Guevara and Ylvisaker (2002) have detailed the model used in the partnership and the logistics of organising the programme. Students are placed primarily in generic non-governmental welfare organisations rather than specialist agencies as these provide for broad-based exposure to a host of pertinent issues such as adoption, foster care, children of the street, HIV/AIDS, residential care, social work in informal settlements and substance abuse.

As one of these organisations is faith-based, this has allowed us to link into contemporary American debates regarding the Bush administration's views on the role of faith-based organisations in welfare service delivery. One placement was a Place of Safety that housed many youths awaiting spunky 70 year old GVSU Faculty member chose to register as a student at University of Natal and did her field placement at The Association for the Aged (TAFTA).

The students have the benefit of an agency supervisor, who attends to the day-to-day hands on experiences of the students and deals with the students' on-the-spot inquiries. Mentoring and debriefing generally took place twice per week with sessions of two to three hours each. These sessions were complemented by students' exposure to other international students as they took lessons on South African history, music and culture. As the main objective of GVSU was that its students would investigate 'comparative social policy issues that would guide practice, or investigate comparative social work practices between the USA and South Africa' (Guevara and Ylvisaker, 2002), formal sessions were offered on the following: the history and development of social welfare policy in South Africa, including the recent policy shifts towards developmental social welfare, HIV/AIDS, domestic violence, children of the street, and elders.

Where possible, representatives from the National government were called into the sessions to address the students. For example, Ashley Theron, the Chief Director from the National Department of Social Development, spoke on the new welfare funding policy,[4] while Ela Gandhi, a Member of Parliament, had the students spellbound as she detailed women's participation in the struggle against apartheid. The value of this is underscored by the fact that women's voices in history are often under-played and lost.

Unfortunately, not all the placements were always successful. In one instance, on account of what would appear to be inadequate planning on the part of the Centre for Social Work at the University of Natal and a non-committed field supervisor, the placement left much to be desired. This was the only time that the task of co-ordinating the field placement was delegated to a colleague who believed that the arrangements could be made through telephone contact. As there was insufficient communication between the university and the field supervisor, the field supervisor was uncertain about the objectives of the placement and our expectations of the agency. The field supervisor, unfortunately, did not take the initiative to clarify these with us; neither did she exercise any common sense or creativity in ensuring a productive experience for the students.

I found that personal visits to the agency are very important in organising field placements. These serve the purposes of informing the agency about individual student's interests; discussing the orientation and the field programme; clarifying the objectives of the placement and the kinds of activities that students should have exposure to; and the expectations and the roles of the university and field supervisors. Equally important is that these visits validate and affirm the contributions that agencies make to the education and training of students. The personal involvement, dedication and willingness to invest in student development on the part of all relevant persons – staff from the home and host institution, field supervisors and university administrators, are central to successful international exchanges.

Two issues are highlighted to reflect the kinds of content that the debriefing and mentoring sessions focused upon. Given the interactive and circular relationship amongst the questions and concerns, and the systemic relationship between the micro- and the macro- factors, it is difficult to separate issues. Following the radical pedagogy of Freire (1970, 1972, 1973), Gramsci (1971, 1977) and Giroux (1983, 1997), action and critical reflection became crucial components of the educational process. All the discussions and debates were held in relation to the students' observations, experiences and work in the field placement context.

Services to Children and Youth

In view of the massive problems of youth in trouble with the law, children of the street, child abuse and the high rates of HIV infection among children and youth much of the discussion centred around questions such as: What are we offering our children and youth? How does the system fail them? The impact of poverty and structural sources of youth alienation and crime was emphasised, as was the phenomenon of demonisation of youth, particularly black youth by an adult population (Williams, 1988; Giroux, 1994, 1997). Under extensive societal pressures, these groups appear to have moved toward a state of moral relativism as described in other parts of the world (Williams, 2002).

The students' field experiences have highlighted the dimensions of 'race', gender and class, with the highest visibility for them being between 'race' and poverty. The relationship between race and poverty is discussed in the section on HIV/AIDS in South Africa. On a positive note, the shift in emphasis to restorative rather than retributive justice[5] in working with children and youth in trouble with the law, and the move toward family preservation and family reunification, as per the policy recommendations of the Inter-Ministerial Committee on Youth at Risk (1996), were discussed and debated.

HIV/AIDS in South Africa

Discussions on HIV/AIDS, as did many other issues, highlighted the systemic relationship between the individual and family, and broader structural issues, including global ones. Reviewing global patterns of HIV infection drew the possible relationship between poverty, lack of social cohesion and inequality and HIV/AIDS. Of the estimated 40 million people living with HIV/AIDS globally, 28.5 million are in sub-Saharan Africa (UNAIDS, 2002). South Africa, with the following features, has the highest HIV/AIDS prevalence (5 million people) in the world:

- Enormous lack of social cohesion (a legacy of laws that deliberately aimed to destroy families during the apartheid past)
- Mistrust of condom use amongst the majority of people as they associate this with the 1970s subtle but concerted effort to reduce the Black population (Smart et al., 2001)
- One of the most skewed income distribution profiles in the world with a Gini Coefficient of 0.65. On average Africans earn 13 per cent of the income earned by Whites, while Asians and Coloureds earn 40 per cent and 27 per cent respectively. An estimated 45 per cent of the population lives in poverty. Almost all of the poor are Africans who live in either rural areas or urban slums/informal settlements (Department of Welfare and Population Development, 1998). The poverty of African people is highly visible in South Africa.

The Jaipur paradigm (Barnett and Whiteside cited in Smart et al., 2001) uses studies to show that the rate of HIV transmission is determined by two key variables: the degree of social cohesion and the overall levels of wealth. Thus, a country like South Africa with low levels of social cohesion and high-income inequality sees a rapid growth of the epidemic.

The relationship between socio-economic, cultural and political factors was also analysed by reviewing provincial rates. KwaZulu Natal (which has a prevalence rate of 32.5 per cent, compared with the national average of 22.4 per cent of the adult population) with relatively little land space is the most densely populated and home to 20.7 per cent of South Africa's population of over 40 million people. It is also one of the poorest provinces, with high unemployment (39.1 per cent) and low literacy levels (22 per cent compared with a national average of 19.3 per cent).[6] It is also the province that suffered the effects of major violence between the Inkatha Freedom Party and the African National Congress prior to the elections in 1994. This violence contributed to a massive displacement of people and the mushrooming of informal settlements. In addition, it is a province with two ports, with a very well developed road transportation system along the main freeways that lead to neighbouring African states.

These features combined with substantial rural features lay the infrastructure for the rapid spread of HIV/AIDS. Cultural practices such as polygamy, dry sex and the role of patriarchy as co-factors in the aetiology of HIV/AIDS have also been the focus of our attention; as have the myths that sleeping with a virgin, or taking traditional medicines could cure HIV/AIDS. What future for South Africa, with an estimated 70,000 children who are born HIV-positive every year and the fastest rate of infection, via sexual contact, being in the age group 15-29 years?

We also discussed the implications of the high rates of infection and death among the most productive members of our society for various sectors of South Africa. The phenomena of child-headed households, the increased vulnerability of women and children, children orphaned on account of HIV/AIDS and the responses of the South African Government, the non-governmental organisation (NGO) sector and of the international community were discussed at length.

We also considered the failures of the South African Government in respect of not making treatment accessible to HIV positive persons, especially the low cost *nevirapine*[7] for prevention of mother to child transmission, and the impact of the dissident views of President Thabo Mbeki on HIV and AIDS, both nationally and internationally. Of all

South Africa's recent high cost (both material and human) blunders, the enigma of anti-retroviral therapy must be its worst. The debates and controversies around *nevirapine* are not new; they have been going on since 1998.

The macro-economic policy shifts from the Reconstruction and Development Programme (RDP) document that reflected ideals of democratic socialism to the adoption of GEAR in June 1996, with the latter's neo-liberal principles were discussed in relation to economic globalisation and its implications for the people of South Africa. The details of this are considered in another paper (Sewpaul, 2001a). This took the discussion to the political thesis of Franz Fanon (1970) who warned about the emergence of the new national elite in post-colonial states (in South Africa post-apartheid as well), which used the new state for capital accumulation and personal gain. Both the students and I, in grappling with the issues, expressed bewilderment about South African's lack of ability or unwillingness to learn from the well-documented lessons from the history of Africa. Using Santayana's adage (Alexander, 1989, p. 8) reminded us 'that those who are not willing to learn from history are condemned to repeat it!'. In this respect, the words of Saul Alinsky appear to have an ominous ring of truth:

'History is a relay of revolutions; the torch of idealism is carried by the revolutionary group until this group becomes the establishment, and then quietly the torch is put down to wait until a new revolutionary group picks it up for the next leg of the run. Thus the revolutionary cycle goes on' (Alinksy, 1972, p. 22).

The discussions on HIV/AIDS brought into sharp focus the global-local discourses, especially with regard to the status of post-colonial states, economic globalisation and the role of the multinational drug companies with regard to patent laws and lack of accessibility to life-saving treatment for people in the Two-Thirds World. Quoting Sacks, Rollins (2000) indicated that the New York Stock exchange had gains of 20 trillion dollars since 1996. A fraction of this gain would make a substantial difference to the HIV pandemic.

However, the motivation to respond adequately, Rollins argues, depends on fiscal and investment discretion on a global level. Drug companies must become more responsible to the needs of people and trade regulations adjusted to serve communities globally. We also critiqued the roles of the IMF and the World Bank along with the ethics of structural adjustment policies, and the ethics of the power of the G8 countries in determining the economic policies of the Two-Thirds World.

America's role in the subversion of alternative forms of political and economic governance in different parts of world that are well documented (Sunshine, 1996) was also discussed. The United States ideal of capitalist democracy is seen as the only form of acceptable political governance and any deviation from this has been attacked with sanctions, military invasions, open warfare and violence, the threat of withdrawing aid or the actual withdrawal of aid. President Bush's current refusal to lift the embargo against Cuba until Fidel Castro buckles down to America's demands for an alternative form of political governance and a free market ideology is a case in point. This is despite pressures from human rights groups that point to the untold difficulties that the embargo creates for the people of Cuba.

The politicisation of social work, the critical reflection on social work practice and the links between the personal and political aspects of people's lives provided for quite exacting confrontations with self, which were often uncomfortable and anxiety provoking.

Reflection and Integration

I found one of the most poignant students' comments to be in their observation that South African social workers were involved in *survival struggles* and in the *total life world of 'clients'* compared to their American counter-parts.[8] The immediacy of the impact of poverty and structural sources of inequality means that it is almost impossible to ignore the total gestalt of the persons whom we are working with. Family and community outreach and education, material aid, negotiating access to care and treatment, capacity building, skills development and income generation, are as much an integral part of service delivery as is direct counselling and rehabilitation. The commentary on American social work practice by Pozutto merits reproduction:

'... (For) the most part, US social workers envision the social order as a given, largely unchangeable entity ... . Much of the American social work profession has accepted the 'knowledge' that legitimates the American social order. The drive to professionalism was ... an early step in that direction ... . (The) function of much of contemporary social work is to 'normalize' the population ... . (Social) work is a form of social control contributing to the legitimisation of the current social order' (Pozzuto, 2001, pp. 157-158).

The idea is not to provide a simplistic comparison across America and South Africa. Sewpaul (1977) described how social work, as an organised profession, served to maintain the status quo of Afrikaner nationalism during apartheid. On a global level, social work has been criticised for its failure to work towards change that is directed at structural inequalities that keep people in poverty and dispossessed positions (Dominelli, 1996; Dominelli, 1996a; Sewpaul, 1992) and for the entrenchment of control functions inherent in traditional personal-deficiency approaches to welfare. There have been major policy and practice shifts in South Africa, with some very innovative, cost-effective interventions developed by social work practitioners (Sewpaul, 2001b) that need to be acknowledged and validated. While social workers are adept at implementing policy, and appear to understand the impact of structural forces on the lives of people, the challenge is for a greater number of South African social workers to recognise and fulfil their policy making, advocacy and social change roles. In drawing a direct comparison with the United States, Pozzuto (2001, p. 158) goes on to say:

'South Africans know better than this. The transition of the South African government and the current recreation of the civil society show that the social order is not fixed, nor permanent, nor immutable. This is a lesson, a gift, South Africa can provide to the US. South Africans also know that there are competing ways to conceptualise the social world'.

The situation is not as positive or as straightforward as Pozzuto claims. There are marked tensions and contradictions within South African society that present major challenges both for the social work profession and for South African society.

Some of the students' fieldwork experiences offered them an alternative view of professionalism from that of the dominant logical-positivist conception. Logical-positivism, reflecting modernism's technical rationality, favours a linear reductionist approach to assessment and management, sees the practitioner as the 'expert' who prescribes solutions, adopts the 'proof-is-truth' axiom as defined by logical-positivist empiricism, and calls for the practitioner to be uninvolved, detached, value-free and neutral (Sewpaul, 1997, 2001). Such a view of professionalism is incompatible with anti-oppressive practice (Dominelli 1996a).

In describing the students' exposure to alternative views of professionalism, I do not negate the existence of such views in other parts of the world including America. However, it would appear that the existence of these have remained largely invisible in mainstream teaching and practice. There is a need to mainstream alternative conceptions of professionalism, and for a redefinition of professionalism from a feminist perspective (Dominelli, 2002). An emphatic tuning into the life worlds and suffering of people, especially in circumstances of extreme deprivation, poverty and inequality, mean that we cannot remain value-free and neutral. We cannot help but make sense of the lives of people in relation to the structures that surround them, and engage the positive forces of people as we come to terms with our own limitations as professionals and as we confront the major challenges involved in the change process.

Acquiring these insights can form an important part of the international exchange experience. One group of students had the opportunity of being educated by a group of HIV positive women, who I had worked with. A colleague from Minnesota, who spent a brief period at the Centre for Social Work, University of Natal, trained two of the women in English language skills. These women then did a full session with the rest of the group, with the students as participants as well. While the focus was on language acquisition, the messages were about what it means to be living with HIV/AIDS, and a brief, simple lesson on South African politics.

On the same day the students had the opportunity to see the women, who had extensive training in HIV/AIDS counselling, education and outreach in action as they engaged in an HIV/AIDS education programme in a hospital context. The power and credibility of the HIV positive women as peer educators were obvious, and the impact much more than I could have hoped to gain as a professional.[9]

One student cried bitterly during a debriefing session, on account of the emotional trauma as she daily encountered children and adults with symptomatic HIV, and children dying from AIDS; a reality that many South African themselves have difficulty coming to terms with. Linked to this was her major concern of how people back home would possibly understand what she had experienced. While I acknowledged her feelings and concerns, I pointed out that the power for her lay in the lived experience, and that it would be difficult for someone on the outside to fully understand such an experience. In discussing what they could do to make a difference, I often affirmed that they were making a difference simply by their willingness to engage with people on the level that they did. Their affirmation, acceptance, and validation of the people whom they came into contact with were gifts, as might be a change in perspective that they might offer.

However, the major challenge was what could they do when they got back home to de-stigmatise the people of Africa, and to raise awareness about global politics and economics.[10] On account of the general lack of awareness of global politics, and more particularly lack of awareness of American foreign policies and practices, I saw this as a major challenge. Freire (1972, 1973) Gramsci (1971, 1977) and Giroux (1983, 1997) believed that the development of critical consciousness might lead to critical action. Freire's idea of praxis or conscious action involves a dialectical movement from action to reflection and from reflection upon action to a new action (Freire, 1972). Giroux (1983) points out that subjective intentions alone pose little threat to the existing socio-political order. However, social action must be preceded by an awareness that makes the need for such action comprehensible. Awareness represents an important step in getting students to act as engaged and responsible citizens who question the structural basis of social life. One student expressed a great deal of confusion as he cried and said:

'I grew up in America and I was led to believe that we were of value to the world by virtue of being the United States. We were always made to feel so proud to be American. I have come half way across the world to learn about our economic policy and how it might be affecting people in different parts of the world'.

Students like all other people are constructed within particular cultural, social, political and historical relations. Thus, they had difficulty in integrating information and experiences that confronted both self and national identities and loyalties. However, the value of education needs to be questioned if it is not used to challenge dominant paradigms and ideologies. Such confrontation, I believe, is central to one's personal and professional development and to one's commitment to social change. Radical pedagogy confirms that it is the Self that must be the main site of politicisation. It provides scope for students to:

> 'extend their understandings of themselves and the global contexts in which they live ... (and it) affirms the importance of offering students a language that allows them to reconstruct their moral and political energies in the service of creating a more just and equitable order, one that undermines relations of hierarchy and domination' (Giroux, 1997, p. 225).

Conclusion

International exchanges broaden horizons through the challenges provided by field placements, new opportunities for discussion, debate and reflection, and the destabilising experiences that the students undergo. These question their taken-for-granted assumptions and may require them to rethink things that they believe they have known. My own biography and the influence of the emancipatory pedagogy of Freire (1970, 1972, 1973), Gramsci (1988, 1971, 1977) and Giroux (1983, 1994, 1997) were powerful factors that influenced my work with the students, and in offering alternative conceptions of professionalism and social work practice.

The emphases on global and local discourses, around 'race', gender, poverty and HIV/AIDS served to heighten awareness of local struggles, the strengths and limitations of national policies and responses, the impact of American foreign policies and of international macro economic institutions and transnational companies on South Africa's development opportunities. However, these need to be viewed against the tensions and contradictions inherent in South African society.

These contradictions, tensions and resistance are evident in the confluence of various competing paradigms and epistemological approaches to life. While policy documents contain rhetoric reflecting politically correct values of justice, equality and people-centred development, it is modernism's managerial and market-related discourses that have become dominant in the practical sphere of life. The capitalist macro-economic strategy adopted by Government does not augur well for a country with the highest rate of inequality in the world.

Recent trends indicate that the gini coefficient within Black communities is almost as high as the national norm. This is on account of the very rapidly emerging black middle-class, which has not altered the quality of life for the masses of people. Fanon (1970) cogently elucidated the dynamics of such phenomena in respect of deepening discontent. As wealth and material goods are no longer seen to belong to the *other* – the colonial whites, they are seen to be more accessible yet unattainable. When members of one's own reference group succeed, one's own deprivation becomes more pronounced. Thus, it is not poverty per se but poverty linked to inequality that constitutes a greater source of discontent. In the face of such poverty and inequality, it is unfortunate, and perhaps to South Africa's peril, that it has reneged on its earlier promise of democratic socialism.

Despite some major shifts in social policy and social work practice in South Africa, the dominant influence of logical-positivist rationality and professionalism, our over-reliance on Western directives (for example, the move toward managerialism and the competences-based approach to social work), and our willingness to adopt the kind of demeaning dependency that Nettleford (1995) mentions, all pose threats to our ability to develop critical discourses. They also challenge our sense of agency and our subject locations within our historical, cultural, economic and global contexts.

Our agency and subject positions are also challenged by the contested spaces of control and struggle in South Africa. While sites of contestation and struggle were clear in the past, this is no longer so. Trade unions and various groups of civil society, that effectively align themselves with the new democratic order, also find themselves in a *war of position* (Gramsci,

1971) with the South African government in respect of issues such as globalisation, neo-liberal economics, privatisation and access to health and welfare services.

In this respect South Africa does, indeed, have a lesson for the rest of the world – a meaningful democracy is an on-going process of struggle for human rights, justice, freedom and human dignity. We have arrived at a relatively peaceful democracy from one of the most oppressive and demeaning pasts. We need to remember that if democracy is to remain meaningful, we have to place *humanity* at the centre of a democratic state in a globalising world and have human need and human struggles take precedence over the market and profit. To achieve this objective, we need to be prepared to engage in wars of position both within and across national boundaries.

Notes

1. Given the limitations of the dichotomies mentioned, and the linear modernist implications of First and Third Worlds, I prefer the concept 'Two-Thirds World'. The concept reflects, numerically, the majority of the world's population who live in poverty and deprivation and does not imply any evaluative criteria with regard to superiority/inferiority.

2. I am indebted to the Faculty in the School of Social Work, Grand Valley State University, Grand Rapids, Michigan for the opportunity of spending a three-month paid sabbatical there. It has been an invaluable experience in helping me broaden my horizons.

3. These concepts are problematic as they reflect the traditional bio-medical model, which support the notion of the person as a passive recipient of services with the social worker or educator as 'expert' who knows best, and an implication of a hierarchical 'worker-client' relationship characterised by a so-called neutrality. It is antithetical to the holistic biopsychosocial health model which views people as active agents in change processes and structures, and to empowerment based practice which calls for active involvement, rather than a detached neutrality on the part of practitioners and educators. However, in the absence of a more suitable alternative, I have continued to use these concepts.

4. I discussed the language and intent of the document, which coheres with management and market-related discourses, and detailed the possible implications of the new policy in a paper on *Globalisation and Social Welfare in South Africa*. I presented this paper at the British Academy Seminar Series on 'Globalisation and Social Work' at the University of Southampton, U.K., in November 2000.

5. Restorative justice reflects the following: a belief that crime violates people and relationships; making the wrong right; seeking justice between victims, offenders and communities; people are seen to be the victims; emphasis on participation, dialogue and mutual agreement; is oriented to the future and the development of responsibility. This is opposed to retributive justice, which reflects that crime violates the State and the offender; the State as victim; an authoritarian, technical and impersonal approach; and orientation to the past and guilt.

6. I obtained population figures and rates of unemployment and illiteracy obtained from *Statistics South Africa* (1996).

7. Nevirapine is registered in South Africa for use in the prevention of mother to child transmission of HIV/AIDS. The South African Government has been using cost, safety and lack of infrastructure as reasons for not providing *nevirapine* on a universal basis, except at 18 research sites. One dose of *nevirapine* is administered to the mother during labour and one dose is given to the baby within 72 hours of birth. The cost of the treatment is about $US 3-00 and its success rate in preventing mother to child transmission is about 50 per cent. This means that of the estimated 70,000 children born HIV-positive each year in South Africa we could be saving about 35,000 of them. The Government lost the last Constitutional Court hearing on the subject and was ordered to provide *nevirapine* to all HIV-positive pregnant women in hospitals and clinics that have the capacity to do so.

8. The placement choices for students might reflect a bias in that the more progressive organisations that generally reflect the policy shifts in welfare post-1994 are selected for exchange students.

9. The work with the women are detailed in two papers: Sewpaul, V and Rollins, N (1999) 'Operationalising Developmental Social Work: The Implementation of an HIV/AIDS Project', *Social Work/Maatskaplike Werk*,

35(3), 35(3), pp. 43-54, and Sewpaul, V and Mahlalela, T V (1998), 'The Power of the Small Group: From Fear to Disclosure, *Agenda*, 39, pp. 34-43.

10. Although this was not expected, staff at the agencies and I were very grateful for the efforts of the three students (Sara, Kevin and Catherine) who were part of the 2001 group, who on returning home held a charity concert and raised funds for the placements that they were at. The Faculty member and students of the 2002 group presented these funds to the agencies.

23 The Cultivation of Global Citizenship through International Student Exchanges: The Hong Kong Experience

CECILIA L.W. CHAN and ERNEST W.T. CHUI

Introduction

The development of globalisation is driven by economic forces. Although the term itself is used and interpreted in diverse and multifarious ways, it nonetheless denotes the pervasive trend towards international exchanges of people, cultures, activities, and, perhaps most crucially, in business and finance. Globalisation has also had an impact on the educational and academic fields by engendering exchanges of scholars and students and promoting collaborative and comparative research projects involving colleagues from other countries. Hong Kong, a cosmopolitan city strategically located as a gateway from the West to China and Southeast Asia, is in a good position to promote all types of international exchanges.

The University of Hong Kong (HKU), the first university to have been founded in this former British colony, has fulfilled its historical mission to form a bridge between China and the rest of the world, and is therefore a focal point for projects which demonstrate the merits of international exchanges in academia. Within HKU, the Department of Social Work and Social Administration (the Department) is particularly committed to realising this mission in the specific field of social work education.

This chapter highlights the Department's experience, over the past 50 years, of activities such as student exchanges, study tours, and overseas placements, which have contributed to the cultivation of 'global citizenship' among the students.

Global Citizenship and International Social Work

The pervasive wave of globalisation has virtually torn down national boundaries and fostered increased levels of interaction between nations and peoples in terms of various aspects of modern life. Economically, booms and slumps in a particular country may have repercussions in others, especially where the financial markets are concerned.

Environmentally, the 'greenhouse effect' and the transmission of pollutants from one country to another affects the whole world. In terms of politics, international divides have accentuated hostilities and even led to the polarisation of rival countries, and culturally, the easy and efficient penetration of telecommunications means that mass culture in one country can now leave its imprint on others, especially amongst young people.

Globalisation has contributed to the increasing interconnectedness of people in different parts of the world. However, it has also led to new challenges and problems on a transnational scale, such as ethnic diversification in societies due to mass migration, growing poverty and economic inequalities, violations of human rights, and pandemic diseases such as AIDS (Hokenstad and Midgley, 1997). These problems cannot be solved by individual states, but require the concerted efforts of international and regional groupings, usually targeting a particular issue (Lyons, 1999).

Although the impact of globalisation on labour markets and the economy has been widely discussed, recognition of its relevance to welfare and the development of responses by social care professionals is relatively recent (Lyons, 1999). In fact, social workers, as professionals and as citizens, must also be aware of global matters in order to understand and resolve the problems they face in working with clients and communities (Healy, 2001, p. 105). They have to understand that virtually all aspects of their clients' lives, such as health, security, and well-being, are now directly affected by global interdependence.

Such interdependence in the environment, cultural, and welfare domains has led to greater similarities in the social problems experienced in the various countries of the world and in the policies developed to combat them. This has resulted in what has been called 'homogenisation in social policy' (Healy, 2001) whereby nations around the world shape and reshape their social policies according to trends elsewhere. This has created a substantial shared agenda for knowledge and action.

As a result of this agenda social workers, as well as taking care of their clients within their national boundaries, must also take up the idea of 'global citizenship'. This concept may be thought of as taking responsibility for understanding how the world works (economically, politically, socially, culturally, technologically, and environmentally), participating in the community at a range of levels from the global to the local, and generally acting to make the world a more equitable and sustainable place (Oxfam, 1997, p. 2, cited in Lyons, 1999, p. 151). Such global responsibility is connected to the growing importance of international civil society – the activities of non-governmental bodies and of the world's citizenry, independent of government.

Closely related is Pratt's (1989) concept of 'humane internationalism' which denotes the acceptance, by citizens of the industrialised states, that they have ethical obligations towards those beyond their borders and that these in turn impose obligations upon their governments (cited in Healy, 2001). Lorenz (1994) applies the term 'committed citizenship' to the global role that social workers can play in integrating rights and humanitarian obligations through action (cited in Healy, 2001).

More specifically, 'global citizenship' encompasses such principles as antiracism, equal opportunities, multiculturalism and intercultural learning, and concerns about human rights and the environment (Oxfam, 1997, p. 6, cited in Lyons, 1999, pp. 151-152). It also includes the principles of distributive justice, combined with ecological imperatives (Lister, 1998, cited in Lyons, 1999, p. 151). In practical terms, social development, human rights, multiculturalism and cultural competence, social exclusion and inclusion, security, and sustainability (Healy, 2001) are particularly salient concepts for global work.

Here, the concept of 'international social work' becomes particularly important. Robert Barker defined *'international social work'* as 'a term loosely applied to (1) international organisations using social work methods or personnel, (2) social work co-operation between countries, and (3) the transfer between countries of methods or knowledge about social work' (1995, p. 194, quoted in Johannessen, 1997, p. 153). International social work education is seen as offering the chance to develop new paradigms or interventions and to enhance understanding of cultural differences and structural oppression (Lyons, 1999). In summary, social work practitioners striving to adopt an international perspective or orientation should cultivate an interest in international affairs, instead of focusing only on local issues.

Specifically, social workers with global perspectives should take responsibility for helping to make progress towards world peace, the alleviation of poverty, and the protection of human rights, and demonstrate their concern about the problems caused by poverty, deprivation, exploitation, and injustice. These ideas echo the tenets of 'global citizenship' mentioned above whilst remaining grounded in the general emphasis of the social work profession on human welfare, justice, and equality.

One of the major challenges for international social work is the exposure to cultural diversity which comes with increased contact between different countries and societies. It is important to differentiate here between two of the principal approaches to diversity: namely, cultural pluralism and multi-culturalism.

'Cultural pluralism' emphasises the unique attributes or experiences of distinct social groups in isolation from each other and has the aim of creating mutual understanding. 'Multi-culturalism', on the other hand, explicitly recognises the interrelationships between various racial, ethnic, national and cultural groups and highlights the multiple dimensions that define social life (Healy, 2001).

International social workers have to strive towards being 'reflective practitioners' (Schon, 1983). They should be comfortable reflecting on their personal biases and be willing to resolve their own prejudices. They have to be equipped with cultural competence and techniques for combating racism (Healy, 2001).

Such competencies are grounded upon an awareness of the importance of culture in shaping people's beliefs and behaviour, and an appreciation of the unique problem-solving approaches embodied in various customs, history, and traditions. This ties in neatly with non-judgmentalism, one of the fundamental social work values: international social workers must strive to find meaning, refrain from passing judgment, listen to different voices, and monitor messages from the silent majority.

This mentality is also congruent with the professional principles of acceptance, humility, and respect for differences in other people's values and priorities. In fact, such culture-sensitive practice is also a rebuttal of the 'professional imperialism' (Midgley, 1981), which might originate from ethnocentrism, preconceptions, stereotypes, biases, or over-generalisations about particular ethnic groups, cultures, religions, or lifestyles.

Only by equipping ourselves with the above conceptual vocabulary and the corresponding cultural competence can we as social workers position ourselves in a rapidly changing world marked by complicated networks of interconnection. Here, social work education has an indispensable role to play in equipping students with the required tools. International exchanges by social work schools can enhance faculties' and students' ability to achieve this, warranting the promulgation of various types of international student exchanges. What follows is a brief review of the experience of the University of Hong Kong in promoting such international exchange for social work students.

International Student Exchanges: Experiences from Hong Kong University

The Social Work Department of the University of Hong Kong has more than 50 years of expertise in professional social work education. As the first social work training institute in Hong Kong, HKU has taken the lead in promoting international exchanges for its teaching staff and students. Since the late 1960s, the Department has promoted international exposure for its students by organising cultural exchanges and study tours to the Southeast Asian countries.

Cultural Exchange and Study Tours

The government's Social Welfare Department established the 'Social Work Training Fund' as a result of two reports by Dr. Eileen

Younghusband on social work education in Hong Kong in 1969 and 1971. This provided funding support for students to go on study tours.

In 1976, a group of MSW students went to visit rural development projects in the Philippines. Three of the male students visited a remote village on a hillside, where one mother asked her three daughters to stand in a line and invite the visitors to take any one of them back to Hong Kong with them: rural life was so hard that she would rather risk offering her daughters to strangers than continue the struggle for survival. The young men were flattered but shocked. They shared this story with many people after their return to Hong Kong and their awareness of the critical problem of poverty and its adverse impact on families was increased.

One of the authors, Cecilia, went to Thailand for a summer internship project as a social work student for ten weeks in the mid-1970s. She witnessed a stark gap between rich and poor people. During that time, political upheaval resulted in a military takeover in Bangkok in which many students were killed or arrested. Student activists were put into prison and the rest had to hide in the mountains.

Another study tour which she undertook to India, Nepal and Bangladesh, at that time, the poorest countries in the world, also revealed the prevalence of poverty and human suffering. In India, she saw malnourished children running around on the streets and sick people in the Home for the Dying Destitute run by Mother Teresa and her Catholic sisters; hundreds of people sat by the side of the pavement staring into emptiness, as they could find neither work nor food. She also witnessed the disparity of income and its effects: the rich people were strong and tall while the poor were feeble and short.

In another incident, walking into a village in Nepal, the villagers jumped into the river because they believed that foreigners were 'unclean'. Infant mortality was high. International organisations were not allowed to provide social services nor run schools, but they could run clinics and hospitals. Traffic had to stop if a cow happened to stand in the middle of the street, waiting there until it decided to move on. Little Goddesses were trained to be autistic human statues, sitting on a chair all day long to be worshipped by the people. All these incidents demonstrated to Cecelia the influence of cultural and religious knowledge in the lives of people in other parts of the world.

By witnessing poverty and desperation in other countries, Cecilia reflected upon her ignorance of the world's cultural, religious, economic, and political realities. By learning about other cultures and the problems faced by other countries, we can reflect on our own culture and appreciate strengths and virtues in Chinese culture and society of which we had not been aware. All these experiences illustrate the merits of international exposure for students.

In more recent years, the Department has continued to promote participation in overseas study tours for its students. For instance, in 2001, we succeeded in obtaining a private donation to subsidise five students' membership of an international student exchange programme – 'Social Work Education from an International Perspective', which was organised by the University of Lapland in Finland. The students had to prepare cultural performances and present details of Hong Kong's welfare system to the other participants. By working hard on this project, they gained a more in-depth understanding of Chinese culture and Hong Kong.

Social Service Projects in China

In an affluent city like Hong Kong, social work students are not generally aware of the realities of poverty, deprivation, and malnutrition. Going to China is a convenient and inexpensive way to give them exposure to this situation. The Chinese government refused international aid for a long time, until the great flood in 1991. Since then, individuals and organisations have raised funds to alleviate poverty and build schools in remote rural areas in China.

In 1994, the Social Work Society, a student body of the Department, started an ongoing buddy scheme with children in Tsingyun, a poor, mountainous area in Guangdong Province. They have raised funds in Hong Kong and visit the village schoolchildren every year, bringing with them stationery and books. The children enjoy the games and the chance to meet our students. The students are also empowered as they manage the whole project, raise money, and build a long-term relationship with the children in China.

Summer Block Placement in China

In 1985, the Department started its first collaboration with Zhongshan University in Guangzhou, China. Guangzhou was chosen because of its physical proximity to Hong Kong and also because the two cities share the same dialect, so there is no problem with communication. HKU teachers taught in Zhongshan University, whilst some of the students conducted their ten-week summer block placement in Guangzhou, contributing to the establishment of social service projects in local neighbourhoods and social services organisations.

Economic reforms in rural areas have been ongoing since the Open Door Policy was brought in by China in 1979. However, urban reforms were only just beginning to take place in 1985. Social services were delivered by the Communist Party, the Labour Union, the Women's Federation, and the Communist Youth League.

There were no trained social workers in these organisations, and our social work students took the role of expert advisers, helping them to set up new services in Guangzhou. An MSW student was placed in the research department of the Guangzhou Women's Federation in 1986. She trained the women cadres in how to conduct research and was subsequently appointed as advisor to the Federation, remaining there for ten years.

Moreover, our students have contributed to the establishment of innovative services in Guangzhou. One student helped the Communist Youth League to set up a youth counselling hotline, whilst another established a neighbourhood service centre for discharged mental patients. Some students were placed in non-governmental and church organisations, organising self-help groups for parents of children with mental disabilities.

As well as contributing to the formation of new service units and introducing professional social work concepts, while on placement, students also learnt a lot about the hitherto unfamiliar socio-political structure of the Chinese socialist government.

Their research contributed to our understanding of the socialist welfare system in Guangzhou. In fact, the Hong Kong schools of social work, led by HKU, have been recognised as providing consultation on curriculum development and research opportunities which have made important contributions to the development of Chinese social work education (Garber, 1997, p. 167). Apart from these specific examples, through these various experiences, not only did the Hong Kong students develop a better understanding of Chinese cultural and administrative systems, but they also established a stronger sense of Chinese identity.

However, there were also times when we were confronted with the reality of the extremely tight control on information and data rights in China during the 1980s. An MSW student, who had participated in Chinese university students' democratic movements during his undergraduate days in Hong Kong, was placed in a youth organisation in a factory in Guangzhou.

Suddenly, people stopped offering him information and support and effectively disassociated themselves from him. He found that the authority had discovered his pro-democracy record. When he began collecting information on employment security, he was actually summoned to the police station and warned. This illustrates the students' lack of training and political sensitivity when operating outside the Hong Kong system.

International Summer Block Placement

Starting in 1997, the Department embarked upon a trial overseas placement programme, reaching a bilateral exchange agreement with the Department of Social Work and Psychology of the National University of Singapore. A collaborative project was also established with the University of Sydney to arrange placements in Australia for social work students. Ever since then, the Department has gradually expanded this programme, extending its coverage to Canada, the United States, and Taiwan, and going from having two students in 1997 to sixteen in 2002.

The beneficiaries of this programme have included students enrolled in both Bachelor and Masters' courses. The Department subsidises the students' administrative expenses and has solicited the University's and the Alumni Association's support in offering them scholarships. Students can either formally register as 'exchange' or 'temporary' students in the host universities, or simply visit them as guests.

Accommodation takes a variety of forms, such as renting rooms in student hostels, living with local host families, or staying with friends or relatives. These provide different experiences for the students in terms of developing an understanding of people's way of life in the host countries. Placement agencies have either been identified by the corresponding social work departments, or have been referred by former Hong Kong social work colleagues who have migrated to the host nations.

Students are supervised either by university faculties or agency supervisors affiliated to relevant social service agencies. A wide variety of agencies offer these placements, ranging from those serving Chinese migrants, health centres, and youth service agencies, to provincial government welfare departments.

Students gain a lot of positive experiences from their overseas placements. In one particular example, an MSW student had the chance to work with a gay group in Vancouver, an experience she would never have had from a placement in Hong Kong. In her report, she recorded her critical self-reflection in terms of re-examining her own biases against gay and lesbian people, and her uneasiness with the social work principles of non-judgmentalism and unconditional acceptance.

In another case, a student was placed with a social services agency in Vancouver, and was assigned to work with Asian migrants. Through interviews with several clients from various Southeast Asian countries, she noticed differences in attitudes towards seeking help as well as in family and gender roles.

Two students working in the Vancouver Ministry of Children and Family were interviewed by a local radio to share their experiences of working in a foreign country. This really was a memorable experience for the students because they would not normally have had the chance to enjoy doing this in Hong Kong.

Two students were placed in a retirement community in Colorado Springs in the USA. In this example, the students raised their awareness of the problems faced by the ageing population in an affluent society. They also enjoyed many positive experiences of relating and working with seniors in a residential setting. One of their peers worked in another retirement settlement in Colorado Springs. She admitted having had some preconceptions about elders before taking up the placement, but ended up with good memories of living and working with those senior residents. Upon her return to Hong Kong, she shed tears when recounting these experiences.

Another student, placed in Singapore, had the chance to participate in a programme celebrating the national day of Singapore. She was thus directly exposed to the prevalence of national spirit amongst the Singaporeans, an idea which she had seldom, if ever, experienced in Hong Kong, given the lack of development of national sentiment in its colonial history. In addition, she had an extraordinary opportunity to be part of an international conference of the Asia-Pacific Association of Social Work Education (APASWE). This provided an eye-opening chance for her to experience a 'close encounter' with the international social work community.

In various other cases, students were briefed before they left Hong Kong to take the chance to share their views with overseas social work colleagues about Hong Kong's social policies and problems, and the influence of Chinese culture upon professional practice. In anticipation of such challenges, students prepared themselves by working together to read, browse the internet, and discuss the concepts amongst themselves. These helped them to have a solid grasp of the situation in Hong Kong and to critically appraise their understanding of their own cultural heritage.

All of these individual examples reveal the genuine merits of such international placement programmes in facilitating personal growth and professional development for individual social work students.

Overseas Students' Exposure Programme in Hong Kong

As well as themselves visiting other countries and cities, our students can learn more about Hong Kong through receiving visitors from abroad. Study tours and exposure programmes for students from US universities take place in our Department, each lasting for one to two weeks. As we teach in English, the American students can sit in our classes, attend seminars, visit agencies, and also go into China. Students from our Department participate in discussions and sharing sessions with the visitors.

In order to convey the basics about life in Hong Kong to our visitors and our own students have to equip themselves with information about their own societies. Through responding to questions, they become more aware of cultural differences and give more thoughts to ideas and practices that are generally taken-for-granted.

There are now several universities, like the National University of Singapore and University of Queensland, which regularly send visitors to our Department. Hong Kong is a geographically convenient Asian city which can provide easy access to many other major Asian cultures. The visiting students can also take short trips into China. As the Department has developed strong links with universities and social service organisations in China, some overseas students actually carry out their placement in Chinese cities. Again, this illustrates the importance of Hong Kong's strategic position in promoting multilateral exchanges.

Web-based Course on Comparative Social Policy

Using our academic staff's rich international network in social work, a web-based course on comparative social policy has been launched in collaboration with three universities in Japan, Austria, and Hong Kong. Students of the respective universities communicate via the internet to share their understanding of and views on their nations' social policies. This is a good example of the usefulness of technology in enhancing international exchanges by overcoming physical barriers.

Factors Conducive to Promoting International Student Exchanges

Given the pervasiveness of globalisation, universities have come to be aware of the need to respond by incorporating an international perspective into their strategic developmental plans. This paves the way for a more concerted effort towards promoting international exchange for students, helped by contextual factors conducive to supporting the concept in general, as well as those pertinent to social work in particular.

First amongst these factors is the economic development of host countries. For example, China has demonstrated the impact of a gathering economic momentum which has enabled its people to enjoy tourist visits abroad and its university students to undertake studies overseas.

Secondly, a necessary, if not sufficient, condition for exchange is that the city or even the entire country can adopt a cosmopolitan outlook or, better still, a modern infrastructure in terms of telecommunications, international transportation networks, laws, and policy mechanisms. There should also be promotion of teaching and learning of foreign languages, so as to enable understanding and appreciation of foreign cultures. This infrastructure can enable efficient flows of personnel, information, and materials, as well as ensuring protection for individuals through mechanisms such as the provision of visa approval for students and teachers.

Ideally, in this connection, inter-governmental liaison and bilateral agreements should be reached, so as to arrive at a mutual understanding in facilitating student exchange. In our experience at HKU, it has sometimes been necessary to convince the host country that our placement students will not adversely affect the local employment conditions. In some instances, formal approval or 'exemption of employment authorisation' has had to be obtained before the students can be officially allowed to commence their placements in social service agencies.

Thirdly, there needs to be government support for higher education institutes in promoting international exchange programmes. Funding bodies should recognise such programmes as part and parcel of university education and provide earmarked grants to enable universities to support them. The establishment of scholarships may also help students, especially those from disadvantaged sectors, to enroll in international programmes.

HKU has joined the *Universitas 21* along with 16 other universities from the Asia-Pacific region and elsewhere. As a result, HKU has set up a special fund and designated a special administrative section to support faculties, departments, and students through inter-university collaboration and student exchanges.

Indeed, increasing levels of international funds are becoming available for academic staff to serve as 'visiting scholars' in overseas universities for a specific period of time. This gives teachers a chance to assimilate the latest knowledge and practices of foreign countries and bring their insights back home, serving as a type of 'innovation diffusion' to stimulate transformations or adaptations of practices. Closely connected to this trend are the various models of distance education which may be used to enhance international learning. In particular, web-based courses have expanded the options in distance education and international exchanges could benefit from these (Healy, 2001).

This leads to the fourth factor, namely the availability of information technology (IT) by which to facilitate information transfer and assimilation. In this regard, the promulgation of computer technology, both 'hard' and 'soft'-ware, is a necessary precondition. This is affected by the problem of the 'digital divide', which requires sufficient resources to be deployed so as to enable equal access to IT facilities by students from various socio-economic and ethnic backgrounds. With such access, students can easily obtain relevant information on overseas universities and various programmes to plan their further studies.

Looking specifically at promoting international social work education, there are organisations, such as the International Association of School of Social Work (IASSW), the International Federation of Social Workers (IFSW), and others, which promote international exchanges amongst social work academics and practitioners. Through international conferences, workshops, seminars, and the like, experiences can be shared, knowledge can be disseminated, and collaborative efforts promoted. There is also an increasing number of colleges and universities identifying globalisation as part of their mission statements, meaning that the internationalisation of social work is now a strategy that can enhance the credibility of the profession within the larger academy (Healy, 2001).

Limitations and Lessons to be Learned

Although there are many factors which are favourable to international exchanges in general and international social work education in particular, there are also various obstacles. Again, these can relate to general conditions at the country or society level, or to higher education and social work education in particular.

International collaboration and exchanges have to be grounded on positive relationships between countries, governments, and participating organisations. However, the various polarisations, such as the north-south divide, developed versus developing countries, and ideological antagonism, can also give rise to constraints in cultivating international exchanges. The prevalence of parochialism and ethnocentric dispositions amongst people and even institutions may also cause concern.

The 'clash of civilisations' (Huntington, 1996) may have an impact upon participants engaging in such international exchanges, causing them to experience a range of negative effects from misunderstandings, disharmony, discontent, and suspicion, to hatred and even overt conflict.

On a more practical level, students from less developed countries may find it difficult to meet their expenses in a country with a much higher standard of living. At the university level, there can be problems related to the lack of a viable mechanism of credit transfer amongst participating institutions. Without the assurance of continuity in their studies, taking part in international exchange programmes may lead to students having to incur extra costs in time and money.

Avoiding this would require an accreditation system or mechanism involving the authorities of both higher education institutes and professional associations in various countries, the co-ordination of which is a formidable challenge. In fact, there is a host of obstacles, as an international survey of higher education in the 1980s revealed; lack of a full curriculum, lack of financial resources, a view that the work is not relevant to graduates' jobs, rigid curriculum requirements, a faculty which is unprepared to teach international content, lack of curriculum materials, and lack of institutional legitimacy for such ventures (Healy, 2001, p. 249).

As well as these problems, there are other conditions that are essential to success; goal interdependence (the identification of common interests and a mutual resource exchange whereupon each partner contributes resources valued by the other), frequent contact and communication between partners, positive attitudes and behaviours from the personnel involved, high levels of interpersonal trust and open-mindedness, a willingness to take risks and try new approaches, and sensitivity to organisational and cultural differences (Healy, 2001). This is a demanding 'checklist' of requirements for participating institutions.

In terms of social work education specifically, an issue arises from the fact that social work is defined differently in different countries. Educational standards and content, therefore, vary and because the functions of social workers are different, the tasks which students are expected to be able to do at one institution may not always fit perfectly with those which the partner university requires (Healy, 2001).

In our own experience of placements at HKU, for example, our Bachelor degree students are not allowed to do clinical practicum in North American social service agencies, since such work is normally restricted to students at Master's level. However, in Hong Kong, holders of a Bachelor of Social Work degree can register and practice in various settings, ranging from clinical to community-based services.

Students also require sufficient preparation, emotionally as well as in terms of values, knowledge, and skills. They should be inspired by the post-modern concept of tolerating difference, rather than holding on to a preconceived, dominant paradigm, and be able to develop the humility to respect and appreciate others and accept their own limitations and weaknesses.

However, in an increasingly uncertain and insecure world, students, just like older adults, may be influenced by pragmatic or even opportunistic concerns, looking for short-term benefits and immediate returns in their academic and career pursuits. They may prefer to avoid undertaking international programs or courses that demand a substantial contribution of time and money, the results of which may not yield immediate or tangible career returns.

Conclusion

'The World is Getting Smaller' was the name of a folk song in the 1970s. It still holds true today and vividly exemplifies the increasing challenge of globalisation. Humankind is living on 'mother Earth' or in the 'global village'. People around the world, irrespective of their ethnicity, economic condition, religion, and so on, have to face the same problems: problems which may have originated in a particular part of the world, but which now have an impact everywhere.

As a result, we all have to shoulder the responsibility of coming together to tackle those problems with joint efforts. Social workers, as constituent members of this world community, cannot evade this responsibility of global citizenship. And, as Healy (2001) asserts, the values of world-mindedness and global social work competence must evolve so as to position the profession for the task of assuming its responsibilities in this global era.

Although social work practice is basically culture-bound and grounded upon the local, indigenous context, there is still merit in attempting to enhance practice through international or cross-cultural perspectives. This means that there is a need to promote international exchanges by social work practitioners and also by students preparing themselves to enter such practice.

As postulated by Lyons (1999), international exchanges have been a source of practical and/or moral support to educators and practitioners, validating their efforts and providing a renewed energy and direction to educational programmes. Such exchanges provide new challenges and are an essential response to the realities of global politics and economics (Lyons, 1999). In another respect, too, international exchanges offer a potentially important way to energise social work's response to global realities.

These exchange programmes can provide experiential learning and expand the community of social workers who recognise their international commitment (Hokenstad and Midgley, 1997). They can help students develop an appreciation of global problems and trends, and of comparative perspectives on social work, contributing to a refocusing of the core values of social work which reiterates its concerns with human rights and social justice. Exchanges can also enhance the development of theoretical frameworks for analysis and action at macro- as well as mezzo- and micro- levels (Lyons, 1999).

Taking account of the vital importance of international exchanges in promoting international social work, the priorities for the immediate future should be the promotion of increased opportunities for exchanges, the strengthening of international associations, and the establishment of institutional affiliations (Hokenstad and Midgley, 1997). It will also be important to institutionalise the international programme and curriculum within universities (Healy, 2001) and between collaborators.

The Department of Social Work and Social Administration of the University of Hong Kong has attempted to explore various mechanisms for promoting international exchange for its students at both Bachelor and Master's levels. The Department and its students and staff have achieved some success and learned some important lessons as a result of these activities.

Strategically placed as the 'door to China' and a place where 'east meets west', Hong Kong rightly occupies a pivotal position in facilitating such international exchanges. This is particularly important in relation to China, whose social work education has yet to be developed, and other parts of the world where the profession is in its infancy. Having a history to draw upon in developing exchanges with other partners is an invaluable asset. It enables those of us at the University of Hong Kong to use the lessons that we have learnt elsewhere wisely.

24 Conclusions
LENA DOMINELLI and WANDA THOMAS BERNARD

Sending students on overseas placements broadens their horizons and causes them to reflect upon the taken-for-granted assumptions that carry them through daily practice at home. This book has highlighted the importance of preparing adequately for international exchanges, securing clear and non-exploitative agreements among participating partners, and monitoring progress regularly. Many different things can go badly. But they can also go well. Appropriate preparation assists greatly in securing desirable outcomes to the exchange.

The experiences of those writing in this book has indicated that only the effective management of difficulties, good-will, a commitment to partnership and a shared value system have enabled participants within international exchange schemes to stay on the positive side of what often appears as a thin line between standing on firm ground and falling into chaos. Success becomes part of a cycle that spawns further gains and increases the worth of becoming involved in promoting international social work despite participants finding that they have to engage in such work on top of their usual workloads.

Valuing the Experience

Outcomes

Each chapter in the book has elucidated those elements of achievement that those engaged in a particular experience have perceived to be important in retelling their stories to others. These contributions have not written according to a standard pro-forma to ensure that each author's voice remains unique. Yet, despite this, a number of common themes recur in different accounts.

As explicated in this book, an important component in the story of the success of the *European Union–Canada Project* is grounded in the contribution it made to the individual growth and professional development of those taking part. These positives were also echoed in the contributions emanating from other projects. Like the others, these have also emphasised shifts in ways of knowing and doing which have provided new ontological outlooks through which previous, present and future practice might be evaluated. Additionally, for those in the European Union–Canada Project, their capacity to realise the Project's goals have produced a number of outcomes that went well beyond those initially anticipated by the participants. These have included:

- Exchanges that involved
  - faculty/academic staff
  - practitioners
  - students on assessed placements
- A Project Website
- Five conferences
- One International Child Welfare (Web-based) Course, entitled *Child Welfare across Borders*
- Three books
  - *Community Approaches to Child Welfare* (edited by Lena Dominelli)
  - *Valuing the Field* (edited by Marilyn Callahan, Sven Hessle and Susan Strega)
  - *Broadening Horizons: International Student Exchanges in Social Work* (edited by Lena Dominelli and Wanda Thomas Bernard)

Similar outputs have resulted in the other projects that are described in this volume.

That the European Union–Canada Project succeeded beyond expectations impacted on participants' views of it. The majority verdict was that the experience of studying overseas was a worthwhile opportunity and one that those participating in it wished to see extended to others in the future. Their aspirations included setting up practitioner exchanges to enhance practice on the ground. Below, we consider the key benefits that participants brought to our notice.

Value to Students

The students identified the value of the Project to them as a significant life event that changed their ways of thinking about themselves, appreciating difference and understanding the work they did in practice. They describe these as itemised below. Having been on the Project, they claim that they were able to:

- learn about other cultures;
- reflect reflexively on their own culture;
- learn another language (some students);
- develop new friendships;
- acquire new knowledge and skills, not only with regards to professional social work, but also with respect of their own personal growth;
- understand themselves and others better; and
- reconsider their options regarding their area of professional practice.

Value to Practice Teachers/Field Supervisors

Practice teachers involved in the Project were very enthusiastic about its continuation and felt that their involvement in the Project was extremely useful in encouraging them to rethink their own approaches to practice and innovate. As a result, their practice benefited. Additionally, those who travelled overseas with the Project were able to learn about practice in other countries directly. They did so by visiting other agencies working in the child welfare arena. The benefits they focused upon included their being able to:

- reflect on their own practice, both with students and clients
- learn new knowledge and skills, not only with regards to child welfare practice, but about other peoples' cultures and the different legislation that was used to address issues similar to those they faced

- feel valued more by their home institution and
- organise placements (the practicum) more effectively because they were required to respond more closely to individual student needs than was often the case with home students where the colleges often dominated their teaching programme.

Other practitioners in the offices where international students were based also acquired an enthusiasm for the exchanges and felt the benefits of being included in the Project. Many of them became involved in discussions about practice and reconsidered the taken-for-granted routines that would have remained unquestioned but for the presence of the exchange students. Moreover, their attendance at student seminars and Project conference proceedings enabled them to engage in lively deliberations about child welfare practice with other practitioners, students, educators and experts in the field.

Value to Academics/Faculty

Academic staff were able to benefit from having such a Project located within their respective department both directly and indirectly. The Project was discussed at staff meetings and required the involvement of more than the people mentioned on the application form. As a number of colleagues from other countries would visit the participating departments, this allowed for exchanges of curricula and experiences, which would not have occurred otherwise.

Additionally, since these meetings often involved teachers who did not work in the child welfare arena. This meant that broader discussions about social work teaching and training could occur. Of course, all these interactions consumed time, which academics in busy departments never seem to have enough of. Although the demands that the Project made on staff time were not adequately foreseen, people gave it willingly and found themselves learning considerably more than they had anticipated from the experience. At the same time, they found that much of what they learned could be used in their own country.

However, staff continued to experience the tensions between giving time to the Project and getting on with the rest of the many demands placed upon them. As might be expected, these were never completely resolved and proved to be more problematic for some universities than others, depending on the range of other commitments, the support available for international exchange activities, and personal commitments of different levels of staff to this kind of work.

Additionally, staff not directly associated with the Project invariably became involved in its diverse activities. Some of these may have never been involved in teaching social work students, yet they found themselves being called upon to support their learning whether or not these students were part of a cohort who was actually registered with (i.e., paid fees to) their employing institution. Administrators, accountants, secretaries and others contributed to its work to varying degrees, whether or not they had explicitly committed themselves to the Project, thereby providing another source of tensions which surfaced at times.

The academic staff identified the following features as being of high value to them:

- the opportunity to reflect on their own curriculum including both the academic and the practice (field) elements;
- becoming aware of alternative ways of teaching and learning;
- appreciating collaborative opportunities;
- developing new networks;
- acknowledging the wide range of skills that students brought to bear on their experience overseas; and
- learning how to negotiate with funders.

The issues and concerns raised by the participants in the European Union–Canada Project that we have identified above were also evident in the chapters written by the authors who wrote about the other projects considered in this manuscript. And although, the struggles for national liberation in industrialising countries featured prominently in some of these offerings, their stories reflected many similar concerns to those voiced by those conducting exchanges amongst countries in the industrialised West.

These include the desire to tackle oppression and promote the development of autonomous human beings in an interdependent and non-exploitative world. Helping people acquire the capacity to bridge such gaps is one of the strengths of international social work.

Reflecting upon the European Union-Canada Project

The European Union-Canada Project was viewed by all those that participated in it as extremely worthwhile. As a result, they were saddened by the lack of continuation funding following its completion, despite their endeavours to secure additional monies for this purpose.

The shortage of funding opportunities to support future work within the overall European Union-Canada Exchange Programme was seen as a major deficiency of the European Union-Canada Programme for Co-operation in Higher Education and Training by all participants in the Project. Whilst the Project participants recognised the funders' dilemma of extending their limited resources to as many different partnerships as possible, in reality, it meant that follow-on activities were severely curtailed.

From talking to others working on projects within the overall Programme, and others involved in other international exchanges, we discovered that this fate is a common one. Few projects have been able to obtain continuation funding for the whole of the original network or consortium. Sadly, without such funding, it has proved extremely difficult for participating partners to finance further major programmes of student exchanges, whatever goodwill and commitment, they have had towards that objective.

The lack of funding for student mobility is the greatest casualty of the failure to fund the continuation of future exchanges. Although a few students might be able to take advantage of the existing infrastructure of support by financing their own placement overseas, the majority of students will be unable to do this and so will be deprived of the opportunity to study abroad. Thus, we do not expect large numbers of students to require overseas placements, although we know from feedback from cohorts of students enrolling on our courses after the European Union–Canada Project had terminated, that a number of them would have liked the opportunity to have gone on an international exchange.

Nonetheless, a few students have succeeded in procuring funding that has enabled them to pursue overseas studies without Project funding. However, these have relied more on bilateral agreements between institutions rather than upon the network as a whole, although these opportunities would not have existed if it were not for the network's facilitation of their creation in the first instance.

Future Developments

The amount of grant provided to the Project from its official funders, the European Union and the Canadian government, reflected about one-third of its actual costs. However, this represented the crucial amount that made it possible for the Project to exist and for the student exchanges to take place. The scarcity of funding for international student exchanges raises the issue of how a key dimension of the work of this particular Project and others like it might be continued in the future. The range of possibilities is mixed. Some activities will continue on an ad hoc basis, although the Project as a whole will not.

The future of the Project is more assured in terms of the dissemination of the experience, particularly through its publications which include three books. Other outputs such as the Project website, the web-based international course, *Child Welfare across Borders*, will contribute to this endeavour for a period for money is necessary to continue developing and upgrading these initiatives. Nonetheless, the computer and web-based technologies have allowed the Project to reach other audiences further afield and thereby engage with students, practitioners and academics not directly involved in its work.

Connecting with others external to the Project was an explicit aim of the international child welfare course. Additionally, it was hoped that it would act as a medium whereby people located in their own countries could begin to think about practice in other countries and engage in dialogue that would serve to enhance social work practice with children in a number of different geographical areas.

Moreover, the Project has resulted in several research projects, some of which have been externally funded. These will enable some of the academic staff of the partner institutions to continue working together. Several partners have also entered into bilateral agreements to continue working together and find in this a rich source of future collaborative activities.

Conclusions

Many of the insights gained during the European Union-Canada Project are evident in the writings of the authors who have rooted their experiences in other countries. Despite differences in geography, culture, traditions, language, social, political and economic systems, the commonalities encountered are remarkable. Part of these common elements can be attributed to social work educators' and practitioners' commitment to social work values that include social justice, their willingness to struggle to ensure peoples' well-being, and the desire to reflect these ideals in their practice with students.

In closing, we would like to identify the following items as those that need particular attention in any international exchange programme. We do not prioritise them in any particular order, but we think they all need considerable thought. Moreover, the partners involved in the exchange have to reach specific agreement on how to deal with the issues that emanate from them. They are:

- Egalitarian values and vision
- Common principles and agreed procedures
- Collaboration with partners on a mutually beneficial basis
- Structures of and for collaboration
- Promote clients as citizens
- Engaging the team as a whole
  - practitioners
  - academics
  - students
  - administrators
- Curricula development and innovation
  - practice
  - academic

- Assessment structures and agreement to achieve equivalence without homogenisation
- Preparation of students
- Support of students
  - home
  - overseas
- Communication
  - home
  - overseas
- Funding
  - short-term
  - long-term
- Other practicalities
  - immigration and visa requirements
  - travel arrangements
  - accommodation
  - travel insurance
  - health insurance

Other than preparing for these practicalities and any contingencies that might arise, those organising the exchange need people who get on well with each other, and a dose of good luck. Having fortune on your side is useful, for example, in having steady exchange rates and financial markets that do not suddenly eat away a major portion of your purchasing power. Fluctuating exchange rates consumed a considerable proportion of the funding of the European Union–Canada Project and exacerbated the inadequate funding that was an integral aspect of this international exchange.

International social work holds the promise of enabling social work educators, practitioners and students to work across various social and geographic divides to promote human well-being and create a more egalitarian and sustainable future. Realising its potential is challenging and fraught with a range of physical, social, political and economic obstacles. These barriers become more complex and intractable as the forces of globalisation impact upon the welfare policies that are promoted by the nation-state. However, with goodwill, commitment, collective organisation and lots of hard work, most of the obstacles that appear at the micro-level can be overcome. Eliminating structural barriers will require collective action and will take longer to bring about. However, international social work has a significant role to play in creating a world geared to meeting human needs.

Bibliography

Adams, A. and Shardlow, S. (eds) (2000) *Fundamentals of Social Work in Selected European Countries*. Lyme Regis: Russell House Publishing.

Adams, A., Erath, P. and Shardlow, S. (eds) (2001) *Key Themes in European Social Work*. Lyme Regis: Russell House Publishing.

Addams, J. (2002) *Twenty Years at Hull House*. New York: Signet Books.

Alexander, N. (1989). 'Liberation Pedagogy in the South African Context', in Critocos, C. (ed.) *Experiential Learning in Formal and Non-formal Education*. Durban: Media Resource Centre: Department of Education: UND.

Alinsky, S. (1972). *Rules for Radicals*. New York: Vintage Books.

Alperson, M. (1997) *The International Adoption Handbook: How to Make an Overseas Adoption Work*. New York: Henry Holt.

Aronson, J. et al. (1998) *Ieder Vluchtelingenkind is een Misbruikt Kind*. Research Proposal, Hogeschool West Brabant, Breda, the Netherlands.

Avison, D. and Wood-Harper, A.T. (1990) *Multivie: An Exploration in Information Systems Development*. Henley on-Thames: Alfred Waller.

Barker, R. (1995) *The Social Work Dictionary*. Washington, D.C.: NASW.

Barlow, C. and Whittaker, W. (2002) *An India-Canada Field Education Partnership: Opportunities and Challenges*. Paper presented at the Congress of the International Association of Schools of Social Work, Montpellier, France, July.

Barlow, C., Whittaker, W. and Sammon, S. (2002) *India-Canada Field Education Partnership: Opportunities and Challenges*. Paper presented at the International Association of Schools of Social Work Congress, Montpellier, France, July.

Belsky, J. and Vondra, J. (1993) 'Lessons from Child Abuse: The Determinants of Parenting', in Gibbons, J. (ed.) *The Children Act, 1989 and Family Support: Principles into Practice*. London: HMSO.

Bisman, C.D., Hardcastle, D.A., and Cree, V.E. (2000) *Social Work Education and Training in a Global Economy*. Paper presented at the IFSW/IASSW World Congress, Montreal.

Blumenthal, P. (1995) *Academic Mobility in a Changing World: Regional and Global Trends*. London: Jessica Kingsley.

Bolea, P.S., McFall, J., Schott, E. and Freddolino, P. (1999) *International Field Placements: Creating Global Opportunities*. Paper presented at Annual

Program Meeting of the Council on Social Work Education, San Francisco, CA.

Brauns, H.J. and Kramer, D. (1988) *Social Work Education in Europe: A Comprehensive Description of Social Work Education in 21 European Countries.* Frankfurt: Deutsche Verein für Öffentliche und Privat Fürsorge.

Brindle, D. (2000) 'Care Less', *The Guardian*, 27 January.

Brown, A. and Bourne, I. (1976) *The Social Work Supervisor.* Buckingham: Open University Press.

Brown, M.J. (1997) 'Preparing Social Work Students for a Corrupt Work Environment', *Maatskaplike Werk/Social Work*, 35(3), pp. 282-284.

Burr, V. (1995) *An Introduction to Social Constructionism.* London: Routledge.

Callahan, M. and Dominelli, L. (1996) *International Exchanges in Social Work.* Presentation to the European Union – Canada Exchange Programme Application.

Callahan, M. (1993a) 'The Administrative and Practice Context: Perspectives from the Front Line', in Wharf, B. (ed.) *Rethinking Child Welfare in Canada.* Toronto: McClelland and Stewart Inc.

Callahan, M. (1993b) 'Feminist Approaches: Women Recreate Child Welfare', in Wharf, B. (ed.) *Rethinking Child Welfare in Canada.* Toronto: McClelland and Stewart Inc.

Callahan, M., Hessle, S. and Strega, S. (eds) (2000) *Valuing the Field: Child Welfare in an International Context.* Aldershot: Ashgate.

Canadian Association of Social Workers (1994) *Social Work Code of Ethics.* Ottawa: CASW.

Cannan, C. (1996) 'The Impact of Social Development and Anti-Exclusion Policies on the French Social Work Professions', *Social Work in Europe*, No. 3, 2, pp. 1-4.

Care of Abusers (Special Provisions) Act/LVM (1998) Ministry of Health and Social Affairs. Sweden. Stockholm: Cabinet Printing Works.

Care of Young Persons (Special Provisions) Act/LVU (1998) Ministry of Health and Social Affairs. Sweden. Stockholm: Cabinet Printing Works.

Carter, D. (1997) 'Digital Democracy or Information Aristocracy', in Loader, B. (ed.) *The Government of Cyberspace.* London: Routledge.

CCETSW (1995a) *Assuring Quality in Social Work Education, Training and Assessment: a Framework for Approval, Review and Inspection.* London: CCETSW.

CCETSW (1995b) *Assuring Quality for Practice Teaching, Rules and Requirements and Guidance on Evidence Indicators for the Practice Teaching Award.* London: CCETSW.

Chetty, D. (1999) 'Social Work in South Africa: Historical Antecedents and Current Challenges', *European Journal of Social Work*, 2(1), pp. 67-76.

Children and Family Services Act (1997) Province of Nova Scotia. Halifax: Queen's Printer.

Clarke, J. and Newman, J. (1997) *The Managerial State*. London: Sage.

Clarkson, E.M.R. (1990) 'Teaching Overseas Students in Great Britain', in *International Social Work*, 33, pp. 353-364.

Coetzee, J.K. (2001) 'A Micro Foundation for Development Thinking', in Coetzee, J.K. et al. (eds) *Development: Theory, Policy and Practice*. Cape Town: Oxford University Press.

Conversations, seminars and/or information sessions with Mia Garphult and others, Framnäs School and Therapy Centre; Eva Holmsberg-Herrström, Stockholm University; Tommy, Supervisor, Kista Child Protection Unit; Thomas Goldberg, Akademiker SSR Förbundet; Bengt Forssman, Maria Ungdom.

Cutler, T. and Waine, B. (1994) *Managing the Welfare State: The Politics of Public Sector Management*. Oxford: Berg.

Davidson, A. (1977) *Antonio Gramsci: Towards an Intellectual Biography*. London: Merlin Press.

Davies, T. (1998) *Open Doors: International Exchanges of Students*. New York: Basic Books.

Deacon, B., Hulse, M. and Stubbs, P. (1997) *Global Social Policy: International Organisations and the Future of Welfare*. London: Sage.

DeJong, P. and Miller, S.D. (1995) 'How to Interview for Client Strengths', in *Social Work*, 40(6), November.

Department of Health (2001) 'General Social Care Council Implementation', London: Department of Health.

Department of Welfare and Population Development (1998) *White Paper on Population Policy*. Pretoria: Government Printers.

Detroit News, 1 September 1997.

Dominelli, L. (1989) 'Betrayal of Trust: A Feminist Analysis of Power Relationships in Incest Abuse and its Relevance for Social Work Practice', in *British Journal of Social Work*, No. 19, pp. 291-307.

Dominelli, L. (1992) *Opportunities or Opportunism? Recent International Developments in Europe*. Paper presented at the IASSW-IFSW Joint World Congress in Washington, D.C., July.

Dominelli, L. (1996) 'Deprofessionalising Social Work: Anti-Oppressive Practice, Competencies and Postmodernism, *British Journal of Social Work*, 26, pp. 153-175.

Dominelli, L. (1996a) 'The Future of Social Work Education: Beyond the State of the Art', *Scandavanian Journal of Social Welfare*, 5, pp. 194-201.

Dominelli, L. (1996b) 'Opportunities or Opportunism', in Healy, L (ed.) *Challenges*. Proceedings from the IASSW 1992 Congress in Washington, D.C.

Dominelli, L. (1997) *Anti-Racist Social Work*. London: BASW/McMillan. Second Edition.

Dominelli, L. (1998) *Anti-Racism, Culturally Competent Social Work and Internationalism*. Paper presented at the CSWE International Commission Conference on Anti-Racism, Ann Arbor, Michigan, December.

Dominelli, L. (1998) 'Globalisation and Gender Relations in Social Work' in Lesnick, B. (ed.) *Countering Discrimination in Social Work*. Aldershot: Ashgate.

Dominelli, L (ed.) (1999) *Community Approaches to Child Welfare: International Perspectives*. Aldershot: Ashgate.

Dominelli, L. (2000) 'International Comparisons in Social Work', in Pierce, R. and Weinstein, J. (eds) *Innovative Education and Training for Care Professionals*. London: Jessica Kingsley Publishing.

Dominelli, L. (2001) 'Globalisation: A Myth or Reality for Social Workers' translated as 'Globalizacija: mit ili stvarnost za socijalne radnike?', in *Revija za Socijalnu Politiku*, 3-4, 2001, pp. 259-266.

Dominelli, L. (2002) *Anti-Oppressive Social Work Theory and Practice*. New York: Palgrave.

Dominelli, L. (2002a) *Feminist Social Work Theory and Practice*. New York: Palgrave.

Dominelli, L. (ed.) (1999) *Community Approaches to Child Welfare*. Aldershot: Ashgate.

Dominelli, L. (forthcoming) *Social Work: Practice for a Changing Profession*. Cambridge: Polity Press.

Dominelli, L. and Hoogvelt, A. (1996) 'Globalisation, Contract Government and the Taylorisation of Intellectual Labour', in *Studies in Political Economy*, 49, pp. 71-100.

Dominelli, L. and Hoogvelt, A. (1996a) 'Globalisation and the Technocratisation of Social Work', in *Critical Social Policy*, 16(2), pp. 45-62.

Drower, S. (1999) 'Directions form the East? Reflections on a Visit to Asian Social Work Training Institutions', in *Maatskaplike Werk/Social Work*, 35(3), pp. 237-249.

Dubois, M. and Ntetu, A. (2000) 'Learning Cultural Adaptation through International Social Work Training', *Canadian Social Work*, 2(2).

During, S. (1995) 'Postmodernism or Postcolonialism Today', in Ashcroft, B., Griffiths, G. and Tiffen, H. (eds) *The Post Colonial Studies Reader*. London: Routledge.

Dustin, D. (2000) 'Managers and Professionals: Another Perspective on Partnership', *Managing Community Care*, 8(5), pp. 14-20,

Erath, P. and Hamalainen, J. (2001) 'Theory in Social Work', in Adams, A., Erath, P. and Shardlow, S. (eds) *Key Themes in European Social Work*, Lyme Regis: Russell House Publishing.

Erath, P., Hamalainen J. and Singh, H. (2001) 'Comparing Social Work from a European Perspective: Towards a Comparative Science of Social Work', in Adams, A., Erath, P. and Shardlow, S. (eds) *Key Themes in European Social Work*. Lyme Regis: Russell House Publishing.

Esping Andersen, G. (1999) *Social Foundations of Post-industrial Economies*. Oxford: Oxford University Press.

Estes, R. (1999) 'Information Tools for Social Workers: Research in the Global Age', in. C.S. Ramanathan and R.J. Link (eds) *All Our Futures: Principles and Resources for Social Work Practice in a Global Era*. Toronto: Brooks/Coles.

Family Violence Unit (1999) *The Family Violence Prevention Initiative*. Halifax: Family Violence Unit.

Fanon, F. (1970) *The Wretched of the Earth*. Harmondsworth: Penguin Books.

Fook, J., Ryan, M. and Hawkins, L. (2000) *Professional Expertise – Practice, Theory and Education for Working in Uncertainty*. London: Whiting and Birch, Ltd.

Freeman, M. (ed) (1996) *Children's Rights*. Dartmouth: Dartmouth Publishing Co.

Freire, P. (1970) *The Pedagogy of the Oppressed*. Harmondsworth: Penguin Books.

Freire, P. (1972) *Cultural Action for Freedom*. Harmondsworth: Penguin Books.

Freire, P. (1973) *Education for Critical Consciousness*. New York: The Seabury Press.

Galper, J. (1975) *The Politics of Social Services*. New Jersey: Prentice-Hall.

Garber, R. (1997) 'Social Work Education in an International Context', in Hokenstad, M.C. and Midgley, J. (eds) *Issues in International Social Work: Global Challenges for a New Century*. Washington, D.C.: NASW Press.

Garber, R. (2000) *The World Census of Social Work Education*. Toronto: IASSW. Also available from the IASSW website at <http://www.iassw.soton.ac.uk>.

Gastavsson, N. and Segal, E. (1994) *Critical Issues in Child Welfare*. London: Sage.

Giddons, H. (1993) *The Children Act 1989 and Family Support: Principles into Practice.* London: HMSO.

Gilbert, N. (1997) *Combatting Child Abuse: International Perspectives and Trends.* Oxford: Oxford University Press.

Gilroy, J. (1999) 'Critical Issues in Child Welfare: Perspectives from the Field', in Dominelli, L. (ed.) *Community Approaches to Child Welfare.* Aldershot: Ashgate.

Gilroy, J. (2000) 'The Changing Face of Child Welfare: Perspectives from the Field', in Callahan, M., Hessle, S. and Strega, S. (eds) *Valuing the Field.* Aldershot: CEDR/Ashgate.

Giroux, H.A. (1983) *Theory and Resistance in Education: A Pedagogy for the Opposition.* London: Heinemann Educational Books.

Giroux, H.A. (1994) 'Living Dangerously: Identity Politics and the New Cultural Racism', in Giroux, H.A. and McLaren, P. (eds) *Between Borders: Pedagogy and the Politics of Cultural Studies.* New York: Routledge.

Giroux, H.A. (1997) *Pedagogy and the Politics of Hope: Theory, Culture and Schooling.* Colorado: Westview Press.

Gjelten, T. (2001) *NATO: Becoming a Rusty Relic.* Great Decisions Seminar Series. Unpublished paper presentation. Ford Museum, Grand Rapids: Michigan.

Glastonbury, B. and La Mendola, W. (1992) *The Integrity of Intelligence.* Basingstoke: Macmillan.

Gould, N. and Harris, A. (1996) 'Student Imagery of Practice in Social Work and Teacher Education: A Comparative Research Approach', in *British Journal of Social Work*, 26, pp. 223-237.

Gramsci, A. (1971) *Selections from the Prison Notebooks*, edited and translated by Hoare, A. and Smith, G.N., London: Lawrence and Wishart.

Gramsci, A. (1977) *Selections from Political Writings 1910-1920.* London: Lawrence and Wishart.

Gramsci, A. (1988) *Gramsci's Prison Letters*, translated by Henderson, H. Edinburgh: Zwan Publications.

Griffiths, R. (Sir Roy) (1988) *Community Care: Agenda for Action (The Griffiths Report).* London: HMSO.

Guevara, J.A. and Ylvisaker, R. (2002) 'Two Models for International Collaboration to Create Service Learning Opportunities', in Asomoah, Y., Healy, L.M. and Hokenstad, M.C. (eds) *Models of international Collaboration in Social Work Education.* Washington: NASW Press.

Hallet, W. (1995) 'Child Abuse: An Academic Overview', in Kingston, P. and Penhale, B. (eds) *Family Violence and the Caring Professions.* London: Macmillan.

Hantrais, L. and Letablier, M. (1996) *Families and Family Policies in Europe.* London: Addison Wesley and Longman.

Harris, K. (1991) 'Teenage Mothers and Welfare Dependency: Working Off Welfare', in *Journal of Family Issues*, No. 4(12), pp. 492-518.

Hasenfeld, Y. (1987) 'Power in Social Work Practice', in *Social Services Review*, No. 61(3), pp. 48-67.

Hayes, P. (1996) 'The European Agenda: Social Work and Social Work Education', in Ford, P. and Hayes, P. (eds) *Educating for Social Work: Arguments for Optimism.* Aldershot: Avebury.

Healy, L.M. (2001) *International Social Work: Professional Action in an Interdependent World.* Oxford: Oxford University Press.

Hegar, R and Hunzeker, J. (1988) 'Moving Towards Empowerment-Based Practice', in *Public Child Welfare Social Work*, November/December, pp. 20-30.

Hessle, S. and Vinnerljung, B. (2000) *Child Welfare in Sweden – An Overview. Stockholm Studies in Social Work, No 15.* Stockholm: Stockholm University, Department of Social Work.

Hick, S. (1999) 'Learning to Care on the Internet: Evaluating an Online Introductory Social Work Course', *New Technology in the Human Services.* Southampton: University of Southampton.

Hokenstad, M.C., Khinduka, S.K. and Midgley, J. (1992) 'The World of International Social Work', in M.C. Hokenstad, S.K. Khinduka, and J. Midgley (eds), *Profiles in International Social Work.* Washington, DC: The National Association of Social Workers.

Hokenstad, M.C. and Midgley, J. (1997) 'Realities of Global Interdependence: Challenges for Social Work in a New Century', in Hokenstad, M.C. and Midgley, J. (eds) *Issues in International Social Work: Global Challenges for a New Century.* Washington, D.C.: NASW Press.

Hokenstad, M.C. and Midgley, J. (eds) (1997) *Issues in International Social Work: Global Challenges for a New Century.* Washington, D.C.: NASW Press.

hooks, b. (1989) *Talking Back.* Boston: South End.

HRDC Labour Division (1996) *Poverty.* Ottawa: National Council of Welfare.

Huntington, S.P. (1996) *The Clash of Civilizations and the Remaking of World Order.* New York: Simon and Schuster.

Husband, C. (1995) 'The Morally Active Practitioner and the Ethics of Anti-Racist Social Work Practice', in Hugman, R. and Smith, D. (eds) *Ethical Issues in Social Work.* Routledge: London.

Ife, J. (1989) *Rethinking Social Work.* London: Addison, Wesley and Longman.

Ife, J. (2000) 'Localised Needs and a Globalized Economy: Bridging the Gap with Social Work Practice', in *Social Work and Globalisation – Special Issue.* Ottawa: Canadian Association of Social Workers.

Ife, J. (2002) *Human Rights and Social Work: Towards Rights-Based Practice*, Cambridge University Press, UK.

Interview with Dutch Refugee Council (VVN) Centre Coordinator, 31 May 1999.

Interview with Immigration and Naturalization Departmental Centre Coordinator, 25 June 1999.

Interview with medical clinic nurse, 3 June 1999.

Interview with worker of the Opbouw Foundation, 2 June 1999.

Jenson, J. (1989) 'Different but not 'Exceptional: Canada's Permeable Fordism', *Canadian Review of Sociology and Anthropology*, 20(1), pp. 69-94.

Johannessen, T. (1997) 'Social Work as an International Profession: Opportunities and Challenges', in Hokenstad, M.C. and Midgley, J. (eds) *Issues in International Social Work: Global Challenges for a New Century.* Washington, D.C.: NASW Press.

Johnson, L. and Barnhorst, D. (1991) *Children, Families and Public Policy in the 1990s.* Toronto: Thompson Educational.

Jordon, B. (1998) *The New Politics of Welfare.* London: Sage Publications.

Jordan, B. (2000) *Social Work and the Third Way – Tough Love as Social Policy.* London: Sage.

Jordan, B. with Jordan, C. (2002) *Social Work and the Third Way – Tough Love as Social Policy.* London: Sage. Second Edition.

Kasiram, M. and Partab, R. (2001) *Partnering for Success: Marrying Social Work with Religion and Culture.* Paper presentation at the 24th International HERDSA Conference, Newcastle, Australia.

Kendall, K.A. (1998) *IASSW First Fifty Years, 1928-1978, A Tribute to the Founders.* Alexandria, VA.: IASSW and CSWE. First published in 1978.

Kendall, K.A. (2002) *The Origins of Social Work in Europe.* Alexandria, VA.: CSWE.

Khan, P. and Dominelli, L. (2000) 'The Impact of Globalisation on Social Work in the UK', *European Journal of Social Work*, Vol. 3, No. 2, pp. 95-108.

Kirton, D. (2000) *'Race', Ethnicity and Adoption.* Buckingham: Open University Press.

Kitchen, B. (1995) 'Children and the Case for Distributive Justice between Generations in Canada', *Child Welfare*, 74(3), May/June, pp. 58-69.

Klineberg, T. (1976) *International Educational Experiences.* New York: Sage.

Langan, M. and Day, L. (1992) *Women, Oppression and Social Work – Issues in Anti-Discriminatory Practice.* London: Routledge.

Lawrence, S. and Reverda, N. (2000) 'The Recognition and Accreditation of European Postgraduate Programmes', *Social Work in Europe*, 7(2), pp. 33-35.

Ledrer, V.M. and Neal, M.B. (eds) (1999) *Working and Caring for the Elderly: International Perspectives*. London: Routledge.

Lister, R. (1997) *Citizenship: Feminist Perspectives*. London: Macmillan.

Lipsky, M. (1990) *Street Level Bureaucracy*. New York: Russell Sage Foundation.

Loader, B. (ed.) (1997) *The Government of Cyberspace*. London: Routledge.

Loader, B. (ed.) (1998) *Cyberspace Divide*. London: Routledge.

Lombard, A. (1999) 'Transforming Social Work Education in South Africa: A Contextual and Empowerment Issue', in *Maatskaplike Werk/Social Work*, 35(2), pp. 97-112.

London Metropolitan University (2002) *Mission Statement*. London: UNL.

Longres, J. (1986) 'Marxist Theory and Social Work Practice', in *Catalyst*, No. 4, pp. 13-34.

Lorenz, W. (1994) *Social Work in a Changing Europe*. London: Routledge.

Lynn, E. (1999) 'Value Bases in Social Work Education', in *British Journal of Social Work*, 29(6), pp. 939-953.

Lyons, K. (1999) *International Social Work: Themes and Perspectives*. Aldershot: Ashgate.

Lyons, K. and Ramanthan, C.S. (1999) 'Models of Field Practice in Global Settings', in C.S. Ramanthan and R. Link (eds) *All Our Futures: Principles and Resources for Social Work Practice in a Global Era*. Belmont, CA: Brooks/Cole.

Madge, N. and Attridge, K. (1996) 'Children and Families', in Munday, B. and Ely, P. (eds) *Social Care in Europe*. London: Prentice Hall.

Majewska-Galeziak, A. (1998) 'Educating for Social Work in Poland: Challenges of the Transformation Period', in *European Journal of Social Work*, 1(1), pp. 95-100.

Mama, R.S. (2001) 'Preparing Social Work Students to Work in Culturally Diverse Settings', in *Social Work Education*, 20(3), pp. 373-382.

Marchak, M. (1987) *Ideological Perspectives in Canada*. Toronto: McGraw Hill.

Martin, E. (1999) *Changing Academic Work*. Buckingham: SRHE and Open University Press.

Mayadas, N., Watts, T., and Elliott, D. (1997) *International Handbook of Social Work Theory and Practice*. New York: Greenwood Press.

Mazibuko, F. (1996) *Social Work and Sustainable Development: The Challenges for Practice, Training and Policy in South Africa*. Paper given at Joint World Congress of IFSW and IASSW, Hong Kong, July.

McKendrick, B. (1998) 'Social Work Education and Training: From Preparing for Apartheid Society to Training for a Developing Democracy', in *Maatskaplike Werk/Social Work*, 34(1), pp. 99-111.

McLanahan, S. (1994) 'The Consequences of Single Motherhood', in *The American Prospect*, No. 18, pp. 48-58.

McLaughlin, J., Rosen P., Skinner, D. and Webster, A. (1999) *Valuing Technology Organisations, Culture and Change*. London and New York: Routledge.

Menachery, J. and Mohite, A. (1998) 'Whither Social Work Education', in *Maharashtra: The Indian Journal of Social Work*, 62(1), pp. 106-120.

Midgley, J. (1981) *Professional Imperialism: Social Work in the Third World*. London: Heinemann.

Midgley, J (1990) *International Social Work: Learning from the Third World*, National Association of Social Workers Press, Washington, USA.

Midgley, J. (1999) 'Social Development in Social Work: Learning from Global Dialogue', in C. Ramanathan, C.S. and Link, R.J. (eds) *All Our Futures: Principles and Resources for Social Work Practice in a Global Era*. Belmont, CA: Brooks-Cole.

Midgley, J. (2000) 'Globalization, Capitalism and Social Welfare: A Social Development Perspective', in Rowe, B. (ed.) *Social Work and Globalization*. Ottawa: Canadian Association of Social Workers.

Ministry of Finance (1996) *Growth, Employment and Redistribution: A Macro-Economic Strategy*. <www.gov.za/reports/1996>.

Ministry of Health and Social Affairs (1998) *Social Services Act and Care of Young Persons (Special Provisions) Act/LVU and Care of Abusers (Special Provisions) Act/LVM*. Stockholm: The Printing Works of the Cabinet Office and Ministries.

Mulally, B. (1997) *Structural Social Work: Ideology, Theory and Practice*. Oxford: Oxford University Press. First published in 1993.

Murray, C. (1994) *The Underclass Revisited*. London: Institute of Economic Affairs.

Naidoo, S. (2001) *The Social Work Profession in South Africa*. Unpublished Doctoral Study. Quo Vadis: University of Durban-Westville.

Nettleford, R. (1995) *Outward Stretch, Inward Reach: A Voice from the Caribbean*. New York: The Macmillan Press Ltd.

Noble, C. (1999) 'The Essential yet Elusive Project of Developing Field Education as a Legitimate Area of Social Work Inquiry', in *Issues in Social Work Education*, 19(1), Spring, pp. 2-17.

Ntusi, T.M. (1998) 'Professional Challenges for South African Social Workers: Response to Recent Political Changes', in *Maatskaplike Werk/Social Work*, 34(4), pp. 380-383.

Parton, N. (ed.) (1996) *Social Theory, Social Change and Social Work*. London: Routledge.

Parton, N. (1997) *Child Protection and Family Support: Tensions, Contradictions and Possibilities*. London: Routledge.

Payne, M. (1995) *Social Work and Community Care*. London: Macmillan.

Philp, M. (1979) 'Notes on the Form of Knowledge in Social Work', *Social Work and Sociological Review*, 27(1), pp. 83-111.

Pierce, R. and Weinstein, J. (eds) (2000) *Innovative Education and Training for Care Professionals*. London: Jessica Kingsley Publishing.

Platt, D. (2000) *Modern Social Services: A Commitment to People. The 9th Annual Report of the Chief Inspector of Social Services*. London: Department of Health.

Pozutto, R. (2001) 'Lessons in Continuation and Transformation: The United States and South Africa', in *Social Work/Maatskaplike Werk*, 37(2), pp. 154-164.

Pringle, K. (1998) *Social Welfare in Europe*. Oxford: Oxford University Press.

Pringle, K. and Harder, M. (eds) (1997) *Protecting Children in Europe: Towards a New Millennium*. AAlborg: Aalborg University Press.

Province of Nova Scotia (1990) *The Children and Family Services Act*. Halifax: The Queen's Printer.

Rafferty, J. (1997) 'Critical Comments: Shifting Paradigms of Information Technology in Social Work Education and Practice', *British Journal of Social Work*, 27, pp. 959-974.

Ravetz, J. (1998) 'The Internet, Virtual and Real Reality', in Loader, B. (ed.) *Cyberspace Divide*. London: Routledge.

Razack, N. (2002) *Transforming the Field: Critical Anti-Racist and Anti-Oppressive Perspectives for the Human Services Practicum*. Halifax: Fernwood Publishing.

Rees, S. and Rodley, G. (eds) (1995) *The Human Costs of Managerialism: Advocating the Recovery of Humanity*. London: Pluto Press.

Ritzer, G. (2000) *The McDonalization of Society*. New York: Pine Forge Press.

Rollins, N. (2000) 'AIDS 2000: A Conference for Children', Editorial in *Social Work/Maatskaplike Werk*, 36(4), pp. ix-xi.

Rowlings, C. (2000) 'Social Work Education and Higher Education: Mind the Gap', cited in Salustowicz, P. (ed.) *Education for Social Work in Times of Globalisation – Internalisation and Academisation as Responses to*

Globalisation. Paper presented at the IFSW/IASSW World Congress, Montreal.

Royce, D., Dhooper, S. and Rompf, E. (1996) *Field Instruction: A Guide to Social Work Students*. Lexington: University of Kentucky, Longman Publishers, USA.

Sallnäs, M. (2000) *Barnavårdens institutioner (The Child Welfare Institutions)*. Dissertation. Stockholm: Stockholm University, Department of Social work

Salomon, A (1937) *Education for Social Work: A Sociological Interpretation Based on an International Survey*. New York: International Committee of Schools of Social Work with the Russell Sage Foundation.

Sarago, E. (1993) 'The Abuse of Children', in Dallos, R. and McLaughlin, E. (eds) *Social Problems and the Family*. London: Sage.

Schon, D. (1983) *The Reflective Practitioner: How Professionals Think in Action*. New York: Basic Books.

Sewpaul, V. (1992) 'Primary Care: The Challenge to Social Work Educators', in *Social Work/Maatskaplike Werk*, 28(3), pp. 20-28.

Sewpaul, V. (1997) 'The RDP: Implications for Social Work Practice and Social Welfare Policy Development in South Africa', in *Social Work/Maatskaplike Werk*, 33(1), pp. 1-9.

Sewpaul, V. (2001) *The Caribbean – South African Diaspora: Towards Locally Specific Social Work Education and Practice*. Unpublished keynote address presented at the Conference of the Association of Caribbean Social Work Educators (ACSWE), in Nassau, The Bahamas, August 2001.

Sewpaul. V. (2001a) 'Economic Globalization and Social Policy Reform: Social Work Curricula in the South African Context', in *Social Work/Matskaplike Werk*, 37(4), pp. 309-323.

Sewpaul, V. (2001b) 'Models of Intervention for Children in Difficult Circumstances in South Africa', in *Child Welfare*, LXXX (5), pp. 571-586.

Sewpaul, V. and Mahlalela, T.V. (1998) 'The Power of the Small Group: From Fear to Disclosure', in *Agenda*, 39, pp. 34-43.

Sewpaul, V. and Rollins, N. (1999) 'Operationalising Developmental Social Work: The Implementation of an HIV/AIDS Project', in *Social Work/Maatskaplike Werk*, 35(3), pp. 43-54.

Skolnik, L., Wayne, J. and Raskin, M. (1999) 'A Worldwide View of Field Education Structures and Curriculum', in *International Social Work*, 42(4), pp. 471-483.

Slater, P. (1996) 'Practice Teaching and Self-Assessment: Promoting a Culture of Accountability in Social Work', in *British Journal of Social Work*, 26, pp. 195-208.

Smith, M. and Kollock, P. (eds) (1999) *Communities in Cyberspace*. London: Routledge.

Social Services Act (1998) Ministry of Health and Social Affairs, Sweden. Stockholm: Cabinet Printing Works.

Starbuck, L. and Egan, R. (2000) 'Field Education in a Market-Place World', in *Advances in Social Work and Welfare Work Education*, 3(1), pp. 152-160.

Statutes of Nova Scotia (1990) *Nova Scotia Children and Family Services Act*. Halifax: Queen's Printer.

Sunshine, C.A. (1996) *The Caribbean: Survival, Struggles and Sovereignty*. Washington, D.C.: EPICA.

Tait-Rolleston, W. and Barlow-Pehi, S. (2001) 'A Maori Social Work Construct', in Dominelli, L., Lorenz, W. and Soydan, H. (eds) *Beyond Racial Divides: Ethnicities in Social Work*. Aldershot: Ashgate.

Taylor, I. (1999) 'Critical Commentary', in *British Journal of Social Work*, 29(1), pp. 175-180.

Tesoriero, F. and Rajaratnam, A. (2001) 'Partnerships in Education: An Australian School of Social Work and a South Indian Primary Health Care Project', in *International Social Work*, 44(1), pp. 31-41.

The National Post, 10 February, 1999.

The Task Force on the Child as Citizen (1978) *The Child as a Citizen in Canada*. Ottawa: Canadian Council on Children and Youth.

Tsang, A.K.T., Yan, M.C. and Shera, W. (2000) 'Negotiating Multiple Agendas in International Social Work', in Rowe, B. (ed.), *Social work and Globalization*. Ottawa: Canadian Association of Social Workers.

UNAIDS (2002). *Epidemic Update*. July.

United Nations Convention on the Rights of the Child. New York: United Nations.

Universitas 21 homepage (2002) <www.universitas.edu.au/introduction.html>.

University of Durban-Westville (1991) *Mission Statement*. Quo Vadis: UDW.

USA Today, 18 May 1996.

Waldman, J. (1999) *Help Yourself to Learning at Work*. Lyme Regis: Russell House Publishing Ltd.

Washington, J. and Paylor, I. (1998) 'Europe, Social Exclusion and the Identity of Social Work', in *European Journal of Social Work*, 1(3), pp. 327-338.

Waters, M. (1995) *Globalization*. London: Routledge.

Weinstein, J. (1996) 'Education and Training for Social Work: A Response to Tony Novak', in *Social Work Education*, 15(3), pp. 34-39.

Welch, J. (1999) 'How to Cut Down your Hours', *The Guardian*, 1 May, p. 2.

Wellman, B. and Gulia, M. (1999) 'Virtual Communities as Communities', in Smith, M. and Kollock, P. (eds) *Communities in Cyberspace*. London: Routledge.

Wharf, B. (1993a) 'The Constituency/Community Context', in Wharf, B (ed.), *Rethinking Child Welfare in Canada*. Toronto: McClelland and Stewart Inc.

Wharf, B. (1993b) 'Rethinking Child Welfare', in Wharf, B. (ed.) *Rethinking Child Welfare in Canada*. Toronto: McClelland and Stewart Inc.

Wichterich, C. (2000) *The Globalized Woman: Reports from a Future of Inequality*. London: Zed Books.

Williams, C., Soydan, H. and Johnson, M. (eds) (1998) *Social Work and Minorities: European Perspectives*. London: Routledge.

Williams, L.O. (1988) *Partial Surrender: Race and Resistance in the Youth Service*. London: The Falmer Press.

Williams, L.O. (2002) *Adolescents and Violence in Jamaica*. New York: UNICEF.

Young, I. (1990) *Justice and the Politics of Difference*. New Jersey: Princeton University Press.

Youngblood, I. and Belsky, J. (1990) 'Social and Emotional Consequences of Child Maltreatment' cited in Darmstadt, G. (ed.) 'Community-Based Child Abuse Prevention', in *Social Work*, No. 35(6), pp. 487-489.

Younghusband, E. (1958) *Training for Social Work – Third International Survey*. New York: United Nations.

Youth LIVE. *Information Brochure*.

Author Index

Subject Index

abuse, 39-42, 49-50, 59, 66,
70-71, 76-5, 80, 84-5, 87, 89,
90, 104-105, 108, 110-11,
114, 116-18, 121-21, 124-5,
127, 133, 135, 164, 177, 179,
189, 202, 235, 248-3, 321,
323
academic, 4, 7, 10-12, 15-24, 53,
152, 156-8, 163, 167, 182-3,
194, 216-18, 222, 225, 243-4,
248, 252, 254, 258, 261-6,
282, 291, 301-392, 304,
306, 336, 348-51, 355, 358,
360-61
academic staff, 4, 7, 10-12, 15-8,
21, 243-4, 248, 348-9, 355,
358, 360
acceptance, 120, 125, 146, 207,
330, 338-9, 346
accommodation, 17, 19, 66-7,
95, 107, 147, 170, 173,
177-8, 180, 226, 252,
275, 319, 362
accountants, 358
accreditation, 22, 157, 160, 350
action, 28, 38, 50, 56, 57, 63, 72,
74-5, 85, 91, 95, 110, 112,
115, 125, 192, 194, 198, 228,
275, 306-17, 323, 329-30,
338, 352, 364

administration, 19, 169, 199,
285, 321
administrative, 159, 206, 223,
257, 266, 304, 344-5, 349
adult, 12, 114, 118-7, 158, 283,
290, 308, 313, 323-4
adult education, 313
adult learners, 283, 290
advocacy, 28, 100, 109, 328
African, 54, 113, 250, 289, 291,
295-6, 297, 301-302, 309,
311, 316, 318-21, 324-32,
335
African National Congress, 325
age, 5, 29, 50-9, 53, 67, 85, 94,
98, 132, 185, 190-91, 197,
209, 217, 282, 308, 325
ageing, 17, 182, 346
agency, 4, 9, 22, 33, 57, 61, 66,
67-8, 70, 72-8, 83, 102, 107,
107-10, 113, 116-29, 140,
142, 144, 152, 165-7, 170,
172-3, 175, 189, 191-2, 196,
247-50, 254-8, 263-9, 272-8,
311, 321-32, 332, 346
agency cooperation, 192
agency staff, 146, 167, 255, 258,
273, 277
aid, 84, 106, 122, 151, 247, 268,
327, 343

CL